ODJÏB'WE

SMITHSONIAN INSTITUTION
BUREAU OF AMERICAN ETHNOLOGY
BULLETIN 53

CHIPPEWA MUSIC–II

BY

FRANCES DENSMORE

WASHINGTON
GOVERNMENT PRINTING OFFICE
1913

LETTER OF TRANSMITTAL

SMITHSONIAN INSTITUTION,
BUREAU OF AMERICAN ETHNOLOGY,
Washington, D. C., April 29, 1912.

SIR: I have the honor to submit herewith a memoir bearing the title "Chippewa Music—II," by Miss Frances Densmore, and to recommend its publication as Bulletin 53 of the Bureau of American Ethnology. This paper embodies the results of the author's final studies of the music of the Chippewa, or Ojibwa, Indians, and supplements the material published as Bulletin 45. This latter publication has met with high favor among students of primitive music throughout the world, and some of the material contained therein has been adapted and presented by orchestras.

Yours, very respectfully,

F. W. HODGE,
Ethnologist in Charge.

Hon. CHARLES D. WALCOTT,
Secretary of the Smithsonian Institution.

FOREWORD

Chippewa music in its relation to tribal life constitutes one of the subjects dealt with in the present volume, as well as in the writer's first contribution to this study.[1] Not less important is the melodic and rhythmic analysis of the songs, which was begun in the first work and is developed more extensively in the following pages. The native religion of the Chippewa also was considered in Bulletin 45. War forms the keynote of the present memoir, together with the Drum-presentation Ceremony, which is said to have united the Chippewa and the Sioux in permanent peace. In both volumes there are songs of tribal games and dances, and songs "composed in dreams," many of which are the individual songs of forgotten warriors.

The analysis of the Chippewa words and part of the translation are the work of Rev. C. H. Beaulieu, a member of the tribe, and of Rev. J. A. Gilfillan, who for twenty-five years lived on the White Earth Reservation, in Minnesota. Grateful acknowledgment is made also to Mrs. Mary Warren English, of White Earth, and to other native interpreters, whose interest and cooperation have contributed materially to the success of the work.

---

[1] Chippewa Music, *Bulletin 45, Bur. Amer. Ethn.*

CONTENTS

ILLUSTRATIONS

LIST OF SONGS

1. Arranged in Order of Serial Numbers

Songs connected with Odjĭb'we's Personal Experience

Songs of War

Songs of the Drum-presentation Ceremony

Songs of the Lac du Flambeau Reservation

War Songs

[1] S.=Sioux song.

---

[1] See also Nos. (serial) 51, 52, 53, 127.

2. Arranged in Order of Catalogue Numbers

Catalogue No.	Name of singer	Description of song	Title of song	Serial No.	Page
268	Henry Selkirk	Unclassified	"We have salt"	168	291
269	....do	....do	"If I were a son-in-law"	169	292
270	Maiñ'gans	Love song	"Work steadily"	170	293
278	Odjîb'we	For the entertainment of children.	War song of Odjîb'we's childhood.	51	138
279	....do	....do	Song before the boys' fight	52	139
280	....do	....do	Little girls' war song	53	139
281	....do	Pipe dance song	"Little plover"	172	295
282	....do	....do	"Why?"	173	296
283	Na'waji'bigo'kwe	Mîde' song	Mîde' burial song (a)	174	297
284	....do	....do	Mîde' burial song (b)	175	298
285	William Potter	Moccasin game song	(No words)	176	299
286	Mrs. Spears	Love song	"I have found my lover"	177	300
287	....do	....do	"He is going away"	178	301
288	A'jide'gijîg	Dream song	"Into the several heavens"	145	267
289	....do	....do	A song of spring	128	253
290	....do	....do	"Two foxes face each other"	146	268
291	....do	....do	"One bird"	147	269
292	....do	Moccasin game song	(No words)	161	282
293	....do	....do	"The sound of his footsteps"	162	283
294	....do	Dance song	"He killed a man"	165	285
295	....do	Woman's dance song	(No words)	164	285
296	Ki'miwûn	Dream song	"The sky will resound"	148	270
297	....do	Dance song	"The entire world"	167	287
298	....do	Dream song	"One wind"	149	271
299	....do	....do	"An overhanging cloud"	150	272
300	....do	Love song	"I have lost my sweetheart"	157	280
301	....do	....do	"I will not drink"	158	281
302	....do	....do	(No words)	159	281
303	....do	....do	....do	160	282
304	....do	Mîde' song	....do	155	279
305	....do	Moccasin game song	....do	163	284
306	....do	Mîde' song	"The noise of the village"	154	278
307	....do	....do	"Be kindly"	156	280
308	....do	Dream (doctor's) song	"My body lies in the east"	138	261
309	....do	....do	"Sitting with the turtle"	139	262
310	....do	....do	"Carried around the sky"	140	263
311	....do	....do	"The approach of the thunderbirds."	141	264
312	....do	....do	"White-haired raven"	142	265
313	....do	....do	(No words)	143	266
314	Ki'niwûna'nakwad	Dream song	"Heaps of clouds"	151	272
315	....do	....do	(No words)	129	255
316	Gegwe'djibi'tûñ	Southern dance (ca'wûno'ga) song	"I carry it away"	166	286
317	Awûn'akûm'îgîckûñ'	Dream song	(No words)	133	258
318	....do	....do	"Around the sky"	152	273
319	....do	....do	(No words)	144	266
320	....do	....do	....do	134	258
321	....do	....do	....do	130	256
322	....do	....do	"The thunderbirds"	153	274
323	....do	....do	(No words)	135	259
324	....do	....do	....do	131	257
325	....do	....do	....do	136	260

Catalogue No.	Name of singer	Description of song	Title of song	Serial No.	Page
390	Odjíb'we	War song	Song when offering the peace pipe.	45	128
391	....do	....do	Song of an unsatisfied warrior....	5	76
392	....do	....do	Odjíb'we's dream song	1	67
393	Míde'wigi'jíg	....do	A song of indecision	81	185
394	É'niwûb'e	Dream song	Song of the thunderbirds	94	198
395	....do	....do	Song of the hand game	102	208
396	....do	....do	Moccasin game song (a)	103	209
397	....do	....do	Moccasin game song (b)	104	210
398	....do	....do	Song of the deer (a)	95	200
399	....do	....do	Song of the buffalo	99	203
400	....do	Love song	"Go with me"	105	216
401	....do	....do	"Do not weep"	106	217
402	....do	Dream song	Song of the deer (b)	96	200
403	....do	Begging dance song...	Song of the dogs	114	229
404	....do	Southern dance song..	(No words)	119	234
405	....do	....do	"Invite our sweetheart"	120	235
406	....do	War song	Song concerning Gwi'wizäns....	83	187
407	....do	....do	"The Sioux follow me"	84	188
408	....do	Pipe dance song	"O'gima"	171	294
409	....do	War song	Song of the sentry	82	186
410	....do	Moccasin game song...	(No words)	125	240
411	....do	War song	....do	88	192
412	....do	....do	....do	89	192
413	....do	Southern dance song (a)	....do	121	236
414	....do	Southern dance song (b)	....do	122	236
415	....do	War song	"Around the sky"	85	189
416	....do	....do	(No words)	90	193
417	....do	....do	....do	91	193
418	....do	....do	....do	92	194
419	....do	....do	"If he is a warrior"	86	190
420	....do	....do	(No words)	93	195
421	....do	Dream song	Song before a boy goes out to fast..	100	204
422	....do	....do	Song after a boy returns from fasting.	101	205
423	....do	War song	"The sound comes pleasingly"...	63	158
424	....do	....do	"The ravens are singing"	64	159
425	....do	....do	(No words)	65	160
426	....do	....do	"In the south"	87	191
427	Mec'kawiga'bau	Moccasin game song...	(No words)	126	241
428	....do	Divorce song	....do	67	162
429	....do	....do	....do	68	163
430	....do	Love song	"You desire vainly"	107	218
431	....do	....do	"He is gone"	108	219
432	....do	War song	"I am small"	66	161
433	....do	Dream song	Song of the deer dancing	97	201
434	....do	....do	"My shining horns"	98	202
435	....do	Song accompanying the gift of a pony.	(No words)	123	238
436	....do	Song of thanks for the gift of a pony.	....do	124	239
437	....do	War song	Song of Butterfly	80	179
438	....do	Begging dance song...	"Here I come again"	115	230
439	....do	....do	"Maple sugar"	116	231

Cata-logue No.	Name of singer	Description of song	Title of song	Serial No.	Page
440	Mec′kawiga′bau......	Begging dance song ..	"My travels".....................	117	232
441	....do.................	....do...............	Song of thanks for food..........	118	233
442	....do....	Love song..........	"I am thinking of her".........	109	220
443	Dji′siä′sïno′kwe......	....do...............	"Weeping for my love"..........	110	220
444	....do..............	....do..............	"Come, let us sing"..............	111	221
445	Mrs. Gauthier.........	....do..............	Song of an ambitious mother.....	112	222
446	O′gabeä′sïno′kwe......	....do..............	Love song........................	113	225
447	....do..............	For the entertainment of children.	Lullaby..........................	127	241
448	John W. Carl	....do.............	Song of the Game of Silence	179	302
449	Odjïb′we.............	....do.............	Song of the crawfish.............	180	305

Sioux Songs of the Drum-presentation Ceremony

Cata-logue No.	Name of singer	Title of song	Serial No.	Page
S. 1	Mec′kawiga′bau............	Song of departure.....................	54	149
S. 2	....do......................	Song of the chief.....................	55	150
S. 3	....do......................	Song of the speaker...................	56	151
S. 4	....do......................	Song of the owner of the drum.....................	57	151
S. 5	....do......................	Song of the warriors......................	58	152
S. 6	....do......................	Song of giving away the drum....	59	152
S. 7	....do......................	Song of restoring the mourners.....................	60	154
S. 8	....do......................	Song of painting the faces..................	61	155
S. 9	....do......................	Mourners' song...........................	62	156
S. 10	....do......................	Song of the pipe.......................	69	169
S. 11	....do......................	Song of the drum......................	70	170
S. 12	....do......................	Song of the closed door...............	71	172
S. 13	....do......................	First song of the dog feast............	72	173
S. 14	....do......................	Second song of the dog feast..........	73	174
S. 15	....do......................	Third song of the dog feast............	74	175
S. 16	....do......................	Fourth song of the dog feast...........	75	176
S. 17	....do......................	Fifth song of the dog feast.............	76	176
S. 18	....do......................	Sixth song of the dog feast.............	77	177
S. 19	....do......................	Seventh song of the dog feast...........	78	178
S. 20	....do......................	Warriors' song..........................	79	178

Special Signs Used in Transcriptions of Songs

⌐‾‾‾‾‾‾‾‾‾‾‾‾¬ placed above the music indicates that the tones included within the bracket constitute a rhythmic unit.

\+ placed above a note indicates that the tone is sung slightly less than a semitone higher than the proper pitch.

− placed above a note indicates that the tone is sung slightly less than a semitone lower than the proper pitch.

(· placed above a note indicates that the note is prolonged slightly beyond its proper time.

·) placed above a note indicates that the note is given less than its proper time.

• is used in songs transcribed in outline to indicate the pitch of a tone without reference to its duration.

Meaningless syllables are italicized.

Where no words are beneath the notes it is understood that meaningless syllables were used, except in songs whose words were sung too indistinctly for transcription, such instances being described in the analyses.

NAMES OF SINGERS

WHITE EARTH RESERVATION, MINNESOTA

WABA′CĬÑG VILLAGE, RED LAKE RESERVATION, MINNESOTA

LAC DU FLAMBEAU RESERVATION, WISCONSIN

CHIPPEWA MUSIC—II

By Frances Densmore

ANALYSIS OF CHIPPEWA MUSIC

Three questions will be considered in the present section, namely: First, What do the Chippewa sing; Second, How do they sing; and, Third, Why do they sing? The material under analysis in Tables 1 to 22 (pp. 18–33) comprises 340 songs, recorded by the phonograph and transcribed in ordinary musical notation with the addition of a few special signs. The songs were collected on the principal Chippewa reservations in Minnesota and on the Lac du Flambeau Reservation in Wisconsin. All the leading classes of songs in use among the Chippewa are represented: The songs of the Mïde'wïwïn (Grand Medicine), dream songs, war songs, and love songs, songs of the moccasin game, songs of the woman's dance, of the begging dance, and of the pipe dance, songs connected with gifts, songs for the entertainment of children, and a limited number not classified. This collection does not include all the available material, the purpose of the work being to preserve the oldest songs and those connected with tribal history, custom, and ceremony. The songs included in Bulletin 45 of the Bureau of American Ethnology are classified according to geographic distribution, those from each reservation being considered as a group and subdivided according to use. In the present work the principal tabulated analysis is made on the basis of the class or use of the song, the material in Bulletin 45 having been rearranged and combined with material collected at later dates.

Before entering on the analysis of the songs, it is desirable to show that a Chippewa song has identity. This identity was established by the following tests: First, a song was recorded by the same singer at different times; second, a song was recorded by different singers on the same reservation; and, third, a song was recorded by different singers on widely separated reservations, only the titles of the songs being given when the duplications were obtained. These tests were repeated at various times and with a number of songs. In every test a comparison of the phonograms showed the identity of the song, though the renditions were not always uniform in every respect. The rhythm was repeated more exactly than the melody, the latter showing occasionally changes in unimportant progressions or in the number of phrases at the close.   In the course of these comparisons it was shown that an old man repeated with accuracy at intervals of several months a song of very irregular rhythm; it was shown also in one instance that a young man modified the rhythm of an old song, making it conform somewhat to the common rhythms of the white race.

A number of Chippewa songs, as transcribed, have no words. Some of these songs originally may have had words and in a limited number of the love songs the words partake so much of the nature of a soliloquy that they can not conveniently be translated and given with the music.   The words of most of the Chippewa songs are few in number and suggest rather than express the idea of the song. Only in the love songs and in a few of the Mïde' songs are the words continuous.   In the latter the words may be altered slightly, provided the idea remains the same (see Bulletin 45, p. 14).   A similar change of words in a war song is noted in the analysis of song No. 37 in the present work.   A change of words in love songs is described in Bulletin 45 (p. 2).   Although the Chippewa say that the words of a song *may* be changed, it is the experience of the writer that, with the exception of love songs, the words of a song seldom vary in renditions by different singers.   The words of Chippewa songs are frequently changed to conform to the music, syllables being omitted or added, and meaningless syllables introduced between the syllables of a word.   The accent of a word is frequently changed in accordance with the accent of the music, and a word is sometimes accented differently in the several parts of a song.   These and other changes are permissible in fitting the words to the note-values of a song.   A subordination of words to melody, and use of meaningless words and syllables has been noted by Doctor Myers in his study of primitive music.[1]

WHAT DO THE CHIPPEWA SING?

Some peculiarities of Chippewa music are indicated in 22 tables of analysis (pp. 18–33), 14 of which concern the melody and 8 the rhythm of voice and drum.   This section is descriptive of the results of this tabulated analysis.

The first broad division of the material is into songs of major and of minor tonality.   (Table 1.)   The term "key" can not properly be used in this work, as the complete tone-system implied by that term

---

[1] Charles S. Myers, M. A., M. D., The Ethnological Study of Music (in *Anthropological Essays Presented to Edward Burnett Tylor*, etc., p. 236): "The words are commonly sacrificed to the tune. . . . We frequently find that liberties are taken with words, or that meaningless words or syllables are introduced into primitive music.   Yet another cause of the presence of meaningless words lies in the antiquity of the music. The words become so archaic, or their sense was originally so involved or so symbolical that all meaning gradually disappears as the song is handed down from generation to generation."

is not always present. Key is defined by Webster as "a system or family of tones based on their relation to a keynote," also as "the total harmonic and melodic relation of such a family of tones," implying an harmonic as well as a melodic test. In recorded Chippewa songs the relation of the tones to a keynote is usually evident, the tone-material of the key being present, and what might be termed the "melodic relation" being satisfactory, but the sequence of tones in many of the songs is such that the "harmonic relation" is extremely complicated, if, indeed (in some instances), it can be said to exist. Thus most of the songs close with a simple tonic chord, not with tones which can be harmonized by a cadence, and the opening phrases of many major songs are characterized by minor intervals and those of minor songs by major intervals. There are, however, in all the songs, the *rudimentary elements* of key. The persistence of the third and fifth above the keynote, the correct intonation of the octave, and the frequent occurrence of the tonic triad, may be noted. The term "tonality" is employed therefore in this work, its use seemingly being warranted by the definition in the Standard Dictionary (1910): "Tonality, the quality and peculiarity of a tonal system."

In determining the keynote of a song a test by the ear seems permissible and the tonality of the song is determined by the distance of the third and sixth above this keynote. The third occurs in about 97 per cent of the songs under analysis. A song is classified as major in tonality if the third is a major third (two whole tones) above the keynote, and as minor in tonality if the third is a minor third (a whole and a half tone) above the keynote. According to this basis of classification 57 per cent of the songs are major in tonality and 42 per cent minor, while three songs show a change from major to minor or from minor to major by altering the pitch of the third, the keynote remaining the same. These songs are Nos. 189 and 192 in Bulletin 45, and No. 6 of the present work. The sixth occurs in 81 per cent of the songs, and is found to be a minor interval in songs that contain a minor third between the tonic and mediant, and a major interval in songs having a major third between these tones. In contrast with the frequent occurrence of the third and sixth it is found that the seventh occurs in only about 9 per cent of the minor songs. In one-third of these the seventh is a semitone below the tonic, as in modern musical usage (No. 79 of Bulletin 45, and Nos. 36, 100, and 119 of the present work), while in the remainder the seventh is a whole tone below the tonic—the interval which occurs in most of the ecclesiastical modes and in scales formed by the addition of two tetrachords (Nos. 19, 126, and 150, Bulletin 45; Nos. 9, 50, 85, 100, 119, and 124 of the present work).

Having determined the probable keynote of the song, this keynote is used as a basis for further examination, noting in Table 2 the relation of the initial tone to the keynote. Fifty-four per cent of the songs begin on the dominant, indicated as the twelfth in songs having a compass of 12 tones, and as the fifth in songs of smaller range. Next in number are the songs beginning on the octave, which comprise 15 per cent of the entire number.

Table 3 shows the tones on which the songs end. Sixty-seven per cent end on the tonic, and in 90 per cent (indicated in Table 4) the final tone is the lowest tone occurring in the melody. From these characteristics it is not surprising to find, in Table 5, that the largest proportion of songs has a compass of 12 tones and that the next smaller group has a range of an octave. Thus it will be seen that the melodic boundary of a majority of Chippewa songs corresponds to a fundamental tone and its principal harmonic upper partial tones, commonly called overtones.[1] It has been stated already (Bulletin 45, p. 5) that " the phonograph record shows the octave, fifth, and twelfth sung accurately by men who give the other intervals with uncertain pitch," and further observation has confirmed this statement.

Having observed the outlines of the melodies, the tone-material comprised in them may be noted. Table 6 shows that 131 songs, or about 39 per cent of the entire number, contain the tones of the pentatonic, or five-toned, scales, according to the five varieties of the pentatonic scales described by Helmholtz.[2] The tones are the same in all these scales, the difference being in the keynote. The intervals between the tones which comprise the five-toned scales are the same as the intervals between the black keys on the piano. Supposing these tones to constitute the material under consideration, we should have the first five-toned scale according to Helmholtz by using C sharp as the tonic, or keynote; the second five-toned scale by using D sharp; the third by using G sharp; the fourth by using F sharp; and the fifth by using A sharp. This series contains 88 songs on the fourth five-toned scale, more commonly known as the "major pentatonic," or "Scotch scale," and 40 songs on the second five-toned scale, more commonly known as the "minor pentatonic," while two songs (Nos. 51, 2) are on the fifth five-toned scale, and one (No. 116) is on the first five-toned scale. As the fourth five-toned scale occurs in the largest number of songs, we seek to know what groups of tones may have led up to it or in what incomplete form it may be found. It is interesting to note that the next smaller group (the major triad and sixth) comprises 12 per cent of the entire number and contains the tones of the fourth five-toned scale lacking the second. These tones are used in two different ways: (1) The

---

[1] " The ear when its attention has been properly directed to the effect of the vibrations which strike it . . . . becomes aware of a whole series of higher musical tones, which we will call the *harmonic upper partial tones.*"—HELMHOLTZ, *The Sensations of Tone,* translated by Ellis, London, 1885, p. 22.

[2] Ibid., pp. 260, 261.

sixth is used as a passing tone between the tonic and dominant in descending progression (see No. 176), the tonic chord being emphasized; (2) the sixth is combined with the tonic triad above it, forming a minor triad and seventh, which changes to the tonic major triad by the descent of the sixth to the dominant, the song closing with the tonic chord (see No. 147).

We next observe the tone-material of Chippewa songs in its relation to the tones of the diatonic octave and find the seven tones of the diatonic octave in only 6 per cent of the songs. The fifth is present in 338 songs, the only songs in which it does not occur being the two songs (Nos. 51, 52) on the fifth five-toned scale. A similar persistence of the fifth is noted by Doctor Baker in his analysis of 31 Indian songs, the fifth being present in 30 of the songs under his observation.[1] The relative persistence of the fifth and fourth in the songs of the Murray Islanders has been exhaustively studied by Dr. C. S. Myers, who states:[2] "There is good reason to believe that in Murray Island the use of the fourth preceded that of the fifth, but that with the development of the tonic, the note which is a fifth above it is more often used than that which is a fourth above it." The next interval in point of persistence is the third, which occurs in 329 songs, or about 97 per cent of the entire number. The character of the songs from which the third is absent is considered in the analysis of song No. 53. A similar frequency of the third was noted by Doctor Baker, who found the third in 25 per cent of the 31 songs analyzed by him. The presence of the sixth is noted in 276, or about 81 per cent of the Chippewa songs; that of the second in 210, or about 62 per cent; of the fourth in 135, or about 40 per cent; and of the seventh in only 110, or about 32 per cent of the songs. Doctor Baker noted also the seventh as being found in only 8, or 26 per cent, of the songs under his analysis, this being the interval which occurred with least frequency. Thus is noted some similarity between the result of Doctor Baker's analysis of the songs of several Indian tribes and the result of the analysis of Chippewa songs, in which the persistence (or frequency of occurrence) of the tones of the diatonic octave are in the following order: Fifth, third, sixth, second, fourth, seventh.

An interesting group of songs is that classified as "octave complete except seventh and fourth." The omitted tones are the same as those lacking from the fourth five-toned scale, but in this group of songs the third and sixth are minor intervals, making the songs minor in tonality, while in the fourth five-toned scale these intervals are major intervals and the songs therefore major in tonality (see No. 83).

---

[1] Theodor Baker, *Über die Musik der nordamerikanischen Wilden*, Leipzig, 1882; "Tabellen der Intervalle und des Tacts," p. 82.

[2] In *Reports of the Cambridge Anthropological Expedition to Torres Straits*, vol. IV, Cambridge, 1912, p. 260.

The tone-material of most of these songs is diatonic, Table 7 showing that 85 per cent contain no accidentals. In songs containing accidentals the tone most frequently affected is the sixth, this interval being either raised or lowered a semitone in 27, or 8 per cent, of such songs. Accidentals occur more frequently in the love songs than in any other group.

There are next observed the accented tones in their relation to one another, in order to determine whether the songs are harmonic or melodic in structure (Table 8). In making this analysis songs were classified as harmonic in structure if contiguous accented tones bore a simple chord-relation to each other, and as purely melodic if no such relation appeared to exist. According to this basis 83 songs, or 24 per cent, are harmonic in structure (see No. 144), and 222 songs, or 66 per cent of the number, are melodic in structure (see No. 165). Having identified these groups of songs, it was found that certain songs remained which did not properly belong in either group. Thus there are many Chippewa songs which would be classified as harmonic except for one tone, or in some instances two tones; a third group was made therefore to include these songs, which may be termed "intermediate" in structure. Such songs are classified as "melodic with harmonic framework." This group comprises 35 songs, or 10 per cent of the entire number, an example being No. 30, in which the only accented tone not having a chord-relation to a contiguous accented tone is B flat in the fourth measure from the close of the song.

It has been noted that the boundaries of the melodies suggest a chord-relation to the keynote and that the persistence of the third and fifth suggests a chord; it is therefore surprising to note the small percentage of songs which are harmonic in structure.

The next inquiry concerns the progressions in the melody—their direction and the nature of the intervals. Table 9 shows that in 70 per cent of the songs the first progression is downward, and Table 10 that 65 per cent of the entire number of progressions in the songs are downward.[1] It has been noted that in 90 per cent of the songs the last tone is the lowest tone in the song (see Table 4); thus these three tables combine to demonstrate the downward trend of Chippewa melodies.

The nature of the intervals now claims attention in Tables 11 and 12. The interval which occurs most frequently is the second; but this is not of great significance, as the second is often a passing tone or a tone of approach. Next in frequency is the interval of the minor third, comprising 34 per cent of the downward, and 29 per cent of the upward, progressions. This interval has been mentioned

---

[1] The proportion of downward and upward intervals is more uniform in the various classes of songs than any other peculiarity considered in the analysis.

as characterizing the music of other uncultured peoples. Concerning the songs of the Asaba (Niger) people, Charles R. Day states: [1] "A preference for the minor third is rather noticeable, especially at the conclusions." Rev. G. W. Torrance, writing of the Australian aborigines, says: [2] "The songs in compass rarely exceed the distance of a third, and minor intervals predominate." Concerning the Sumatrans William Marsden states: [3] "The Sumatran tunes very much resemble to my ear those of the native Irish and have usually, like them, a flat third; the same has been observed of the music of Bengal." In this connection, it is interesting to note that William Gardiner [4] gives in musical notation the note of the plover and the call, with its answer, of a small beetle, the former being represented by the descending minor third F–D, and the latter l y the descending minor third B flat–G. In these observations it can not be assumed that the intervals heard by the travelers were accurate minor thirds, but that, to the ear accustomed to the musical standards of civilization, the interval of the third was clearly a non-major interval.

In the Chippewa songs it is noted that the percentage of minor thirds, in both ascending and descending progression, is more than twice that of major thirds, a reversal of the statement of tonality, Table 1 showing the songs of major tonality to be about a third more in number than those of minor tonality. This suggests that the relation of the tones in these songs is an interval-relation, not what might be termed a "key-relation," also that the interval is the melodic nucleus of Chippewa song. The minor third is frequently prominent in songs which are major in tonality (see Nos. 140, 141, 151, 163). The major third constitutes a large proportion of the intervals in some songs which are minor in tonality (see Nos. 29, 83, 99). A strong feeling for the interval in melody structure is shown in No. 86, the framework of which consists of two intervals of the fifth, and in No. 82, the framework of which consists of two descending fourths.

In order to determine the feeling for the interval in melody-formation, a test was made which included the 40 songs recorded at Waba′cĭñg, [5] the 50 war songs of Odjĭb′we (pl. 1) recorded at White Earth, and 14 songs recorded by Ē′niwûb′e at Lac du Flambeau. The songs of Odjĭb′we did not show a single instance of "interval-formation," but it was found to characterize 4 (10 per cent) of the Waba′cĭñg songs (Nos. 136, 144, 148, 161), and 3 (21 per cent) of the Lac du Flambeau songs, under observation. From the character of the

[1] *Up the Niger*, by Mockler-Ferryman, with chapter on musical instruments of the natives by Charles R. Day, London, 1892, p. 272.

[2] Music of the Australian Aborigines, in *Journal of the Anthropological Institute of Great Britain and Ireland*, London, 1887, p. 336.

[3] *History of Sumatra*, London, 1811, p. 196.

[4] *The Music of Nature*, Boston, 1838, pp. 232, 246.

[5] The combination *ñg* is pronounced as in the word "finger,"not as in "singer."

songs and the singers at Waba'cĭñg and Lac du Flambeau the material collected there would seem to represent an older culture than the war songs of Odjĭb'we, a factor which adds interest to the result of the test.

Having shown, by analysis, the prominence of the minor third in Chippewa music, and having indicated by reference to authorities its prominence in the music of other uncultured races, it is shown also to be approximately the average interval in Chippewa songs (Table 14). In making this analysis all the intervals were expressed in terms of a semitone and the average interval of progression was found to be 3.1 semitones, or one-tenth of a semitone more than a minor third (Table 13).

In melodic analysis there remains the test to determine the pitch, or musical key, of the songs, which depends for its accuracy on the method of phonographic recording. As the phonograph best adapted to field work at the present time is a machine operated by a spring motor, it is impossible to obtain absolute uniformity of speed, but the following method is used by the writer and gives results of reasonable accuracy. The speed of the phonograph is adjusted to 160 revolutions a minute, and the tone C, sounded by a pitch-pipe of known vibration, is recorded on the blank cylinder, immediately preceding the record of the song. When the transcription of the song is made, the speed of the phonograph is adjusted so that the tone C on the record corresponds with the tone as given by the pitch-pipe. As the last tone is usually the lowest tone and also the tonic, and as 95 per cent of the songs were recorded by men, this table may be regarded as indicating the range of voice among the Chippewa men. Most of the songs are in the major keys of F, G flat, and G. An examination of the songs as transcribed will show that many, perhaps a majority, of the songs end on these tones, in the bass clef.

In considering the rhythm of Chippewa music the instrumental as well as the vocal expression should be observed, most of the songs having been recorded with accompaniment of the drum. Attention is first directed, however, to the rhythm of the song, and the portion of the measure on which the song begins. This indicates whether the "attack" is direct and with emphasis or by a preparatory tone (Table 15). Forty-two of the songs are transcribed in outline, indicating the trend of the melody but not the length of the tones. Sixty-three per cent of the remaining songs begin on the accented part of the measure. This directness in beginning a song is shown also by the fact that in most of the songs the rhythmic unit occurs in the first measure and that the first tone is usually a high tone. The interest of a Chippewa song frequently diminishes as the song proceeds, and in some instances the closing measures contain characterless phrases, repeated indefinitely.

The next feature to be observed is the number of counts in the first measure (Table 16). Deducting the number of songs transcribed in outline, it is to be noted that 50 per cent of the remainder begin in double time and 40 per cent in triple time. In songs indicated as having more than two or three counts in the first measure, there is no secondary accent; thus a measure transcribed with 5 or 7 counts is clearly a unit and could not properly be indicated by a triple measure followed by a double or a quadruple measure. Similar instances of measures containing 5 counts have been recorded by other students of primitive music,[1] and in the music of the Omaha there occur also songs with 7 counts in a measure.

Table 17 shows, however, that the rhythm of the first measure is rarely continued throughout the song. Forty-two songs were transcribed in outline, without time-indication, but in 77 per cent of the remainder the rhythm (or number of counts) in the first measure does not continue throughout the song. The transcriptions show in many instances a change of time with almost every measure. In No. 121 the measures in double and triple time alternate throughout the song. No. 39 contains double, triple, and quadruple time. In No. 81 the double rhythm is interrupted by only one triple measure, which gives character and a certain "swing" to the rhythm of the song as a whole. This wide variation in measure-lengths might suggest improvisation, but these measure-lengths were determined by accents that were unmistakable and that showed no change in the several renditions of the song, even when slight changes were made in the melody. A single exception occurs in a song recorded at White Earth (No. 144), which so closely resembles one recorded at Waba'cĭñg (No. 176) that it may be inferred they are different versions of the same song, though one is in double and the other in triple time.

Turning to the rhythm of the drum (Table 18), the accented double rhythm is found not so prominent as in the vocal expression. One hundred and sixteen of the songs were recorded without the drum. Deducting this number, 43 per cent of the remainder are found to have a triple rhythm. This characterizes a large majority of the dream songs and the songs of various dances and is closely allied to the drum-rhythm of the moccasin game song. The songs showing a triple drum-rhythm are songs which aroused little mental or physical

---

[1] Among the Omaha: A Study of Omaha Indian Music, by Alice C. Fletcher, aided by Francis La Flesche. With a Report on the Structural Peculiarities of the Music by John Comfort Fillmore, A. M.; *Archæological and Ethnological Papers of the Peabody Museum, Harvard University,* Cambridge, Mass., 1893, vol. 1, No. 5; songs Nos. 6, 111, 137, 140.
Among the Kwakiutl: Franz Boaz in *Journal of American Folk-lore,* vol. I, 1888, pp. 51, 59.
Among the Hopi: Benjamin Ives Gilman, *Hopi Songs,* Boston, 1908, p. 117.
Among the Creek and Yuchi: Frank G. Speck, Ceremonial Songs of the Creek and Yuchi Indians, in *Anthropological Publications of the Museum of the University of Pennsylvania,* Philadelphia, 1911, vol. 1 No. 2, pp. 169, 170, 178, 226.
Also among the Sudanese: Heinrich Zöllner, Einiges über sudanesische Musik, *Musikalisches Wochenblatt,* Leipzig, 1885, p. 446.

excitement. The dream songs were undoubtedly composed under abnormal conditions, but no drum was used in their composition and the present study concerns only the manner of their rendition. In this connection it is interesting to note that, according to Beau (1835) and to Barth and Roger (1841),[1] the rhythm "of the adult heart, beating 60 to 80 and acting normally" is a triple rhythm. The exact rhythm described by these authors is found in two of the Chippewa songs— the song of the war messenger and that of his return (Nos. 11, 12). The writer has frequently heard this rhythm when the drummers *began* their performance (see Bulletin 45, p. 6); gradually they changed to that most often recorded on the phonograph, in which the unaccented stroke precedes, instead of follows, the accented stroke.

In all the Mĭde′ songs and in 53 per cent of the war songs there is a drum-rhythm of rapid unaccented strokes, two of which are approximately equal to one metric unit of the melody. It is stated that under certain conditions, "especially a moral emotion or violent physical exertion," the triple rhythm of the heart becomes "allied to a double measure."[2] The collection of additional data may throw more light on a possible connection between the action of the physical organism and the form assumed by primitive musical expression.

The next observation concerns the rhythmic unit, or *motif* (Table 19), which appears to constitute the rhythmic nucleus of the song, as the interval forms its melodic nucleus. As a basis for this classification, a rhythmic unit was defined as "a group of tones of various lengths, comprising more than one count of a measure, occurring at least twice in a song and having an evident influence on the rhythm of the entire song." According to this basis of classification it was found that 62 per cent of the songs contain a rhythmic unit, while in many other instances the song itself possesses a rhythmic completeness which constitutes it a unit. One hundred and ninety-one songs contain a rhythmic unit, and in 132 songs (69 per cent) the unit occurs in the first measure, showing, as in Table 15, a directness of "attack."

There are four ways in which a rhythmic unit is used to form a Chippewa song: First, it is continuously and exactly repeated throughout the song (see No. 26); second, it is repeated continuously except for a measure or two having a different rhythm, thus breaking the monotony and giving character to the rhythm of the song as a

---

[1] *Dictionnaire de Physiologie*, Richet, Ch., editor, Paris, Tome IV, 1900, p. 74. "Beau compara un bettement de cœur à une mesure à trois temps, dans laquelle le premier temps serait occupé par le premier bruit, le deuxième par le deuxième bruit, le troisième par le grand silence. . . . D'après Barth et Roger le rhythme représente une sorte de mesure à trois temps, dans laquelle le premier bruit occupe le tiers environ; le petit silence, à peu près un sixième; le deuxième bruit, un sixième; et le grand silence, le dernier tiers."

[2] Ibid., p. 75 (signed by Lahousse). "Si, au contraire, les battements du cœur sont accélérés, le silence diminue et l'on n'a plus qu'une mesure qui se rapproche de la mesure à deux temps. . . . C'est surtout quand une émotion morale, ou violent exercice physique agissent sur le cœur de l'homme, ou quand il est le siège de certains états pathologiques."

whole (see No. 132); third, it is repeated continuously except for a middle section, which contains the words and is in a different rhythm (see No. 1); and, fourth, the repetitions of the rhythmic unit are freely interspersed with measures having no rhythmic interest (see No. 118). There are also five songs in which the rhythmic unit is continuously repeated except at the close of the song (see No. 4).

In addition to the use of the rhythmic unit in repetition, there is an equally important use of it as a basis for the rhythm, the unit appearing either in separated phrases or with a change of accent (see No. 90). This change of accent or other modification sometimes produces a second or (in one instance, No. 157) a third·rhythmic unit which is repeated several times. Songs numbered 17, 47, 121, and 123 contain two rhythmic units, the second being formed from the first and constituting an answering phrase. A similar structural peculiarity was noted by Fillmore, who states: "Having invented his original motive, which is commonly striking in its rhythmic form and highly characteristic, the Indian composer proceeds to build his song out of modified repetitions of this motive." [1]

Among the 191 Chippewa songs containing a rhythmic unit there is only one duplication, Nos. 192 and 195 in Bulletin 45 containing the same unit. In the 20 Sioux songs of the Drum-presentation Ceremony the percentage is much larger, as the second rhythmic unit in song No. 73 of the present series is similar to the unit occurring in No. 77. There is, however, a division of a count ♪ ♩ ♩ which occurs in Chippewa songs recorded on a reservation showing Sioux influence, and which is found also in Sioux songs. This division of the count occurs in 15 per cent of the songs recorded at Waba′cǐñg (Nos. 131, 153, 157, 159, 161, 163), and is found in only five other songs of the entire collection. The same phrase is found in 10 per cent of the Sioux songs of the Drum-presentation Ceremony (Nos. 54, 62), and also in about 10 per cent of the Sun-dance songs of the Teton Sioux recorded by the writer at Standing Rock, North Dakota, in 1911. The Chippewa at Waba′cǐñg are in frequent communication with the Sioux of North Dakota, parties from these tribes visiting each other at their various festivals. The Chippewa at Waba′cǐñg are also composing music at the present time to a greater extent than those on other reservations. It is interesting to note that the correspondence between the music of the Chippewa and the Sioux, which may be attributed to contact of the two tribes, is rhythmic, not melodic.

Further evidence of the rhythmic unit as a nucleus of Chippewa song is found in the fact that some songs were repeated in sections,

---

[1] John Comfort Fillmore, Primitive Scales and Rhythms, in *Memoirs of the International Congress of Anthropology*, Chicago, 1894, p. 175.

the singer using the phrases in varying order, apparently as his fancy prompted him. This is noted in the analysis of No. 105, and was observed especially in the love songs. No. 100 affords an example of a song the entire rhythm of which constitutes a unit that is complete in itself and can not be divided. Such a song would become, in its repetitions, the rhythmic unit of an extended musical performance.

Finally, there is observed the speed of voice and drum, as indicated by a Maelzel metronome, the number representing the number of beats per minute. The method of adjusting the phonograph to secure uniform speed in recording and in playing a song has been already described. Table 20 shows the metric unit of the voice, the indication being usually for the time of a quarternote, though in some instances a half-note, or even an entire measure-length, was the only unit by which the tone-values could be determined. It will be noted that the largest percentages of speed occur on the numbers 96 to 104 M. M., this group being a somewhat clearer indication of the natural tempo of Chippewa song than the average speed of the entire collection (107 M. M.), as the latter is slightly affected by songs whose peculiar structure necessitates a very large or a very small unit of measurement. The metric unit is particularly slow in songs of controlled excitement (see No. 30).

Table 21 shows the metric unit of the drum, the highest percentages being between 104 and 112 and the average speed 109. Both these tests show the speed of the drum to be greater than the speed of the voice, though a proportion between the two is not evident.

The comparative speed of voice and drum is further shown in Table 22, the songs in which the drum is slower than the voice being about half the number of those in which the metric unit is the same, and less than half the number of those in which the drum is faster than the voice. The independence of the vocal and instrumental expressions is further shown by the fact that the tempo of the voice may change but the tempo of the drum remains the same, a peculiarity which is noted in the analysis of No. 168.

There may be instances in which the metric units of voice and drum are in the ratio of two to three, but the writer does not recall an instance in Chippewa music in which drum and voice coincided on the first count of the measure, one showing two and the other three pulses, or metric units, during the measure, although this "two-against-three rhythm" has been found in the music of other Indian tribes and among many other primitive peoples. Fillmore gives an instance of a Bala Bala (Bellabella) Indian song containing a 2–4 rhythm in the voice and a 5–8 rhythm in the drum, the two coinciding on the first of each measure.[1] In Chippewa music,

---

[1] John Comfort Fillmore, *Primitive Scales and Rhythms*, p. 173.

however, the two expressions seem to be entirely distinct. Even when voice and drum have to the ear the same metric unit, the drum slightly precedes, or in some instances follows, the voice. Bulletin 45 (p. 6) contains a description of a phonograph record in which the metric units of voice and drum are so nearly alike that the same metronome indication was used for each. At the beginning of the record the drumbeat was slightly behind the voice, but it gained gradually until for one or two measures drum and voice were together; the drum continued to gain until at the close of the record it was slightly in advance of the voice. An independence of rhythm of voice and drum was noted by Doctor von Hornbostel,[1] and also by Doctor Myers.[2]

Further consideration is given the rhythm of Chippewa songs in Bulletin 45 (p. 18).

How do the Chippewa Sing?

The manner of Chippewa singing varies with the nature of the song and the skill of the singer. A nasal drawling is always used in the love songs, but in no other songs. This is not a loud tone, and it remotely suggests the call of an animal. The songs of the Mĭde′wĭwĭn (Grand Medicine) contain meaningless syllables, which are distinctly pronounced and in most instances are given similarly in the various renditions of a song. These syllables are frequently interpolated between parts of a word and sometimes bear resemblance to syllables of the words. In these songs the words are mispronounced more often than in others, being changed to fit the music, which is the essential element of the song (see Bulletin 45, p. 14). In other classes of songs the vocables are throaty sounds, which differentiate the tones but can not be expressed in letters. It is said that "one must have an Indian throat to sing the songs properly." A Chippewa does not move the lips in giving these vocables, but seems to produce them by a contraction of the glottis; the tone lengths are, however, entirely distinct and rarely vary in the repetitions of the song. In addition to these styles of singing, which are universal, there is a vibrato, or wavering tone, which is cultivated among the younger singers and is considered an evidence of musical skill (see Bulletin 45, p. 4). A similar phase of musical culture was noted by the writer among the Sioux of North Dakota.

---

[1] Erich M. von Hornbostel, Über die Musik der Kubu (aus dem Phonogramm-archiv des psychologischen Instituts der Universität Berlin, Frankfurt am Main, 1908, phonogramme 15a).

[2] Charles S. Myers, M. A., M. D., The Ethnological Study of Music (in Anthropological Essays Presented to Edward Burnett Tylor, etc.), p. 237: "Not infrequently the accents or measures in the melody are opposed to those in the accompaniment." P. 238: [In polyphonic music of primitive peoples] "different simultaneous rhythms are allowed full scope for independent development. . . . Such 'heterophonic' music surely demands of the native audience the same oscillations of attention as occur in us when we listen to two persons talking simultaneously."

Concerning accuracy of intonation according to the piano scale, there is wide variance among singers, as well as in some instances, among the several intervals sung by the same person. The transcriptions of these songs should be understood as indicating the tones produced by the singers as nearly as it is possible to indicate them in a notation which is familiar by usage and therefore convenient for observation.[1] A few additional signs are used and the peculiarities which can not be expressed graphically are noted in the descriptive analyses of the songs. Where a variation from the piano scale was marked and was repeated in the several renditions of a song, it is indicated by the sign + or − above the note, showing the tone to have been persistently sung less than a semitone above or below the note transcribed. In five records a faulty intonation at the beginning of a song was corrected in the latter part (see Nos. 54, 129, 133, 146, 164).

In the rendition of Indian music the writer finds tones which correspond to intervals of the piano scale and occasionally, in the same song, other tones whose pitch varies so constantly and by such minute gradations that they have no equivalent in that scale. Tones of the former class are capable of transcription in ordinary musical notation; those of the latter can adequately be shown only by a sound-wave chart, but, in the present work, are transcribed by the notes they most nearly approximate in pitch. Minute gradation of tone in Indian song has given rise to the statement that Indians habitually use intervals of eighths or quarter tones. Intervals smaller than a semitone are familiar to every student of Indian music, but before it can safely be assumed that they form a fixed part of a musical system it should be proved by mechanical tests that they can be accurately repeated. Such proof is believed to be lacking at the present time. It is the opinion of the writer that these minutely graded tones are survivals of a less differentiated vocal expression. In the present analysis of Indian music we observe the tones on which a purely natural vocal expression crystallizes and first coincides with that system of tones which has gradually developed in the musical history of the white race.

In the early part of the investigations a few phonograph records were made which were found to be "musically incoherent," the tones having no clear relation to one another or to a keynote. On inquiry it was always found that the men who sang these songs were not considered good singers by the members of the tribe. In a repetition of the song by a "good singer" the trend of the melody was the same, and the intervals were such that the melody "made musical sense," con-

---

[1] Helmholtz, *The Sensations of Tone*, translated by A. J. Ellis, London, 1885, pt. 3, p. 260. Translator's footnote: "All these [scales] are merely the best representatives in European notation of the sensations produced by the scales on European listeners."

tained a keynote, and could be expressed with reasonable accuracy in musical notation. In recording several hundred songs there have been a few instances in which singers have tried to improvise parts of songs which they could not remember and have even "made up songs as they went along." These attempts were readily discovered and the records discarded, together with the efforts of those who, like some members of the white race, "could not carry a tune." Indians distinguish clearly between competent and incompetent singers, and when the purpose of the writer's work was fully understood they recommended only such of their number as were good singers.

The management of the breath by a Chippewa singer is radically different from that of a member of the white race. This is indicated by the fact that rests occur in only 13 (4 per cent) of the songs, about half of these being songs of the Mïde' ceremonies, which are characterized by forcible ejaculations. The Chippewa sing almost continuously for several hours at a time, each song being repeated an indefinite number of times. In some instances the measure which connects the song and its repetition is a complete measure and is so indicated in the transcription, but in many others the song is completed as transcribed and the singer at once begins the repetition, disregarding uniformity of measure-lengths.

The accénts are clearly given and never vary in the repetitions of the song. By these accents the measure-lengths of the transcription are determined. In many instances it was necessary to reduce the speed of the phonograph greatly in order to discern a metric unit or any note-value on which a transcription could be based, but when this metric unit was discovered it could easily be traced throughout the song and its repetitions, and could be heard clearly when the original speed of the phonograph was restored. In the writer's experience the metric unit and the measure-length are practically without variation in the repetitions of Chippewa songs, and the note-values are changed only when words are introduced, or occasionally in the closing phrases of a song, which are often without special interest or importance.

The songs are usually accompanied by the drum, though the rattle is frequently used with Mïde' songs and the songs connected with the use of medicine. The musical instruments of the Chippewa are described in Bulletin 45 (p. 11), and will be considered also in the group analyses of the songs in the present volume.

WHY DO THE CHIPPEWA SING?

Investigation of the origin and use of Chippewa songs leads to the conclusion that most of them are connected, either directly or indirectly, with the idea of reliance on supernatural help. This idea rarely assumes the form of direct address, though one song

(No. 156) contains the words "Be kindly, my manido'," and in some of the Mïde' songs a manido' (spirit) animal or bird is represented as speaking—"I am a spirit to be able to become visible, I that am a male beaver" (Bulletin 45, No. 34), and "I am about to alight that you may see me" (ibid., No. 41).

It is said that in the old days all the important songs were "composed in dreams," and it is readily understood that the man who sought a dream desired power superior to that he possessed. A song usually came to a man in his "dream"; he sang this song in the time of danger or necessity in the belief that by so doing he made more potent the supernatural aid vouchsafed to him in the dream. Songs composed, or received, in this manner were used on the warpath, in the practice of medicine,[1] and in any serious undertaking of life. Thus there are many dream songs among the songs of war, of the Mïde', and of the moccasin game, in addition to the group of dream songs in the classified analysis. An instance of a warrior's success connected with the singing of a dream song is shown in No. 42, and of a warrior's defeat attributed to the failure of supernatural help, in No. 8.

In addition, to songs connected with dreams and with triumphs gained by supernatural aid, there are love songs, and songs of physical activity (as the social dances) and of the home life (as the songs for the entertainment of children). Almost without exception the love songs are songs of disappointment and longing, though a few love-charm songs are included among those of the Mïde' (Bulletin 45, Nos. 71–76).

The words of 248 songs are transcribed; one-third of this number contain mention of some manifestation of nature, the number and percentages of this group being as follows:

	Number	Percentage
Songs concerning animals	30	36
Songs concerning birds	17	21
Songs concerning the sky	17	21
Songs concerning water	11	13
Songs concerning clouds	4	4.5
Songs concerning the wind	4	4.5

Noting the large number of songs containing mention of animals, it is interesting to consider whether animals may have seemed to the Indian better fitted than himself to cope with natural conditions. The animals mentioned in the songs are the otter, beaver, weasel, marten, crawfish, rattlesnake, large bear, fox, deer, and dog; there is also (on a reservation showing Sioux influence) one reference to the horse and the buffalo. The birds mentioned are the crow, loon, owl,

---

[1] Compare Aleš Hrdlička, Physiological and Medical Observations Among the Indians of Southwestern United States and Northern Mexico, *Bulletin 34 of the Bureau of American Ethnology*, Washington, 1908, pp. 222–227, 243, 244.

raven, plover, eagle, "thunderbird," and "water-birds." Reference to water occurs principally in songs of the Mïde'wïwïn, the emblem of that organization being a shell, and all its traditions being associated with water and with aquatic animals.

A spontaneous outburst of melody, giving expression to either joy or sorrow, does not characterize Chippewa songs; indeed, the nature of the songs is more frequently objective than subjective, more often connected with accomplishment than with self-expression.

A comparison between the content and the tonality of the songs may now be undertaken. As we are accustomed to connect a minor key with the idea of sadness, it is interesting to inquire whether the same mode of expressing sadness obtains in Chippewa songs. First, it is observed that, apart from the love songs, there are few songs of sorrow. The series of 340 songs contains 142 in minor tonality, of which only 20 (14 per cent) are songs of sadness, comprising practically all the songs of this character. Among the 85 Mïde' songs there are only two songs of sadness (Nos. 174, 175); these are burial songs. Many Mïde' songs mention sickness, but always with an affirmation that it will be cured by supernatural means. Six of the 88 war songs contain the idea of distress (Bulletin 45, Nos. 120, 150; present collection, Nos. 10, 17, 34, 36). It will be noted that two of these refer to the grief of the enemy (Nos. 10, 34), and in one a condition of distress is relieved by the use of medicine; the three which may be considered songs of unlightened sadness are the songs of the departure of warriors (No. 150, Bulletin 45; No. 17 of the present work) and the song of the warrior left to die on the battlefield (Bulletin 45, No. 120). In a similar instance (No. 33) the song of the wounded man left to die is distinctly major in tonality.

Among the 30 love songs 11, or more than 33 per cent, are songs of sadness and minor in tonality. Of the unclassified songs only one contains the idea of distress, with a minor tonality—this is the song of the little boy who was afraid of the owl (Bulletin 45, No. 121). Two-thirds of the moccasin game songs are minor in tonality; in this connection it may be noted that the result of the moccasin game was always a matter of uncertainty.

Most of the Chippewa songs are major in tonality, and most of the old songs were "dream songs" used in the Mïde', the practice of medicine, and the pursuit of war, the essential nature of a "dream" being associated with the idea of reliance on supernatural help. In contrast with the large proportion of major songs, and of dream songs of various classes, it is found that a minor tonality is used, practically without exception, in songs directly expressing sadness, distress, or uncertainty. These observations may have a bearing on the further study of the psychology of Indian song.

TABULATED ANALYSIS OF 340 SONGS [1]

MELODIC ANALYSIS

TABLE 1.—TONALITY

	Mïde' songs		Dream songs		War songs		Love songs		Moccasin game songs		Woman's dance songs		Begging dance songs		Pipe dance songs		Songs connected with gifts		Songs for the entertainment of children		Unclassified songs		Total	
	No.	Per cent.	No.	Per cent.	No.	Per cent.	No.	Per cent.	No.	Per cent.	No.	Per cent.	No.	Per cent.	No.	Per cent.	No.	Per cent.	No.	Per cent.	No.	Per cent.	No.	Per cent.
Major tonality	68	72	39	76	44	50	12	40	6	33	3	30	5	72	2	67	1	12.5	4	50	11	52	195	57
Minor tonality	27	28	12	24	44	50	18	60	13	67	7	70	2	28	1	33	6	75	4	50	8	38	142	42
Beginning major, ending minor																	1[2]	12.6			1[3]	5	2	
Beginning minor, ending major																					1[4]	5	1	
Total	95		51		88		30		19		10		7		3		8		8		21		340	

TABLE 2.—FIRST NOTE OF SONG—ITS RELATION TO KEYNOTE

	Mïde' songs		Dream songs		War songs		Love songs		Moccasin game songs		Woman's dance songs		Begging dance songs		Pipe dance songs		Songs connected with gifts		Songs for the entertainment of children		Unclassified songs		Total	
	No.	Per cent.	No.	Per cent.	No.	Per cent.	No.	Per cent.	No.	Per cent.	No.	Per cent.	No.	Per cent.	No.	Per cent.	No.	Per cent.	No.	Per cent.	No.	Per cent.	No.	Per cent.
Beginning on the—																								
Thirteenth			1	2	3	4																	4	1
Twelfth [6]	1		6	12	3	4																	10	3
Octave	34	36	20	39	23	26	11	37	7	36	1	10	2	28	1	33	1	12.5	1	12.5	7	33	105	33
Fifth [6]	32	34	7	13	11	12	5	16	4	21	4	40	3	43					1	12.5	3	14	72	21
Eleventh	1	1									1	10									1	5	3	1
Fourth [7]	1	1	2	4	2	2													1	12.5			7	2
Tenth			4	8	14	16			1	5.5	1	10			2	67	1	12.5			2	10	24	7
Third [8]	1	1	3	6													1	12.5			2	10	10	3
Ninth	5	5	1	2	7	8	2	7					1	14			1	12.5			1	5	16	5

Second [9]	6	6				1	5.5	1	10	1				1	12.5		2	25		1	12.5
Octave	11	12	7	13	24	27	10	33	2	11	2	20	1	14		2	25		2	10
Seventh	2	2			1	1	7		1	5.5	1									2	10
Tonic	2	2			1		2		3	16						4	50			
Total	95		51		88		30		19		10		7 [a]		3		8		8		21

9	3
51	15
6	2
13	4
340	

TABLE 3.—LAST NOTE OF SONG—ITS RELATION TO KEYNOTE

Ending on the—																				
Tonic	60	63	62	70	66	16	84	7	70	3	43	3	100	4	50.0	6	75	16	76	229	67
Fifth	25	26	19	22	27	3	16	2	20	3	43			3	37.5	2	25	4	20	75	22
Third	10	11	7	8	7			1	10	1	14			1	12.5			1	5	36	11
Total	95		88		30		19		10		7		3		8		8		21	340	

[1] The writer gratefully acknowledges her indebtedness to Dr. Aleš Hrdlička, curator of physical anthropology, United States National Museum, for valuable suggestions regarding the methods employed in these tables of analysis; also to Mr. C. K. Wead, examiner, United States Patent Office, for assistance in determining certain bases of classification.

[2] No. 189, Bulletin 45 (same keynote throughout song).
[3] No. 67, present work (same keynote throughout song).
[4] No. 192, Bulletin 45 (same keynote throughout song).
[5] Songs beginning on the submediant and having a compass of less than 13 tones.
[6] Songs beginning on the dominant and having a compass of less than 12 tones.
[7] Songs beginning on the subdominant and having a compass of less than 11 tones.
[8] Songs beginning on the mediant and having a compass of less than 10 tones.
[9] Songs beginning on the supertonic and having a compass of less than 9 tones.

MELODIC ANALYSIS—continued

TABLE 4.—LAST NOTE OF SONG—ITS RELATION TO COMPASS OF SONG

	Bulletin 45		Present work		Total		Serial Nos., Bull. 45	Serial Nos., present work
	No.	Per cent.	No.	Per cent.	No.	Per cent.		
Songs in which final tone is—								
Lowest tone in song	166	*90*	141	*90*	307	*90*	....	*179*
Highest tone in song	....		1	*1*	1	*1*	....	
Immediately preceded by—								
Fifth below	1		....		1	*1*	49	
Fourth below	3	*2*	6	*4*	9	*3*	60,132,160	36,49,120,121,169,172
Major third below	1		1		2	*1*	88	99
Minor third below	4	*3*	3	*2*	7	*2*	17,56,57,59	99,125,154
Whole tone below	3	*2*	2	*1*	6	*2*	19,126,150	9,50,124
Whole tone below with fourth below in a previous measure	....		1		1			100
Whole tone below with sixth below in a previous measure	....		1		1			173
Songs containing a fourth below the final tone	1	*1*	2	*1*	3	*1*	124	47,90
Songs containing a minor third below the final tone	1	*1*	2	*1*	3	*1*	92	166,175
Total	180	......	160	......	340	......		

NOTE

In Bulletin 45 all songs containing tones below the final tone end on the tonic, except Nos. 87, 88, 92, which end on the fifth.

In the present work all songs containing tones below the final tone end on the tonic, except No. 125, which ends on the fifth.

[1] A similar peculiarity is noted in the songs of the Murray Islanders, analyzed by Dr. C. S. Myers (in *Reps. Cambr. Anthr. Exped. Torres Strait*, vol. IV, Cambridge, 1912. p. 260), who states, "The tonic is almost invariably the lowest tone in the melody."

TABLE 5.—NUMBER OF TONES COMPRISING COMPASS OF SONG

Range of—	Mide' No.	Mide' %	Dream No.	Dream %	War No.	War %	Love No.	Love %	Moccasin game No.	Moccasin game %	Woman's dance No.	Woman's dance %	Begging dance No.	Begging dance %	Pipe dance No.	Pipe dance %	Songs w/ gifts No.	Songs w/ gifts %	Entertainment of children No.	Entertainment of children %	Unclassified No.	Unclassified %	Total No.	Total %
Four tones	12	13	1	2											1	33							14	4
Five tones	4	4	1	2	1	1	1	3											1	12.5			8	2
Six tones	8	8	2	4	3	4	11	37									1	12.5	3	37.5			28	8
Seven tones	21	22	8	16	10	11	4	13	4	21	4	40	1	14	2	67	2	25	2	25	2	10	60	18
Eight tones	3	3			7	8	3	10	3	16	1	10	2	29			1	12.5	1	12.5	6	29	27	8
Nine tones	6	7	7	14	10	11	1	3	1	6	1	10	1	14			3	37.5	1	12.5	1	5	32	9
Ten tones	4	4	7	14	12	14	5	17	6	32	4	40	2	29							5	24	45	13
Eleven tones	36	37	19	37	28	32	1	3	1	6			1	14			1	12.5			2	10	89	26
Twelve tones	1	1	6	11	16	18	4	14	4	21											3	14	34	10
Thirteen tones					1	1															2	10	3	1
Fourteen tones																								
Total	95		51		88		30		19		10		7		3		8		8		21		340	

TABLE 6.—TONE MATERIAL

	Mide' No.	Mide' %	Dream No.	Dream %	War No.	War %	Love No.	Love %	Moccasin game No.	Moccasin game %	Woman's dance No.	Woman's dance %	Begging dance No.	Begging dance %	Pipe dance No.	Pipe dance %	Songs w/ gifts No.	Songs w/ gifts %	Entertainment of children No.	Entertainment of children %	Unclassified No.	Unclassified %	Total No.	Total %
First five-toned scale	11	12			12	14	3	10					1	14					2	25			1	
Second five-toned scale			1	2					6	33	3	30					2	25	2	25	2	10	40	12
Fourth five-toned scale	20	21	25	49	25	28	3	10	2	11	2	20	1	14	1	33	2	25			6	29	88	26
Fifth five-toned scale			1	2	1	3	1	3	1	5.5													2	
Major triad									1	5.5													4	1
Major triad and seventh	1												1	14	1	33							1	
Major triad and sixth	20	21	13	26	3	4		16	3	16	1	10	1	33	1	33	1	12.5			1	5	42	12
Major triad and fourth			3	12		4					1	10						12.5			1	5	2	12

MELODIC ANALYSIS—continued

TABLE 6.—TONE MATERIAL—continued

	Mīde' songs		Dream songs		War songs		Love songs		Moccasin game songs		Woman's dance songs		Begging dance songs		Pipe dance songs		Songs connected with gifts		Songs for the entertainment of children		Unclassified songs		Total	
	No.	Per cent	No.	Per cent	No.	Per cent	No.	Per cent	No.	Per cent	No.	Per cent	No.	Per cent	No.	Per cent	No.	Per cent	No.	Per cent	No.	Per cent	No.	Per cent
Major triad and second	1	1			2	2																	3	1
Minor triad	1	1																					1	
Minor triad and seventh			1	2	1	1	1	3									1	12.5	1	12.5	1	5	3	1
Minor triad and sixth	3	3	5	10	2	2	2	7	1	5.5													6	2
Minor triad and fourth					6	7					1	10									1	5	18	6
Minor triad and second	3	3			3	4											1	12.5					1	
Octave complete	6	6	1	2	11	13	5	17	1	5.5	1	10	1	14							2	10	19	6
Octave complete except seventh	13	14	1	2	1	1	1	3	1	5.5			2	28			1	12.5	1	12.5	1	5	32	9
Octave complete except seventh and sixth [1]	1	1			1	1	4	13	1	5.5	2	20											6	2
Octave complete except seventh and fourth [1]	1	1			1	1	1	3	1	5.5													4	1
Octave complete except seventh and third	1	1	1	1	1	1	1	3	1	5.5											3	14	11	3
Octave complete except seventh and second	5	5	5	5	4	4	1	3	2	1	1	10	1	14									15	4
Octave complete except sixth	3	3	3	3	4	4			1	1													1	
Octave complete except sixth and fourth	1	1																					1	
Octave complete except sixth and second	1	1			3	4	1	3															5	2
Octave complete except fourth					1	1																	1	
Octave complete except fourth and third					1	1																	1	
Octave complete except fourth and second							1	3															1	
Octave complete except third							5	17															1	
Octave complete except second	2	2			3	4																	10	3
Minor third and fourth					2	2									1	33							3	1
First, second, and fifth tones																					1	5	1	

(Continuation of preceding table)

Songs containing—	95		51		88		30		19		10		7		3		8		8		21		340	
First, second, fourth, and fifth tones	3	*3*			3	*3*	2	*7*									1	*12.5*	1	*12.5*			1	
First, second, fifth, and sixth tones	3	*3*			3	*3*											1	*12.5*	1	*12.5*			6	*2*
Other combinations of tones	3	*3*																			2	*10*	9	*3*
Total	95		51		88		30		19		10		7		3		8		8		21		340	

TABLE 7.—ACCIDENTALS

Songs containing—	95		51		88		30		19		10		7		3		8		8		21		340	
No accidentals	79	*83*	45	*88*	74	*84*	20	*66*	18	*94*	9	*90*	6	*86*	3	*100*	7	*87.5*	8	*100*	19	*90*	288	*85*
Seventh raised a semitone	1	*1*	1	*2*	1	*1*															1	*5*	4	*1*
Sixth raised a semitone	2	*2*	1	*2*	1	*1*	5	*16*															9	*3*
Fourth raised a semitone	1	*1*					1	*3*															2	
Third raised a semitone									1	*5*													1	
Second raised a semitone			1		2		1	*3*															3	*1*
Fourth and seventh raised a semitone							1	*3*															1	
Fourth raised a semitone and second lowered a semitone					1		1						1	*14*									1	
Second raised a semitone and sixth lowered a semitone							1	*3*															1	
Seventh lowered a semitone					1		1	*1*													1		1	
Sixth lowered a semitone	5	*5*	2		6		7		1	*6*	1	*10*											16	*5*
Fifth lowered a semitone	1	*1*					1																1	
Fourth lowered a semitone	1	*1*	1		1																		2	
Third lowered a semitone	2	*2*			2		2	*2*															3	*1*
Second lowered a semitone	3	*3*			2		2	*2*							1	*12.5*							6	*2*
Second, third, and sixth lowered a semitone					1		1	*1*															1	
Total	95		51		88		30		19		10		7		3		8		8		21		340	

¹ These songs are minor in tonality, the mediant being a minor third from the tonic and the submediant a minor sixth from the tonic. In the fourth five-toned scale the seventh and fourth are also omitted, but the corresponding intervals are major and the songs are major in tonality (see analysis of No. 83).

MELODIC ANALYSIS—continued

TABLE 8.—STRUCTURE

	Mide' songs No.	Per cent.	Dream songs No.	Per cent.	War songs No.	Per cent.	Love songs No.	Per cent.	Moccasin game songs No.	Per cent.	Woman's dance songs No.	Per cent.	Begging dance songs No.	Per cent.	Pipe dance songs No.	Per cent.	Songs connected with gifts No.	Per cent.	Songs for the entertainment of children No.	Per cent.	Unclassified songs No.	Per cent.	Total No.	Per cent.
Harmonic[1]	22	23	25	49	17	19	2	7	8	42					1	33	3	38	1	13	4	20	83	24
Melodic with harmonic framework[2]			8	16	22	25							2	28							3	14	35	10
Purely melodic[3]	73	77	18	35	49	56	28	93	11	58	10	100	5	72	2	67	5	62	7	87	14	66	222	66
Total	95		51		88		30		19		10		7		3		8		8		21		340	

TABLE 9.—FIRST PROGRESSION—DOWNWARD AND UPWARD

	Mide' songs No.	Per cent.	Dream songs No.	Per cent.	War songs No.	Per cent.	Love songs No.	Per cent.	Moccasin game songs No.	Per cent.	Woman's dance songs No.	Per cent.	Begging dance songs No.	Per cent.	Pipe dance songs No.	Per cent.	Songs connected with gifts No.	Per cent.	Songs for the entertainment of children No.	Per cent.	Unclassified songs No.	Per cent.	Total No.	Per cent.
Downward	84	88	39	77	59	66	15	50	9	53	5	50	4	57	2	67	4	50	4	50	13	60	238	70
Upward	11	12	12	24	29	34	15	50	10	47	5	50	3	43	1	33	4	50	4	50	8	40	102	30
Total	95		51		88		30		19		10		7		3		8		8		21		340	

TABLE 10.—TOTAL NUMBER OF PROGRESSIONS—DOWNWARD AND UPWARD

	Mide' songs No.	Per cent.	Dream songs No.	Per cent.	War songs No.	Per cent.	Love songs No.	Per cent.	Moccasin game songs No.	Per cent.	Woman's dance songs No.	Per cent.	Begging dance songs No.	Per cent.	Pipe dance songs No.	Per cent.	Songs connected with gifts No.	Per cent.	Songs for the entertainment of children No.	Per cent.	Unclassified songs No.	Per cent.	Total No.	Per cent.
Downward	1,307	67	872	66	1,362	65	721	64	329	63	160	66	111	67	16	64	114	66	95	59	335	64	5,422	65
Upward	630	33	459	34	717	35	412	36	190	37	81	34	55	33	9	36	60	34	66	41	185	36	2,864	35
Total	1,937		1,331		2,079		1,133		519		241		166		25		174		161		520		8,286	

[1] Songs are thus classified if contiguous accented tones bear a simple chord-relation to each other.
[2] Songs are thus classified if only a portion of the contiguous accented tones bear a chord-relation to each other.
[3] Songs are thus classified if contiguous accented tones do not bear a simple chord-relation to each other.

TABLE 11.—INTERVALS IN DOWNWARD PROGRESSION

(Italic figures are percentages)

Interval of a—	1	2	3	4	5	6	7	8	9	10	11	Total
Second	577 *44*	297 *34*	661 *50*	396 *55*	123 *38*	78 *49*	66 *60*	7 *44*	69 *60*	37 *40*	171 *50*	2,472 *42*
Major third	202 *16*	140 *16*	128 *9*	37 *5*	40 *12*	25 *16*	6 *5*	3 *19*	3 *2*	9 *9*	35 *10*	628 *11*
Minor third	480 *36*	363 *41*	463 *34*	174 *24*	108 *30*	41 *25*	29 *26*	4 *25*	31 *28*	27 *28*	104 *30*	1,824 *34*
Fourth	46 *3*	60 *7*	102 *7*	87 *12*	44 *13*	14 *9*	7 *6*	1 *6*	11 *9*	16 *17*	33 *10*	421 *8*
Fifth	2	8 *1*	4	21 *3*	11 *4*	2 *1*	2 *1*	1 *6*		6 *6*	2	59 *1*
Sixth		3	4	2	2		1 *1*					12
Seventh		1			1							2
Octave				2								2
Ninth				1								1
Twelfth				1								1
Total	1,307	872	1,362	721	329	160	111	16	114	95	335	5,422

TABLE 12.—INTERVALS IN UPWARD PROGRESSION

(Italic figures are percentages)

Interval of a—	1	2	3	4	5	6	7	8	9	10	11	Total
Second	218 *35*	98 *22*	278 *38*	176 *43*	62 *33*	29 *36*	24 *44*	2	31 *51*	23 *35*	68 *38*	1,009 *35*
Major third	92 *15*	80 *18*	71 *10*	28 *7*	21 *11*	10 *12*	5 *9*	1	3 *5*	7 *11*	27 *14*	345 *12*
Minor third	178 *28*	174 *38*	219 *31*	69 *15*	45 *24*	21 *25*	10 *18*	2	15 *25*	15 *23*	52 *28*	800 *29*
Fourth	72 *12*	56 *12*	92 *13*	65 *14*	32 *17*	13 *16*	13 *24*		7 *12*	5 *8*	24 *13*	388 *14*
Fifth	44 *7*	35 *8*	34 *5*	47 *12*	13 *7*	4 *5*	3 *5*		3 *5*	5 *8*	8 *4*	196 *7*
Sixth	11 *2*	8 *1*	9 *1*	8 *2*	6 *3*	2 *2*				1	1	47 *2*
Seventh	2		4	2	1							9
Octave	2	4	10 *1*	9 *2*	9 *5*	2 *2*			1	3	3	43 *1*
Ninth	1			1							2	2
Tenth	1											4
Eleventh	3											3
Twelfth		4		7 *2*	1							17
Fourteenth												1
Total	630	459	717	412	190	81	55	9	60	66	185	2,864

MELODIC ANALYSIS—continued

TABLE 13.—AVERAGE NUMBER OF SEMITONES IN EACH INTERVAL

Class of songs	Number of songs	Total number of intervals	Total number of semitones	Average number of semitones in each interval
Mide' songs	95	1,937	5,598	2.9
Dream songs	51	1,331	4,320	3.1
War songs	88	2,079	6,247	3
Love songs	30	1,133	3,888	3.4
Moccasin game songs	19	519	1,841	3.5
Woman's dance songs	10	241	759	3.1
Begging dance songs	7	166	485	2.9
Pipe dance songs	3	25	88	3.5
Songs connected with gifts	8	174	485	2.2
Songs for entertainment of children	8	161	474	3
Unclassified	21	520	1,606	3
Total	340	8,286	25,791	3.1

TABLE 14.—KEY

	Bulletin 45								Present work							
	Major		Minor		Beginning major, ending minor		Beginning minor, ending major		Major		Minor		Beginning major, ending minor		Total	
	No.	Per cent.	No.	Per cent.	No.	Per cent.	No.	Per cent.	No.	Per cent.	No.	Per cent.	No.	Per cent.	No.	Per cent.
Key of—																
A major	10	5							9	5					19	6
A minor			12	6							6	4			18	5
B flat major	6	3							11	7					17	5

Key															Total
B flat minor		1		2		4		6					*2*		6
B major	*1*	1		11		6		7					*2*		7
B minor	*3*	5		9		8						*4*		*5*	17
C major	*3*	6		10		11						*2*		*3*	13
C minor	*2*	3		7		4						*2*		*3*	13
D flat major	*2*	3		6		6						*3*		*5*	17
C sharp minor	*3*	5		2		1		5				*7*		*4*	14
D major	*11*	19		8		10							*2*		*3*	7
D minor	*11*	19		3		4		11				*1*		*3*	12
E flat major	*11*	19		5		17		3						*5*	9
E flat minor	*4*	7				10		2					*9*		17
E major								6		1		*1*		*2*	6
E minor								8					*7*		*9*	5
F major									*1*	1			*3*		29
F minor									*1*	1				*7*	10
G flat major												*2*		*11*	23
F sharp minor													*3*		6
G major														*3*	36
G minor														*5*	11
A flat major													*11*		*3*	17
G sharp minor															8
Beginning major, ending minor															2
Beginning minor, ending major															1
Total		103		75		2				97		62		1	340

RHYTHMIC ANALYSIS

TABLE 15.—PART OF MEASURE ON WHICH SONG BEGINS

	Mĭde' songs		Dream songs		War songs		Love songs		Moccasin game songs		Woman's dance songs		Begging dance songs		Pipe dance songs		Songs connected with gifts		Songs for the entertainment of children		Unclassified songs		Total	
	No.	Per cent.	No.	Per cent.	No.	Per cent.	No.	Per cent.	No.	Per cent.	No.	Per cent.	No.	Per cent.	No.	Per cent.	No.	Per cent.	No.	Per cent.	No.	Per cent.	No.	Per cent.
Beginning on accented parts of measure	25	47	38	74	51	58	17	51	17	89	9	90	4	57	3	100	7	87	4	50	14	67	189	63
Beginning on unaccented parts of measure	28	53	13	26	37	42	13	43	2	11	1	10	3	43			1	13	4	50	7	33	109	37
Transcribed in outline	42																						42	
Total	95		51		88		30		19		10		7		3		8		8		21		340	

TABLE 16.—RHYTHM OF FIRST MEASURE

	Mĭde' songs		Dream songs		War songs		Love songs		Moccasin game songs		Woman's dance songs		Begging dance songs		Pipe dance songs		Songs connected with gifts		Songs for the entertainment of children		Unclassified songs		Total	
	No.	Per cent.	No.	Per cent.	No.	Per cent.	No.	Per cent.	No.	Per cent.	No.	Per cent.	No.	Per cent.	No.	Per cent.	No.	Per cent.	No.	Per cent.	No.	Per cent.	No.	Per cent.
First measure in—																								
2–4 time	22	42	28	55	45	51	15	50	9	47	4	40	5	72	3	100	5	63	6	75	7	33	149	50
3–4 time	20	37	20	39	37	42	13	43	9	47	6	60	1	14			2	25	1	12.5	11	52	120	40
4–4 time	5	9	1	2					1	5.5							1	12			1	5	9	3
5–4 time	2	4	1	2	4	4	1	3													1	5	9	
6–4 time	1	2																					1	
7–4 time	1	2	1	2																			2	
3–8 time					2	2	1	3					1	14									4	
5–8 time																			1	12.5	1	5	2	
2–2 time	2	4																					2	
Transcribed in outline	42																						42	
Total	95		51		88		30		19		10		7		3		8		8		21		340	

Table 17.—CHANGE OF TIME

(Values are given as count (per cent). Columns are the song classes that together make up the total of 340.)

												Total
Songs having a change of time	39 (74)	48 (94)	58 (66)	25 (84)	12 (63)	6 (60)	6 (86)	3 (100)	5 (63)	7 (87)	20 (95)	229 (77)
Songs having no change of time	14 (26)	3 (6)	30 (34)	5 (16)	7 (37)	4 (40)	1 (14)		3 (37)	1 (13)	1 (5)	69 (23)
Transcribed in outline [1]	42											42
Total	95	51	88	30	19	10	7	3	8	8	21	340

Table 18.—RHYTHM OF DRUM

(Values are given as count (per cent). Columns correspond to the same song classes as in Table 17.)

												Total
Eighth notes accented in groups of two [2]			7 (9)				1 (14)	1 (33)	1 (12)			10 (4)
Eighth notes unaccented [3]	35 (95)	19 (38)	30 (42)						5 (63)			89 (39)
Quarter notes unaccented [4]			8 (11)								4 (21)	12 (5)
Half notes unaccented [5]									1 (12)			1
Each beat preceded by an unaccented beat corresponding to third count of a triplet [6]	2 (5)	31 (62)	25 (35)		14 (82)	9 (100)				2 (100)	13 (68)	96 (43)
Each beat followed by an unaccented beat corresponding to second count of a triplet [7]								2 (67)				2 (1)
Each beat preceded by an unaccented beat corresponding to the fourth count of group of four sixteenth notes [8]			2 (3)		3 (18)		6 (86)		1 (12)		2 (11)	14 (6)
Recorded without drum	58	1	16	30	2	1				6	2	116
Total	95	51	88	30	19	10	7	3	8	8	21	340

[1] Excluded in computing percentage.　[2] See No. 3.　[3] See No. 2.　[4] See No. 15.　[5] See No. 189, Bulletin 45.　[6] See No. 19.　[7] See No. 11.　[8] See No. 125.

RHYTHMIC ANALYSIS—continued

TABLE 19.—RHYTHMIC UNIT OF SONG [1]

	Mide' songs		Dream songs		War songs		Love songs		Moccasin game songs		Woman's dance songs		Begging dance songs		Pipe dance songs		Songs connected with gifts		Songs for the entertainment of children		Unclassified songs		Total	
	No.	Per cent.	No.	Per cent.	No.	Per cent.	No.	Per cent.	No.	Per cent.	No.	Per cent.	No.	Per cent.	No.	Per cent.	No.	Per cent.	No.	Per cent.	No.	Per cent.	No.	Per cent.
Songs containing—																								
A rhythmic unit	46	87	26	51	61	70	16	53	6	33	4	40	3	43	2	67	5	62	3	38	14	66	186	62
Two rhythmic units			1	2	2	2	1	3													1	5	4	2
Three rhythmic units							1																1	
No rhythmic units	7	13	24	47	25	28	13	43	13	67	6	60	4	57	1	33	3	38	5	62	6	29	107	37
Transcribed in outline	42																						²42	
Total	95		51		88		30		19		10		7		3		8		8		21		340	

TABLE 20.—METRIC UNIT OF VOICE

Metronome	Mide' songs	Dream songs	War songs	Love songs	Moccasin game songs	Woman's dance songs	Begging dance songs	Pipe dance songs	Songs connected with gifts	Songs for entertainment of children	Unclassified songs	Total	
												Number	Per cent.
44	1											1	
50				1								1	
52	1			2								2	
54	1			1								2	
56			1									1	
60	5			2								9	3
63				2	1						1	4	1

M. M.												Total	
66	1		1	3	1							5	2
69	3	1	3		1				1			8	3
72	5	3	2	3					1	1	1	16	5
76	2	1	4	2						1	2	11	4
80	2	1	4						1	1	1	11	4
84	4	3	2	2	3						1	14	5
88	1		6	4	1						2	15	5
92	2	2	6	2	3	1					1	16	6
96	2	6	6		2	1	3			3	2	22	7
100	3	4	6		1	1	2		2		1	18	6
104	4	6	7		1	3				2		20	7
108	3	9	4	1		2						18	6
112		3	5		1							18	6
116	1	5	4		1						2	10	8
120	2		3			1	1	1			2	14	5
126	1		5									7	2
132		2	1	1							1	3	1
138	1		1									2	
144	1	1	3						1			7	2
152	3	1	1	1							1	5	2
160	1		3					1				9	3
168	5		7	1	2			1			2	13	4
176	2	1										3	1
184												3	1
192	1		2			1	1	1	1	1	1	5	2
200			1	2				1	1	1		6	2
208												2	
Tempo rubato												²2	
Transcribed in outline	37											²37	
Total	95	51	88	30	19	10	7	3	8	8	21	340	

¹ For the purpose of this analysis a rhythmic unit is defined as "a group of tones of various lengths, comprising more than one count of a measure, occurring at least twice in a song, and having an evident influence on the rhythm of the entire song."

² Excluded in computing percentage.

NOTE.—Average metric unit of voice in 301 songs, 107 M. M.

RHYTHMIC ANALYSIS—continued

TABLE 21.—METRIC UNIT OF DRUM

Metronome	Mide' songs	Dream songs	War songs	Love songs	Moccasin game songs	Woman's dance songs	Begging dance songs	Pipe dance songs	Songs connected with gifts	Songs for entertainment of children	Unclassified songs	Total Number	Total Per cent
72		1	1						1			1	
76		2	2									2	
80			2		1		1		1	1	3	9	4
84		2	3				3					4	2
88			6		1		1				2	8	2
92	5		5								2	15	7
96	4	3	6			1		2	1		3	15	7
100		8	12			1			2		1	15	7
104	1	5	11		1				3			26	11
108	4	7	7		3	1					1	25	11
112	4	6	4		4	1	1				1	25	11
116	3	8	4		2	2				1	3	21	9
120	2	4	5		3	2					3	22	10
126	4	1	3									13	6
132	5	2	3		2	1	1					13	6
138	1	1						1				4	2
144	1											2	
152	2											2	1
160			1									1	
176	1											1	
Recorded without drum	58	1	16	30	2	1				6	2	116	
Total	95	51	88	30	19	10	7	3	8	8	21	340	

NOTE.—Average metric unit of drum in 224 songs, 109 M. M.

TABLE 22.—COMPARISON OF METRIC UNIT OF VOICE AND DRUM

	Mide' songs		Dream songs		War songs		Love songs		Moccasin game songs		Woman's dance songs		Begging dance songs		Pipe dance songs		Songs connected with gifts		Songs for the entertainment of children		Unclassified songs		Total	
	No.	Per cent.	No.	Per cent.	No.	Per cent.	No.	Per cent.	No.	Per cent.	No.	Per cent.	No.	Per cent.	No.	Per cent.	No.	Per cent.	No.	Per cent.	No.	Per cent.	No.	Per cent.
Metric unit of voice and drum the same	7	19	18	36	26	36			3	18	5	56	3	43	3	100	4	50	1	50	10	53	80	36
Drum faster than voice	19	51	26	52	32	44			14	82	4	44	3	43			4	50			1	5	103	46
Drum slower than voice	11	30	6	12	14	20							1	14					1	50	8	42	41	18
Recorded without drum	58		1		16		30		2		1								6		2		[1]116	
Total	95		51		88		30	100	19		10		7		3		8		8		21		340	

[1] Excluded in computing percentage.

GROUP ANALYSIS OF 340 SONGS

One purpose of the following analysis is to determine whether there is any evidence of connection between the motive which prompts the singing of a song and the form assumed by the song. For this test the origin and use of the song will be considered. The songs most nearly related in origin are the Mĭde′, the dream, and the war songs, as many songs said to have been "composed in dreams" were used in the ceremonies and practices of the Mĭde′ and also on the warpath. The songs classified as "dream songs" were given as such by the singers. No special use was assigned them, and they were probably used by individuals in dances until they gradually became general throughout the tribe, usually after the death of the composers.

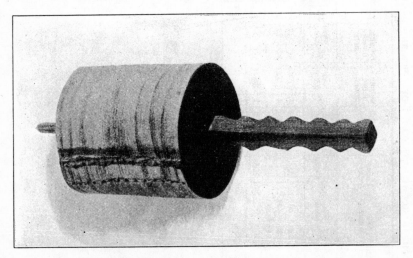

FIG. 1. Mĭde′ rattle.

GRAND MEDICINE SONGS (MĬDE′ NA′GÛMOWĬ′NÛÑ)

This group comprises Nos. 1–90 in Bulletin 45, and Nos. 154, 155, 156, 174, 175, of the present work. The Mĭde′wĭwĭn (Grand Medicine) was the embodiment of the native religion of the Chippewa and has many adherents at the present time (1912), new members being admitted and others advanced to higher degrees in the order. Many characteristics of the Mĭde′ songs are given in Bulletin 45 (pp. 14–20). The musical instruments accompanying the songs are described on pages 11–12, and illustrated in plates 1 and 2, of that work. The Mĭde′ rattles shown in Bulletin 45 are of wood, with sewed covers of untanned hide. In figure 1 above is shown a similar rattle, but made entirely of wood, which formerly belonged to a prominent member of the Mĭde′wĭwĭn at Waba′cĭñg (see p. 251). The principal classes of the Mĭde′ songs are those of the initiation ceremony and those con-

nected with special "medicines." The latter are sung by members
of the Mĭde'wĭwĭn in connection with the use of medicines for the
curing of the sick or the working of charms, and also in the dances
which follow the meetings of members, either for a feast or an initiation. Throughout these songs the element of affirmation is very
strong; indeed, many have a triumphant tone. The idea underlying
them all is the securing of a definite result through supernatural power,
the music being an indispensable factor. In the initiation the desired
end was the transference of "spirit power" to the candidate by the
men and women who were initiating him, also the renewal of the same
power in the members of the order who witnessed the ceremony, and
the prolonging of their lives to old age. In the songs connected with
special "medicines" the purpose to be accomplished was the healing
of the sick and the producing of a certain effect on one or more persons, as in the use of various "charms." Thus it is seen that this
purpose was usually objective, the effect on the singer being only
secondary, that the means of securing benefit was supernatural, and
that the singer had full confidence in its bestowal as well as in its
efficacy.

In the first table of analysis it is noted that 72 per cent of the
Mĭde' songs are major in tonality, this proportion being the same as
in the songs of the begging dance, and exceeded only by the group of
dream songs, which contains 76 per cent of major songs. The proportion of songs beginning on the dominant (either the twelfth or the
fifth) is 70 per cent, the largest of any except the begging dance songs,
which contain 71 per cent, the dream, the love, and the moccasin
game songs ranging from 52 to 56 per cent. Of songs beginning on
the octave, however, the Mĭde' songs contain only 12 per cent, which
is less than the proportion of most groups, and about half that of the
dream and the war songs. Sixty-three per cent end on the tonic,
six groups showing a larger proportion. The feeling for the dominant
is again made evident in the compass of the songs, 50 per cent having
a range of either 12 or 5 tones, which is much larger than in any other
group. In songs having a range of an octave, however, the Mĭde'
songs show only 22 per cent, while the love songs contain 37 per cent
and the pipe dance songs 67 per cent

In tone material the Mĭde' songs are below most other groups in the
number of songs on the five-toned scales, showing only 33 per cent,
while other groups range from 39 to 51 per cent. The Mĭde' songs
show the largest percentage, with one exception, in the songs having
the octave complete except the seventh, namely, 14 per cent of the
number, the allied groups being the war songs with 13 per cent, and
the begging dance songs, which show 28 per cent. In purely melodic
structure this group contains 77 per cent, a larger percentage than any

other except the love songs, woman's dance songs, and songs for the entertainment of children. The proportion of songs having the first progression a downward interval is 88 per cent, which is much larger than in any other group. The percentage of downward progression in the entire group of songs is the same as in the begging dance songs and larger than in any other group. In the number of descending minor thirds this group is exceeded only by the dream songs, and in the ascending minor thirds by the dream and the war songs. The average interval is the same as in the begging dance songs, being 2.9 semitones, the average of the entire series being 3.1 semitones, or a tenth of a semitone more than a minor third. This group is lowest of all in songs beginning on the accented part of the measure, and lower than most groups in songs beginning in 2–4 or 3–4 time.

The drum-rhythm of all these songs is a rapid, unaccented beat which occurs in no other group except the war songs. The proportion of songs containing a rhythmic unit is larger in this than in any other group. Table 22 shows the percentage of songs in which the drum is faster than the voice to be larger in this than in any other group except the dream and the moccasin game songs, the former being 1 per cent and the latter 31 per cent greater.

Here, then, is a group of songs known to be used as a means for accomplishing a purpose, namely, the securing of a definite effect, usually on a person other than the singer, by supernatural power; and the characteristics of this group are found to resemble the begging dance songs more frequently than they do any other group. A prevailing major tonality is noted, and the feeling for the dominant is more marked than for the tonic; the songs open with less directness of "attack" than others, but contain a rhythmic unit more frequently than other groups. The expression is freely melodic, downward in trend, and is characterized by the interval of the minor third. A drumbeat faster than the metric unit of the voice is noted in songs of controlled excitement, and 51 per cent of these songs show this peculiarity. This is evident also in the moccasin game songs, and is found in war song No. 30.

In the Mïde′ songs are found peculiarities which may be connected with the motive and the mental state of the singer: (1) The rhythmic unit suggesting a definite, crystalized idea; (2) the major tonality, a confidence in securing the desired end; (3) a preference for the dominant, the unaccented initial tone, and the freely melodic form, all suggesting an indirect approach; and (4) the rapid drumbeat which is, in many instances, associated with controlled excitement.

For the rhythmic units of the Mïde′ songs see pages 309–313.

DREAM SONGS (INA'BÛNDJĬGAÑ' NA'GŬMOWĬ'NÛÑ)[1]

This group comprises Nos. 108–121 of Bulletin 45 and Nos. 94–104 and 128–153 of the present work. The songs in this group are not composed (in the usual sense of the term) but are said to have "come to the mind of the Indian when he was in a dream." We can not fully understand this dream or trance of the Indian; we can only accept his statement that by isolation and fasting he was able to induce a certain condition in which he "saw a vision" and "composed a song." In the belief of the Indian fasting is a condition essential to certain classes of musical composition. It is a well-known fact that in a condition of inanition the brain enters on a phase of abnormal activity akin to that produced by narcotic stimulants. The composition of songs during or immediately following an abnormal mental state has been noted among other Indian tribes. Thus, for instance, Mr. James Mooney states that "persons taking part in the ghost dance voluntarily sought the trance condition, and on emerging from that condition frequently embodied the story of their vision in a song."

In some instances the Chippewa stated that they sang songs heard in their dreams; thus in the description of No. 112, Bulletin 45, the man said that he "sang a song which he heard the trees singing," and in No. 119, in the same bulletin, he "repeated the song which the crows sang." Nos. 94–99 of the present work are supposed to be the "songs" of the thunderbird, the deer, and the buffalo, which the man saw in his dream. Nos. 1, 102, 103, and 104 of the present work are said to have been learned from manido', which appeared in human form to the dreamer. Mention of the manifestations of nature occur in many dream songs; these are considered on page 16.

It is noted that 16 per cent of the dream songs relate to flight through the air. The sensation of aviation in dreams, due to some disturbance of the nervous equilibrium, is not an uncommon phenomenon.

In the circumstances attending both the composition and the use of the dream songs the underlying idea was that of expectancy and acquirement. To the Indian a "vision" was more to be desired than any material thing. Through the vision he was assured of supernatural aid which would enable him to succeed in life, and the song was one of the means by which he summoned that aid in his hour of need. Considering this idea of acquirement, so closely associated with the dream songs, it is not surprising to find them, in analysis, allied to the woman's dance songs and the songs con-

---

[1] The writer gratefully acknowledges the assistance of Dr. Aleš Hrdlička, curator of physical anthropology, United States National Museum, and of Mr. James Mooney of the Bureau of American Ethnology, in studying the relation between physiological conditions and musical expression.

nected with gifts. One of the principal features of the woman's dance is the presenting of gifts, an invitation to dance being accompanied by a gift. Frequently these gifts are valuable articles, as ponies, rifles, and beaded garments, and the dancers wait with pleasurable expectancy to know what presents will be bestowed on them.

At this dance the writer has often observed the interest with which the Indians watch a man who rises and walks across the dancing circle with an attractive gift in his hand. The feeling is expressed in song No. 177, Bulletin 45, which contains the words, "I have been waiting a long time for you to come over." There is some similarity between this and the mental state of the man who patiently awaits the coming of a supernatural visitant. The songs connected with gifts are sung at the social dances and are frequently interspersed with woman's dance songs. If the gift is so large as to require special celebration these gift songs are used. Some of them accompany the giving and some the receiving of the gift, but all concern an actual event and have not the element of expectancy associated with many of the woman's dance songs.

Among the dream songs the proportion in major tonality is 4 per cent larger than in any other group, comprising 76 per cent, the songs of the Mïde′ and of the begging dance each showing 72 per cent. This group is largest also in songs beginning on the twelfth, the group of love songs ranking next in this respect. The Mïde′, however, contains the highest percentage of songs beginning on the dominant, comprising a large number of songs beginning on that interval but having a compass of less than 12 tones. The number of dream songs beginning on the octave is 1 per cent greater than in the Mïde′ but less than half the proportion shown by the war songs. Further resemblance to the Mïde′ is shown in the ending of the songs, 63 per cent ending on the tonic, as in the Mïde′, though seven other groups show a larger percentage. Thirty-seven per cent of the songs have a compass of 12 tones, as in the Mïde′, the highest proportion except in the woman's dance songs, 40 per cent of which have this compass. In tone material this group shows a difference from the Mïde′ and a similarity to certain other groups, 51 per cent of the songs being based on the five-toned scales while the Mïde′ shows only 33 per cent based on these scales; the allied groups are the woman's dance songs, the songs connected with gifts, and the songs for the entertainment of children, 50 per cent of each being on the five-toned scales. The proportion of songs containing only the tones of the major triad and sixth is the largest except in the pipe dance, constituting 26 per cent of the number. The proportion of songs containing the octave complete except the seventh is only 2 per cent, in contrast with 14 per cent in the Mïde′. The dream songs differ widely in structure from the Mïde′ songs, 49 per cent being harmonic and 16 per cent melodic with harmonic framework (a class in which many songs are harmonic except for one measure); thus, 65 per cent of the dream songs are harmonic in feeling, compared with 23 per cent in the Mïde′ and 44 per cent in the war songs. In the proportion of songs beginning with a downward progression this group is next to the Mïde′, 77 per cent beginning thus. In total number of downward progressions this group shows 66 per cent, the same as the woman's dance songs and the songs connected with gifts. The proportion of minor thirds in both ascending and descending progression is much larger in this than in any other group. The average interval is the same as in the woman's dance—3.1 semitones, this being also the average interval of the entire series. The beginnings of these songs are more direct than in the Mïde′, 74 per cent beginning on the accented part of the measure, contrasted with 47 per cent in the Mïde′, while the proportion of songs beginning in double time is larger than in either the Mïde′ or the war songs, comprising 55 per cent of the number. The time is more variable in this than in any other group except the unclassified songs, 94 per cent of the songs containing a change of time. A triple drum-rhythm is found in 62 per cent, the same percentage as in the songs connected with gifts. A rhythmic unit occurs in a majority of the songs. Both voice and drum have in general a rapid metric unit; in 52 per cent the drum is faster than the voice, a larger proportion than in any except the moccasin game songs.

The structure of the dream songs is more centralized than that of the Mïde′ songs, the harmonic form and the large percentage of songs on the five-toned scales referring the tones distinctly to a keynote. In a general sense it may be said that the Mïde′ songs were used for the purpose of affecting persons other than the singers, while in the dream songs constituting this group (with the exception of the "doctor's songs") the purpose was to secure an advantage more or less personal. The analysis shows that in some respects this group resembles the Mïde′ songs and in other respects shows similarity to the songs of the woman's dance and the songs connected with gifts. The dream songs are even more strongly marked by major tonality than are those of the Mïde′, which they resemble in the prominence of the dominant, but they are different from the Mïde′ and allied to the songs of the woman's dance and the songs connected with gifts, in the harmonic form, the proportion of songs on the five-toned scales, the proportion of upward and downward progressions, the average interval, the accented beginning, and the triple drum-rhythm.

The rhythmic units occurring in the dream songs are given on pages 314–317.

WAR SONGS (MIGA′DIWĬN′ NA′GÛMOWĬ′NÛÑ)

This group comprises Nos. 122–132 and 154–172 in Bulletin 45, and Nos. 1–50, 63–66, and 80–93 of the present work. On the warpath these songs were accompanied by a small drum (see pl. 7). At the dances in the village, preceding the departure and after the return of a war party, a large drum was used and the drummers were seated around it. In recent years the war songs are sung at the social dances of the tribe, accompanied by a drum similar to that used in the Drum-presentation Ceremony (see pl. 18), but, according to the writer's observation, less elaborately decorated.

The war songs are of four kinds—the dream songs of individual warriors, the songs concerning war charms and medicines (these two having a connection with the supernatural element), the songs of the conduct of the war expedition, and those which commemorated its success (the last having no supernatural element). It is said that "in the old days no warrior would have dared sing a war song that was not composed in a dream," referring of course to the first two classes of war songs. The third class includes the songs of the war messenger, the dog feast, and the departure of the war party, and the fourth class includes the songs which were composed by a returning war party or in the victory dances which followed a successful expedition. The boundaries between these classes of songs are not strongly marked, and this division should be understood therefore as general in character.

Fifty per cent of the war songs are major in tonality, the same proportion as in the songs for the entertainment of children. The proportion of war songs beginning on the octave is 27 per cent, the largest of any except the love songs. Seventy per cent of the songs end on the tonic, the same proportion as in the woman's dance, but larger than in the Mĭde′ or in the dream songs. Seventy-six per cent of the songs have a compass of ten or more tones, being exceeded only by the dream and the moccasin game songs, which contain 77 per cent having that range. The percentage of songs on the five-toned scales is less than that of five other groups, but the proportion of songs containing the octave complete except the seventh is larger than in any other group except the Mĭde′ and the begging dance. The sixth lowered a semitone occurs more frequently in this than in any other group. The purely melodic songs comprise 56 per cent, and the allied class of melodic songs with harmonic framework comprise 25 per cent, showing the war songs to be largely melodic in structure, the proportion being exceeded only in the love songs, woman's dance songs, and songs for the entertainment of children. In 66 per cent of the songs the first progression is downward. The number of intervals of a second is much above the average, showing freedom of melodic movement. The average interval is one-tenth of a semitone below the average interval of the entire series of songs. Fifty-one per cent of the songs begin in double time, but this is not steadily maintained, 66 per cent of the songs containing a change of time. The triple rhythm is said to be the drum-rhythm of the victory dance, commonly known as the scalp dance; but this is found in only 35 per cent of the war songs, 42 per cent showing the even beats which characterize the Mïde′ (see footnote, p. 10). Seventy-one per cent contain a rhythmic unit, the largest proportion except in the Mïde′. The metric unit of the voice is rapid, and that of the drum is of medium rapidity; the drum is faster than the voice in only 44 per cent of the songs, the same proportion as in the begging dance and the woman's dance, and much less than in the Mïde′ and the dream songs.

The group of war songs is probably less homogeneous than any other, and its correspondences to other groups are diverse. The relation to the Mïde′ songs seems stronger than any other, being both melodic and rhythmic; there is also a melodic correspondence with the dream songs, the relation to these two groups being attributable to the common element of communication with the supernatural. Both the Mïde′ and war songs are principally melodic in structure, but the feeling is for the dominant in the former and for the tonic and its octave in the latter. Definiteness of idea and assurance of success are suggested by the prominence of the rhythmic unit and the major tonality. The correspondence with the woman's dance may come from the fact that this dance was a favorite one during the periods of peace between the Chippewa and the Sioux. It was said to have been given to the Chippewa by the Sioux. The begging dance also was received from the Sioux, and with that group the war songs show both melodic and rhythmic correspondence. The relation to the moccasin game songs is only in the compass, which may be attributed to the element of excitement in both groups; this element does not affect, however, the tempo of the war songs or the relative speed of voice and drum, as it appears to do in the moccasin game songs. Regarded as a whole, the characteristics of the war songs are control, definiteness, and a strong centralization, the melody tones being referable to a keynote in a greater degree than in many other groups of songs.

The rhythmic units occurring in the war songs will be found on pages 318–325.

LOVE SONGS (SA′GIÏ′DIWĬN′ NA′GŮMOWĬ′NŮÑ)

This group comprises Nos. 133–141 and 163–167 of Bulletin 45 and Nos. 105–113, 157–160, 170, 177, and 178 of the present work, the "love-charm songs" of the Mïde′ not being included. The love songs were unaccompanied by any instrument, but lovers frequently played on a musical instrument commonly called a flute, but similar in construction to a flageolet, being blown at the end instead of at the side.[1] The instrument is called *bĭbĭ'gwûn*. (See pl. 2.) This instrument was procured at Lac du Flambeau, from a middle-aged woman, who said it had belonged to her grandfather. It is 21½ inches long and 1⅛ inches in diameter. A test of the instrument shows its lowest tone to be about a quarter tone above G, second line, treble clef; in the octave above this the tones are clear, but in the second octave the instrument does not respond. It is worthy of note that the fourth produced by this instrument was less accurate than other intervals and that the seventh was very faulty and not a clear tone. Uncertain intonation on the fourth and seventh is noted in Bulletin 45, pages 4–5. The following melody, played on this instrument, was furnished by Rev. C. H. Beaulieu; it is said to be very old.

Attention is directed to the prominence of the subdominant, which has been found to characterize 11 per cent of the love songs (see No. 106).

The love songs of the Chippewa are plaintive in character, usually expressing sadness and disappointment. Thirty of these songs have been recorded and only one of this number is inspired by happiness (No. 177). The words of seven are not transcribed. In most instances the words, which are continuous throughout the melody, were not accurately repeated in the repetitions of the songs, but it has usually been possible to give a free translation indicating the character of the words. Only one love song expresses a promise and one a request, six concern the departure of a lover, and five concern loss and longing. Two express jealousy and offense, two fickleness, and two relate to an attempt to drown disappointment in drink. It has been already stated that the words of the love songs are sometimes impromptu, and that new words are sometimes fitted to old tunes, the general idea remaining the same. Expression by means of a combination of words and music is much more free in the love songs than in any other group, and they may be said to constitute a distinct phase of musical culture and practice.

Although these songs are indicative of an unhappy state of mind, 40 per cent of them are major in tonality. In this group the percentage of songs beginning on the octave is larger than in any other except the war songs. Eighty-six per cent begin on either the tonic, octave, or dominant, nearest to this being the songs of the begging dance, which show 85 per cent, and of the moccasin game, 84 per cent.

[1] Contributions to the History of Musical Scales, by Charles Kasson Wead, in *Report U. S. National Museum*, 1900, p. 426, Washington, 1902.

FLAGEOLET (LOVER'S FLUTE)

The proportion of songs ending on either the tonic or dominant is 93 per cent, larger than in any other group except the pipe dance songs and the songs for the entertainment of children. Ninety-seven per cent of the love songs have a compass of an octave or more, and four songs have a range of 14 tones.

The love songs have the highest percentage among songs containing all the tones of the octave, the begging dance songs ranking next; the omitted seventh, which characterizes the war songs, does not appear in this group, and the octave complete except the second occurs in 17 per cent of the number. The five-toned scales appear less frequently in this than in any other group. In accidentals the sixth is sharped more often than in any other group; the flat third, which we are accustomed to connect with the idea of sadness, does not appear, and the flatted sixth occurs only twice. Two songs have the third omitted, a peculiarity found to exist in several songs concerning women (see analysis of No. 53). Ninety-three per cent of the songs are purely melodic in structure, a proportion much higher than in any group except the woman's dance (100 per cent), the group nearest it being the songs for the entertainment of children, which contains 87 per cent of melodic songs. Half the love songs begin with an upward and half with a downward progression, the proportion being the same in the woman's dance, the gift songs, and the songs for the entertainment of children. The love songs, so eminently songs of sadness, contain a smaller percentage of minor thirds (in both ascending and descending progression) than any other group. The proportion of ascending fifths is much larger than in any other group, and seven ascending intervals of a twelfth are found, showing, as in the preceding Tables, a strong feeling for the dominant. The average interval is 3.4 semitones, the highest except in the moccasin game and the pipe dance songs, two classes comprising songs of a high degree of excitement, in which the average interval is 3.5. In contrast to this the metric unit of the voice is slow. The proportion of songs containing a change of time is much above the average, and most of the songs do not contain a rhythmic unit.

The interval of the twelfth is prominent, showing a feeling for the second overtone as in the Mïde'; it will be recalled that the war songs show the first overtone, which is the octave. Completeness and freedom of expression are suggested by the melodic form, the large compass, and the use of all the tones of the octave; an element of excitement by the largeness of the average interval, and an element of control by the slow metric unit, while a lack of definitely formed thought is suggested by the small percentage containing a rhythmic unit.

For the rhythmic units occurring in the love songs see pages 325–327.

MOCCASIN GAME SONGS (MAKIZĬN'ATA'DIWĬN' NA'GŬMOWĬ'NŬÑ)

This group comprises Nos. 142–145 and 168–176 of Bulletin 45, and Nos. 125, 126, 161–163, and 176 of the present work. It is said that in the old days most of the moccasin game songs were "composed in dreams" but only a few such are included in this series.

The instrument used to accompany these songs is a drum, specimens of which vary but little in size, provided usually with deerskin heads (see pl. 3).[1] With this drum is used an ordinary short drumstick the end of which is wound with cloth. Small pieces of tin are sometimes set in the frame of the moccasin game drum, to add a jingling effect.

In the analysis of these songs may be noted a large proportion in minor tonality, exceeded only by the songs of the woman's dance and the songs connected with gifts. Eighty-four per cent begin on, and all end on, either the tonic or dominant. None of the songs have a compass of less than an octave, resèmbling in this respect the woman's dance and the pipe dance songs. One-third of the songs are on the second five-toned scale, this being the largest proportion in the entire collection, the closest approximation being the woman's dance songs. The several five-toned scales comprise 43 per cent of the entire number, and apart from these the group presents a wide range of tone material. Only one song contains an accidental—the flat sixth. Forty-two per cent of the songs are harmonic in structure, the group being exceeded in this respect only by the dream songs. The percentage of descending minor thirds is below the average, notwithstanding so large a proportion of the songs is minor in tonality, this group resembling the love songs in this respect. The average interval, which is the same as in the pipe dance (3.5 semitones), is the largest in the entire series. Eighty-nine per cent of the moccasin game songs begin on the accented part of the measure, being exceeded in this respect only by the woman's dance songs with 90 per cent, and by the pipe dance songs with 100 per cent. With the exception of the woman's dance and the gift songs this group maintains the time throughout the song more steadily than any other group, a feature which is surprising in view of the excitement of the game. Thirty-three per cent of the songs contain a rhythmic unit, the percentage of songs in the entire series containing such unit being 62. In this the moccasin game songs are seen to be below the average, songs for

---

[1] The instrument here illustrated was obtained at White Earth; it is said to be very old. The cover has been renewed from time to time, the design being duplicated on the new cover, as in the instance of Odjĭb'we's war drum (p. 62). The diameter of the drum shown in plate 3 is 18½ inches, the thickness 2½ inches. A single piece of deerskin forms both heads; this is sewed with strips of hide on which some of the hair remains. Inside the drum are three tightly stretched cords, each provided with small pegs tied at equal distances. At the writer's request the former owner of the drum fastened a cord across an ordinary hoop (pl. 3) in the same manner as the cords are fastened inside the drum. The pegs are tied to the cord and before the cover of the drum is put in place the cord is twisted to increase the tension, permitting the pegs to vibrate against the deerskin.

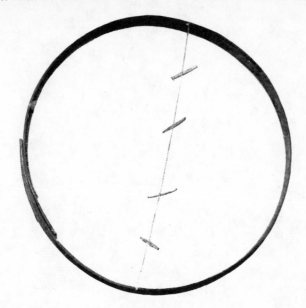

MOCCASIN GAME DRUM

The upper figure shows the arrangement of one of the three cords inside the drum together
with the pegs fastened thereto.

the entertainment of children (38 per cent having a rhythmic unit) ranking next. The rhythmic unit appears to represent a definitely formed thought and conveys that impression to the hearer. In this connection it will be noted that the chief concern of the moccasin game player is to give no clue to his thought, thus mentally eluding his opponents. A wide range is shown in the speed of both voice and drum, and in comparing the metric units of the two it is found that the drum is faster than the voice in 82 per cent of the songs, the percentage for the entire series being only 46.

Thus the moccasin game songs constitute a group which in some phases of analysis shows itself allied to the groups of dance songs (the woman's dance, the pipe dance, and the begging dance), though its songs were never used in dances. This resemblance is in the form of the song, not in the rhythm of the drum, which is peculiar to the moccasin game. It will be recalled that many dream songs and war songs were used in dances and that the phonograph records of those songs show a drum-rhythm similar to that of these three groups of dance songs, but many of the war songs and all the dream songs were essentially personal in character. The social element was strong in the moccasin game and in these three kinds of dances. The woman's dance and the begging dance were open to all the men and women, and the pipe dance is said to have been "the principal good-time dance" of the old Chippewa. In similar if not greater degree a moccasin game was a center of interest in the camp; it is said that "the whole tribe" always gathered around the players, watching the game and betting on the result. Thus the social element may be said to be the point of contact between the moccasin game and the dance groups. A resemblance to the love songs may be noted in the seeming discrepancy between the tonality and the character of the intervals. Perhaps it may be said that these two groups have in common a certain elusiveness and whimsical changeableness. Directness is shown in the accented beginnings of the songs and their endings on the tonic, but this is contradicted by the small percentage of songs containing a rhythmic unit. The rhythm of the drum is the usual moccasin game rhythm (see No. 125).

The rhythmic units occurring in the moccasin game songs are given on pages 327–328.

WOMAN'S DANCE SONGS (IKWE′NIMIWĬN′ NA′GŮMOWĬ′NŮÑ)

This group comprises Nos. 177–185 of Bulletin 45 and No. 164 of the present work.

The woman's dance is a social dance in which an invitation is usually accompanied by a gift. This dance is described in Bulletin 45 (p. 192) and is illustrated in plate 45 of the present work. The dance is said to have been acquired long ago from the Sioux, but the songs in this collection are supposed to have been composed by Chippewa. The drum used to accompany the woman's dance is the large drum similar to that used in the Drum-presentation Ceremony but less elaborately decorated.

Seventy per cent of the woman's songs are minor in tonality, this being the largest proportion of any group except the gift songs, which show 75 per cent. Half the songs begin on the dominant and one-fifth begin on the octave above the tonic. The proportion ending on the tonic exceeds the average of the series. Forty per cent have a range of an octave, and 40 per cent a range of a twelfth, this being the highest percentage in the group. Half the songs are on the five-toned scales, this proportion being the same as in the gift songs and in the songs for the entertainment of children. Only one song contains an accidental, and all the songs are purely melodic in structure, the love songs (93 per cent) being the nearest rivals in this respect. The upward and downward progressions are evenly divided, as in the love songs and in those for the entertainment of children. One-fourth of the intervals, in both ascending and descending progression, are minor thirds. It will be recalled that the moccasin game songs, with almost the same proportion of minor tonality, do not show so great prominence of minor thirds. The average interval is the same as the average for the entire series—3.1 semitones, the same interval being shown by the dream songs. In definiteness of beginning these songs exceed all except the songs of the pipe dance, 90 per cent beginning on the accented part of the measure. Continuity of measure-lengths is greater in this group than in any other, 40 per cent of the songs showing no change of time. The triple drum-rhythm occurs with all the songs. Considering the definiteness of beginning, the large proportion of songs ending on the tonic, and the steadily maintained length of the measures, it is surprising to find that the proportion of songs containing a rhythmic unit is the smallest except in songs of the moccasin game and for entertainment of children. The proportion of songs having the same metric unit of voice and drum is largest except in the pipe dance.

The rhythm of the woman's dance songs is particularly "catchy" and pleasing, but the element of what might be termed intellectuality does not enter into this merrymaking, and perhaps this lack is one of the factors essential to the development of a song from a small group of tones. In tonality we note a correspondence with the gift songs and recall that gifts were an important feature of the woman's dance. Simple pleasure allied this group to that of the pipe dance songs and the songs for the entertainment of children, and some corresponding characteristics are shown by the analysis.

The rhythmic units occurring in the woman's dance songs will be found on page 328.

BEGGING DANCE SONGS (BAGOSAÑ'NINGE'NIMIWĬN' NA'GŬMOWĬ'NŬÑ)

This group comprises Nos. 187 and 188 of Bulletin 45. and Nos. 114–118 of the present work.

The begging dance, like the woman's dance, is said to have been derived from the Sioux. In the writer's observation of this dance among both Chippewa and Sioux the large drum is used; this is carried by two or three men as the begging party goes from tent to tent. This dance is described in Bulletin 45 (p. 171) and its traditional origin is given on page 228 of the present work.

The percentage of these songs in major tonality is 72, the same as in the Mĭde' and 4 per cent less than in the dream songs. Seventy-one per cent begin on the dominant, resembling the Mĭde' songs, in which 70 per cent begin on the dominant. Fourteen per cent only begin on the tonic. The proportion of songs ending on the tonic is 24 per cent below the average (see Tables 2 and 3), indicating a slight feeling for the keynote. The percentage of songs beginning on the ninth is almost double that in any other group. The ninth is usually a tone of approach to the octave. The number of songs on the five-toned scales and the number with the octave complete except the seventh are equal. Only one song contains an accidental, and 72 per cent are purely melodic in structure, this being 6 per cent above the average. The percentage of downward progression is 67, the same as in the Mĭde', and the largest in the entire series. The percentage of ascending fourths is the largest in the series except in the pipe dance. This interval has been found to characterize songs concerning motion; it is considered in the analysis of song No. 22. The average interval of this group is the same as in the Mĭde', and is the smallest in the entire series except in the songs connected with gifts. The percentage of songs beginning in double time is the largest except in the pipe dance and the songs for the entertainment of children, and the time is more steadily maintained than in any except these groups and the unclassified songs. A small proportion of these songs contains a rhythmic unit, the related groups being the woman's dance and the songs for the entertainment of children. The number of songs having the same metric unit of voice and drum is the same as the number in which the drum is faster than the voice.

In the analysis of the Mĭde' songs a similarity between that group and the songs of the begging dance was noted and some correspondence of motive was traced. In the analysis of the begging dance songs are found similarities to the songs of the pipe dance and the woman's dance, the songs for the entertainment of children, and the songs connected with gifts; and some similarity of motive also can be traced between these groups. The purpose of the begging dance was, of course, the securing of gifts. Underlying the other three classes of songs is a strong element of pleasure and simple amusement. The woman's dance, with its exchange of gifts, is greatly enjoyed by the Chippewa, much interest surrounding the "return present," as everyone who is given a present is expected to return one of equal value. The pipe dance is a ludicrous pantomime, and the songs for the entertainment of children usually end in laughter. The element of pleasure is equally strong in the begging dance. The writer has seen a merry party going from tent to tent, singing the begging dance songs. This dance forms the great recreation in a camp. There is the discomfiture of the people who are not prepared with proper gifts of food (the recollection comes to the writer of a woman running after a begging dance party with a pail of maple sugar which she could not find when they were at her tent), and there is the pleasure of forcing people to give who are not disposed to be generous. Added to these factors is the delightful uncertainty as to the nature of the food to be bestowed and the pleasant anticipation of the varied feast to follow. No one acquainted with a Chippewa or a Sioux camp would be surprised at the resemblances shown in this analysis.

The rhythmic units of the begging dance songs are given on page 329.

PIPE DANCE SONGS (OPWA′GŪNINI′MINĬN NÀ′GŪMOWĬ′NŪÑ)

This group comprises Nos. 171, 172, and 173 of the present work. The pipe dance was performed solely for the merriment of the tribe. In its original form it passed out of existence long ago and only a few of its songs remain. The number of songs in this group is so small that the percentages are less significant than in other groups, but some general characteristics of the songs are shown by their analysis.

Most of the songs are major in tonality and begin on the third, but all end on the tonic. One song has a range of but four tones, the only one having a similar range being a dream song. The major triad forms the framework of two-thirds of the songs, none contain an accidental, two-thirds are purely melodic, and the downward progressions are much greater in number than the upward. The average interval is the same as in the moccasin game songs and the element of excitement was probably almost as great in one as in the other. All the songs begin on the accented part of the measure, all begin in double time, and all show a change of time. Two-thirds of the songs contain a rhythmic unit. Considering the element of excitement in the dance, it is surprising to find the metric unit of voice and drum the same in all the songs, none of the other groups showing a percentage of more than 56. This can scarcely be regarded as an original feature of the pipe dance music, but may suggest the mental attitude of the Indian at the present time.

For the rhythmic units occurring in these songs see page 329.

SONGS CONNECTED WITH GIFTS
(MI'GINE, MA'MOYA'NE, NA'GÛMOWĬ'NŮÑ)

This group comprises Nos. 151–153 and 189–191 in Bulletin 45, and Nos. 123, 124 of the present work. These are the songs which accompany gifts, usually the gift of a pony, and are sung by the recipient or giver, together with the singers at the drum. The songs are used in the social dances. Three-fourths of the songs are minor in tonality, and one begins in major tonality but changes to minor by lowering the third and sixth a semitone, the keynote remaining the same. Half of these songs begin on the keynote, and half end on the tonic. Eighty-eight per cent of them have a compass of an octave or more, the allied groups being the moccasin game, woman's dance, and begging dance. Half the songs are on the five-toned scales, as in the woman's dance and the songs for the entertainment of children, and all contain the tonic triad. Only one song contains an accidental and in this the second is lowered a semitone. Sixty-two per cent of the songs are purely melodic in structure. Half begin with a downward progression, the same proportion occurring in the songs of the woman's dance and the songs for the entertainment of children. The minor third constitutes more than one-fourth of the intervals in both ascending and descending progression. The average interval is the smallest in the entire series, being only 2.2 semitones. Eighty-seven per cent of the songs begin on the accented part of the measure, a proportion exceeded only by the songs of the moccasin game, the woman's dance, and the pipe dance. Sixty-three per cent begin in 2–4 time and contain a change of time. The drum-rhythm is that of the social dance. The percentage of songs containing a rhythmic unit is the same as that of the entire series. In half the songs the metric unit of voice and drum is the same, and in half the voice is faster than the drum.

The rhythmic units occurring in these songs are given on pages 329–330.

SONGS FOR THE ENTERTAINMENT OF CHILDREN
(A'DIZO'KE NA'GÛMOWĬ'NŮÑ)

This group comprises Nos. 149 and 197 in Bulletin 45 and Nos. 51–53, 127, 179, and 180 of the present work. Nos. 149 of Bulletin 45 and No. 127 in this volume represent different versions of the same song, recorded on widely separated reservations, which present some differences on analysis. It will be noted that, with the exception of the lullaby, all these songs are characterized by a marked sense of humor and usually mimic the interests and occupations of the tribe.

Half these songs are major and half are minor in tonality; half begin on the tonic and three-fourths end on the tonic. Two songs are on the fifth five-toned scale and two on the fourth five-toned scale, these comprising half the group. From two of the songs the third is omitted (see analysis of No. 53). None of these songs contain an accidental and 87 per cent are purely melodic in structure. Half begin with a downward and half with an upward progression. The minor third is especially prominent in the descending intervals. The average interval is the same as in the war songs, and we note that three of these songs are concerned with a child's game of war and one with war between animals. Half the songs begin on the accented and half on the unaccented part of the measure. Three-fourths begin in 2–4 time and the percentage of songs marked by a change of time is the largest except in the dream songs, the pipe dance songs, and the unclassified songs. Sixty-two per cent contain no rhythmic unit, this proportion being exceeded only in the moccasin game songs. In the rendering of these songs, as well as in those of the moccasin game, a high degree of excitement prevails. Most of the songs were recorded without the drum; in one song drum and voice show the same metric unit, while in another the drum is slower than the voice.

The rhythmic units occurring in these songs will be found on page 330.

UNCLASSIFIED SONGS

This group comprises the following songs: Nos. 146, 147, 148, 150, 186, and 192–196 in Bulletin 45, and Nos. 67, 68, 119–122, 165–169 of the present work. These songs present a wide variety of interest, including songs of the ca'wûno'ga (southern) dance, the divorce ceremony, the friendly visit of one band to another, and a song concerning an historical incident. As the topics of the songs are so diverse it does not seem expedient to consider the group as a unit. The rhythmic units found in the songs are, however, of interest (see pp. 330–332).

MELODIC AND RHYTHMIC RESEMBLANCES BETWEEN SONG GROUPS
(BASED ON TABLES 1–22)

The preceding analysis suggests connection between the idea of the song and its musical form, and also indicates resemblance between groups of songs containing a somewhat similar idea. Tables (pp. 51–58) have been prepared in order that these resemblances may be more conveniently observed. For instance, it will be noted that the Mïde' songs resemble the begging dance songs, the idea common to both being desire for acquirement, in the former for the acquirement of supernatural power and in the latter for gifts of food. Turning to the analysis of the begging dance songs, they are found to be allied to the three groups of songs in which the element of pleasure is strongest—the songs of the woman's dance, the pipe dance, and those for the entertainment of children, the begging dance combining the idea of acquirement with that of pleasure. It may be noted also that the begging dance and the pipe dance songs have in common a large proportion of intervals of the ascending fourth, which have been found to characterize songs concerning motion (see No. 22), and it is recalled that the persons engaged in the begging dance made the circuit of the entire camp and that the pipe dance was a contortion dance. Turning to the analysis of the songs for the entertainment of children, we find that group allied to the pleasure songs and also to the war songs, and recall that one-half the songs of this group relate to mimic warfare or warfare between animals.

From further study of structural resemblances between groups of Indian songs it may be possible to ascertain whether a rhythmic unit is usually found in songs of definitely formed thought, whether a feeling for the tonic and its octave is strongest in subjective songs, and to throw light on other peculiarities suggested as subjects of more extended investigation by this comparative analysis of the content and form of Chippewa songs.

TABULATED ANALYSIS OF RESEMBLANCES

1. MĬDE′ SONGS

General motive of songs: The securing of a definite result through supernatural power, the person affected being usually some one other than the singer.

Melodic resemblances of Mĭde′ songs to—
    Dream Songs
        a, In major tonality
        b, In proportion of songs beginning on octave
        c, In proportion of songs ending on tonic
        d, In compass of twelfth
        e, In first progression downward
    Love Songs
        In purely melodic structure
    Woman's Dance Songs
        In purely melodic structure
    Begging Dance Songs
        a, In major tonality
        b, In proportion of songs beginning on dominant
        c, In proportion of songs containing octave complete except seventh
        d, In proportion of downward progressions
        e, In average interval
    Songs for the Entertainment of Children
        In purely melodic structure

Rhythmic resemblances of Mĭde' songs to—
  Dream Songs
    In proportion of songs in which drum is faster than voice
  Certain kinds of War Songs
    In double drum-rhythm
  Moccasin Game Songs
    In proportion of songs in which drum is faster than voice

2. DREAM SONGS

General motive of songs: The securing of supernatural aid in personal undertakings.

Melodic resemblances of dream songs to—
  Mĭde' Songs
    a, In major tonality
    b, In proportion of songs beginning on octave
    c, In proportion of songs ending on tonic
    d, In compass of twelfth
    e, In first progression downward
  Love Songs
    In proportion beginning on twelfth
  Moccasin Game Songs
    In harmonic structure
  Woman's Dance Songs
    a, In five-toned scales
    b, In compass of twelfth
    c, In proportion of downward progressions
    d, In average interval
  Begging Dance Songs
    In major tonality
  Pipe Dance Songs
    a, In proportion containing major triad and sixth
    b, In songs having compass of four tones
  Songs Connected with Gifts
    In five-toned scales
  Songs for the Entertainment of Children
    a, In five-toned scales
    b, In proportion of downward progressions

Rhythmic resemblances of dream songs to—
  Mĭde' Songs
    In proportion of songs in which drum is faster than voice
  Songs Connected with Gifts
    In triple drum-rhythm

3. WAR SONGS

General character of songs: (1) Dream songs of individual warriors; (2) Songs concerning war medicines; (3) Songs incidental to a war expedition; (4) Songs concerning success on the warpath.

Melodic resemblances of war songs to—
> Mïde′ Songs
>> In proportion of songs containing octave complete except seventh
> Dream Songs
>> In compass
> Love Songs
>> *a,* In proportion of songs beginning on octave
>> *b,* In melodic structure
> Moccasin Game Songs
>> In compass
> Woman's Dance Songs
>> *a,* In proportion of songs ending on tonic
>> *b,* In melodic structure
> Songs for the Entertainment of Children
>> *a,* In equal major and minor tonality
>> *b,* In melodic structure

Rhythmic resemblances of war songs to—
> Mïde′ Songs
>> In double drum-rhythm (of certain classes of war songs)
> Begging Dance Songs
>> In proportion having drum faster than voice

4. LOVE SONGS

General character of songs: The expression of disappointment, loneliness, and sadness.

Melodic resemblances of love songs to—
> Mïde′ Songs
>> In melodic structure
> Dream Songs
>> In proportion of songs beginning on twelfth
> War Songs
>> *a,* In proportion of songs beginning on octave
>> *b,* In melodic structure
> Moccasin Game Songs
>> *a,* In proportion of songs beginning on tonic, octave, or dominant
>> *b,* In average interval

Melodic resemblances of love songs to—
    Woman's Dance Songs
        a, In relative proportion of downward and upward progressions
        b, In melodic structure
    Begging Dance Songs
        a, In proportion of songs beginning on tonic, octave, or dominant
        b, In compass of an octave
    Pipe Dance Songs
        a, In proportion of songs ending on tonic or dominant
        b, In average interval
    Songs Connected with Gifts
        In relative number of downward and upward progressions
    Songs for the Entertainment of Children
        a, In proportion of songs ending on tonic or dominant
        b, In relative proportion of downward and upward progressions

Rhythmic resemblances of love songs to—
    Begging Dance Songs
        In change of time
    Songs for the Entertainment of Children
        In change of time

5. MOCCASIN GAME SONGS

Elements in moccasin game: Controlled excitement, desire for success and gain, pleasure, and confidence in supernatural aid.

Melodic resemblances of moccasin game songs to—
    Dream Songs
        In harmonic structure
    Love Songs
        In number of songs beginning on tonic, octave, or dominant
    Woman's Dance Songs
        a, In minor tonality
        b, In second five-toned scale
        c, In compass
    Pipe Dance Songs
        In average interval
    Songs Connected with Gifts
        In minor tonality

Rhythmic resemblances of moccasin game songs to—
    Mïde' Songs
        In proportion of songs in which drum is faster than voice
    Woman's Dance Songs
        a, In proportion of songs beginning on accented part of
            measure
        b, In time steadily maintained
    Pipe Dance Songs
        In number of songs beginning on accented part of measure
    Songs Connected with Gifts
        In time steadily maintained
    Songs for the Entertainment of Children
        In rhythmic unit

6. WOMAN'S DANCE SONGS

Elements in the dance: Pleasure and securing the gifts offered with
the invitation to dance.

Melodic resemblances of woman's dance songs to—
    Mïde' Songs
        In melodic structure
    Dream Songs
        a, In five-toned scales
        b, In compass of twelfth
        c, In proportion of downward progressions
        d, In average interval
    Love Songs
        a, In melodic structure
        b, In proportion of downward and upward progressions
    Songs Connected with Gifts
        a, In minor tonality
        b, In five-toned scales
        c, In relative number of downward and upward progressions
    Songs for the Entertainment of Children
        a, In five-toned scales
        b, In proportion of downward and upward progressions

Rhythmic resemblances of woman's dance songs to—
    Moccasin Game Songs
        In time steadily maintained
    Pipe Dance Songs
        In number of songs beginning on accented part of measure
    Songs Connected with Gifts
        In time steadily maintained
    Songs for the Entertainment of Children
        In rhythmic unit

7. BEGGING DANCE SONGS

Elements in the dance: Pleasure and acquirement.

Melodic resemblances of begging dance songs to—
 Mīde' Songs
  a, In major tonality
  b, In proportion of songs beginning on dominant
  c, In proportion of songs containing octave complete except
   seventh
  d, In proportion of downward progressions
  e, In average interval
 Dream Songs
  In major tonality
 Love Songs
  In proportion of songs beginning on tonic, octave, or
  dominant
 Pipe Dance Songs
  In number of ascending fourths

Rhythmic resemblances of begging dance songs to—
 Woman's Dance Songs
  In rhythmic unit
 Songs for the Entertainment of Children
  a, In proportion of songs beginning in double time
  b, In rhythmic unit

8. PIPE DANCE SONGS

Elements in the dance: Ludicrous pantomime and contortion.

Melodic resemblances of pipe dance songs to—
 Dream Songs
  a, In proportion of songs containing major triad and sixth
  b, In songs having compass of four tones
 Love Songs
  a, In proportion of songs ending on tonic or dominant
  b, In average interval
 Moccasin Game Songs
  In average interval

Rhythmic resemblances of pipe dance songs to—
 Moccasin Game Songs
  In proportion of songs beginning on accented part of
  measure
 Woman's Dance Songs
  In proportion of songs beginning on accented part of
  measure

9. SONGS CONNECTED WITH GIFTS

Comprising songs which are sung when a gift of considerable value is given or received at a social dance.

Melodic resemblances of songs connected with gifts to—
>   Dream Songs
>>   In five-toned scales
>   Love Songs
>>   In proportion of downward and upward progressions
>   Moccasin Game Songs
>>   In minor tonality
>   Woman's Dance Songs
>>   *a,* In minor tonality
>>   *b,* In five-toned scales
>>   *c,* In proportion of downward and upward progressions

Rhythmic resemblances of songs connected with gifts to—
>   Dream Songs
>>   In triple drum-rhythm
>   Moccasin Game Songs
>>   In time steadily maintained
>   Woman's Dance Songs
>>   In time steadily maintained

10. SONGS FOR THE ENTERTAINMENT OF CHILDREN

Comprising songs of mimic warfare and of warfare between animals—two songs intended only for amusement, and one lullaby.

Melodic resemblances of songs for the entertainment of children to—
>   Mide' Songs
>>   In melodic structure
>   Dream Songs
>>   *a,* In five-toned scales
>>   *b,* In proportion of downward progressions
>   War Songs   .
>>   *a,* In equal major and minor tonality
>>   *b,* In melodic structure
>   Love Songs
>>   *a,* In proportion of songs ending on tonic or dominant
>>   *b,* In melodic structure
>>   *c,* In proportion of downward and upward progressions
>   Woman's Dance Songs
>>   *a,* In five-toned scales
>>   *b,* In proportion of downward and upward progressions

Rhythmic resemblances of songs for the entertainment of children to—
    Love Songs
        In change of time
    Moccasin Game Songs
        In rhythmic unit
    Woman's Dance Songs
        In rhythmic unit
    Begging Dance Songs
        a, In proportion of songs beginning in double time
        b, In rhythmic unit

WAR SONGS OF THE MISSISSIPPI BAND OF CHIPPEWA

Odjĭb'we (pl. 1),[1] the last great warrior of the Mississippi Band of Chippewa in Minnesota, sang the songs which were associated with his own expeditions, related the story of his war parties, and described the war customs of his people, so that the white man might know about them when the last warrior of the Chippewa should have been forgotten. These songs and narratives constitute the greater part of the following chapter.

At the age of 89 Odjĭb'we still possessed a voice of unusual strength and sweetness. The first phonographic records of his songs were made in August, 1909. A second set of records was made two weeks later for purposes of comparison, the songs being accurately repeated. At the expiration of several months the entire material was translated into Chippewa for revision by Odjĭb'we, some new songs were added, and many were sung or recorded a third time. In these repetitions it was noted that certain tones which were shortened or prolonged in the original rendition were similarly shortened or prolonged; also, that a slight sharping or flatting of certain tones was repeated. The records occasionally vary in unimportant melody progressions or in note-values which do not affect the length of the measure, and a few songs show changes in words, Odjĭb'we stating that it is permissible to alter the words, but that the "tune" and the meaning of the words must not be changed.[2] The original record of a song was not played when securing a repetition, hence the identity of the renditions shows how clearly the melody was retained in the mind of the singer.

---

[1] The name of this warrior is identical with the name of the tribe, the word being applied also to a member of the tribe (singular Odjĭb'we, plural Odjĭb'weg). The corrupted form "Chippewa," the only form which seems to have been used in Government publications, has never been adopted by the Indians. Many variants of this name were used by early writers, among those cited being, Achipoés (Perrot, 1671), Ochipoy (York, 1700), Chepeways (Croghan, 1760), Tschipeway (Wrangell, 1839), and Otchipwe (Baraga, 1878). (See Handbook of American Indians, *Bull. 30, B. A. E.*, pt. 1, pp. 280–281.) In the first volume of treaties published by the Government the form "Chippewa" appears. (See Indian Treaties and Laws and Regulations relating to Indian affairs, compiled and published under orders of the Department of War, Washington City, 1826.)

The meaning of the word Odjĭb'we (pronounced Ojib'way) has been a subject of much discussion. (See William H. Keating, in Narrative of an Expedition to the Source of St. Peter's River, vol. 2, p. 151, Philadelphia, 1824; Gov. Alexander Ramsey, in *Report of Commissioner of Indian Affairs*, Washington, 1850, p. 83; and William W. Warren, in History of the Ojib'ways, St. Paul, Minn., 1885, p. 36.) The derivation of the word from a root meaning "to pucker" is established, but the connection of the idea is a matter of dispute. The form of moccasin to which some have attributed the name is shown in plate 36. It is possible that the word Ojibway may have been derived from a place name in the country from which the tribe came many generations ago.

[2] See description of song No. 37, p. 119.

Truly Odjĭb'we was a musician as well as a warrior. More than 70 of his songs were recorded, and these were only part of the melodies at his command. In the long years of his blindness, passed in the Old People's Home at White Earth Agency, Minnesota, he loved to sing. Several of his comrades were there also, and they loved to recall the days when the sweep of the prairie, from horizon to horizon, belonged to the Indian. Niski'gwûn ("ruffled feathers"),[1] who fought beside him in the great struggle at Ca'gobĕns' village, was also there, and how good it was to talk over the old times! And Maiñ'gans ("little wolf"), plate 9, was there, too. Although Maiñ'- gans came from Mille Lac, he had lived at White Earth for almost a generation. He, too, loved the old ways and the old songs. Maiñ'gans is a cripple, his feet having been frozen when he was a boy, yet he is remarkably active. He attributes his rugged strength to the constant use of a native remedy called the bi'jĭkiwûck' ("cattle herb medicine"). This is a kind of medicine used by warriors in the old days, and Maiñ'gans, as his contribution to the war chapter of Chippewa music, described this medicine for the writer, secured specimens of the herb, and sang the songs connected with its origin and use. On one occasion Niski'gwûn was present when Odjĭb'we was recording songs and added to the collection his own dream song and one or two others. The songs of the mĭ'nĭsĭno'wûck ("island herb medicine") were sung by Na'waji'bigo'kwe ("woman dwelling in the midst of the rocks"), who well remembers when the herbs were dug to make this medicine for the departing warriors. Few persons on the White Earth Reservation are more skilled than she in the lore of native medicines. Personal reminiscences were given also by Meja'kigi'jĭg (see footnote, p. 83), Ma'djigi'jĭg ("moving sky"), and A'kiwĕn'zi ("old man"), all of whom took part in the wars against the Sioux, the two last named fighting under Odjĭb'we's leadership. These persons furnished the material in this section.

Odjĭb'we died in April, 1911. Many of the songs herein preserved were known only to him. He stood alone, his preeminence unques- tioned by his tribe throughout northern Minnesota. His hand was never lifted against the white man, but when war was glory he led his people to victory over the Sioux. May he rest in peace.

The final battles in the hereditary warfare between the Chippewa and the Sioux were fought in central Minnesota. This warfare, which began before the tribes became known to the whites, had its origin at the time of the westward migration of the Chippewa (Ojibwa), who found their progress barred by the Dakota, a Siouan tribe. The conflict continued with intervals of peace until brought to an end by the removal of the Minnesota Sioux by the United States Government.

---

[1] See pp. 77-79.

HOLE-IN-THE-DAY

On August 19, 1825, a treaty was negotiated at Prairie du Chien, Michigan Territory,[1] in which the Chippewa and the Sioux agreed on a line of demarkation between their territories. This line (surveyed in 1835) extended diagonally across what is now the State of Minnesota from near the site of the present town of Moorhead to a point on the Saint Croix River a few miles above Stillwater.[2] In spite of the agreement, however, the war parties of both tribes continued to range freely across the boundary line. The last great fight took place in the Minnesota Valley, May 27, 1858, near the site of the present town of Shakopee (see p. 76), but minor encounters between warriors of the two tribes are said to have occurred for some years afterward. Brower makes the following statement:[3]

The last formidable Sioux war party, precipitated against the Ojibway nation of Indians, of which there is definite knowledge, proceeded from the Valley of Minnesota River to the Valley of Crow Wing River via Long Prairie, Minn., in June, 1860. · · · There were about 150 painted, bedecked, and ornamented Indians in the party.

War between Indian tribes was an occupation rather than a calamity. It can not be said to have been strictly tribal in character, according to our understanding of the term, since any prominent warrior might persuade his comrades to join him and organize an expedition. There were periods of peace, but as the maintenance of peace depended largely on the self-control of the individual warrior, outbreaks were of frequent occurrence. Often one fight ended an expedition, the warriors returning satisfied if they had taken even one or two scalps. The motive for organizing a war party was usually revenge for a kinsman's death. This motive is inadequately expressed by the word "revenge," for it involved the idea that the death of a Sioux "restored" the man who had been killed by a Sioux. Underneath all other motives lay tribal pride. War was a game whose terrible tally must be kept in favor of the Chippewa. To this end war parties were planned and for this purpose they went forth to strike the quick blow, departing as stealthily as they had come.

Odjĭb'we was leader of the Chippewa warriors during the time of Bû'gonegi'jĭg (Hole-in-the-day), plate 4,[4] the last great chief of the tribe, who was assassinated in 1868. The two men were cousins and theirs was an alliance of the second generation, as the father of Odjĭb'we was brother of the first Bû'gonegi'jĭg and led his warriors against the Sioux. Bows and arrows were used in Odjĭb'we's earlier battles and neither Sioux nor Chippewa rode upon horses.

1 Statutes at Large, vol. 7, p. 272.
2 *Eighteenth Ann. Rep. Bur. Amer. Ethn.*, part 2, map 33.
3 J. V. Brower and D. I. Bushnell, jr., *Mille Lac*, St. Paul, Minn., 1900, p. 97.
4 From picture (numbered 67) in collection of photographs of North American Indians, in *Descriptive Catalogue of the Photographs of the United States Geological Survey of the Territories for the years 1869 to 1873, inclusive,* by W. H. Jackson, Washington, 1874.

In generalship Odjĭb'we was distinguished for sound judgment and steadiness of purpose rather than for reckless daring. His war expeditions were successful and he boasted that he was never wounded by the Sioux.

Odjĭb'we's prowess won for him the right to wear 11 war-honor feathers, each indicating that he had taken a Sioux scalp; these were eagle feathers and were worn upright in a band around the head (pl. 5). The writer saw Odjĭb'we wearing this decoration in a dance several years before his songs were recorded. Three of the feathers are notched, and the right to wear these was acquired by killing and scalping Sioux; the unnotched feathers indicated that he had scalped Sioux who had been killed by other warriors. The dots of rabbit skin on the feathers indicate the number of bullets in his gun at the time of securing the scalp.[1] Bits of once bright ribbon are at the tip of each feather. Odjĭb'we stated that "four feathers could be counted for the death of each Sioux; one was worn by the man who killed him, one by the man who scalped him, and the others by men who assisted in the scalping."

Odjĭb'we was entitled to wear also a skunk skin badge (pl. 6) on his right arm. This signified that he once caught a wounded Sioux by the arm, the incident being related in connection with song No. 3. His war club (pl. 7), of birch, has a knot for the head. According to Odjĭb'we, he had despatched two Sioux with this club. After the wars were over he allowed his friends to blacken it and to decorate it with brass nails. The Chippewa war drum was called ogĭ'tcĭda dewe'igûn ("drum of the braves"). The frame of Odjĭb'we's drum is 17½ inches in diameter; it is made of wood with metal rim. The frame is apparently not of native manufacture, but Odjĭb'we said it was the original. He said that in time of war it frequently became necessary to renew the cover on the drum, but the design was always duplicated on the new cover. The cover shown in the illustration is comparatively recent. The design on Odjĭb'we's war drum (pl. 7) was explained as follows in the language of the interpreter:

There was a man who invented the use of the drum among the Indians. The lightning is a picture of his dream, and the sound of his drum was like the rumble of the thunder. When We'nabo'jo was wandering around he always sent Mĭcĭ'kĕn ("large turtle") on his errands; so the large turtle came to be considered a great warrior. When Mĭcĭ'kĕn went to war he had Mĭskwa'des ("small snapping turtle") as his oc'kabe'wĭs (messenger). That is why the picture of the lightning and the turtle is on the war drum. The Indians fought with bows and arrows, so a picture of a bow and arrow is also on the drum.

Odjĭb'we's war shirt was of scarlet flannel (pl. 8). After the wars with the Sioux were ended Odjĭb'we kept it in a bag woven of cedar

---

[1] All the war paraphernalia of Odjĭb'we, including these feathers, are now in the National Museum at Washington.

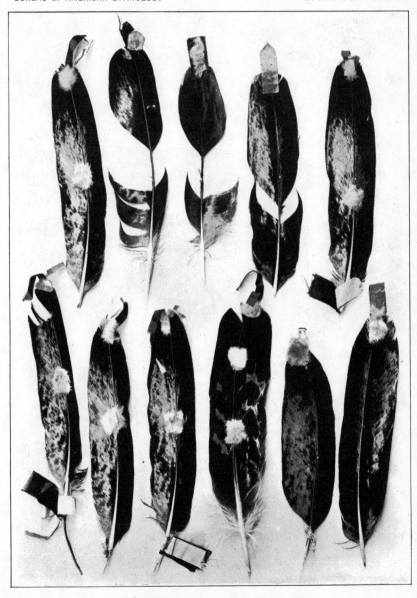

ODJÍB'WE'S WAR-HONOR FEATHERS

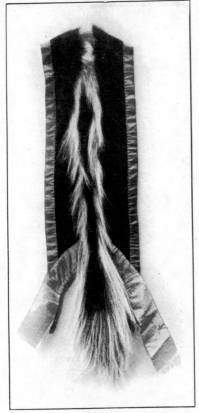 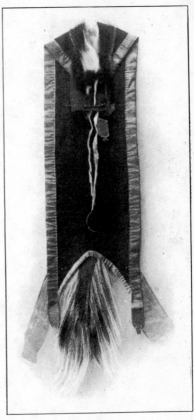

FRONT   BACK

ODJIB'WE'S WAR-HONOR BADGE

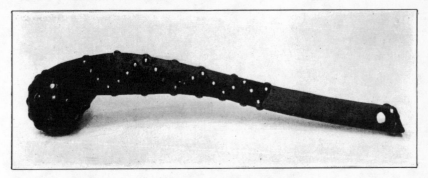

ODJÏB'WE'S WAR CLUB AND WAR DRUM

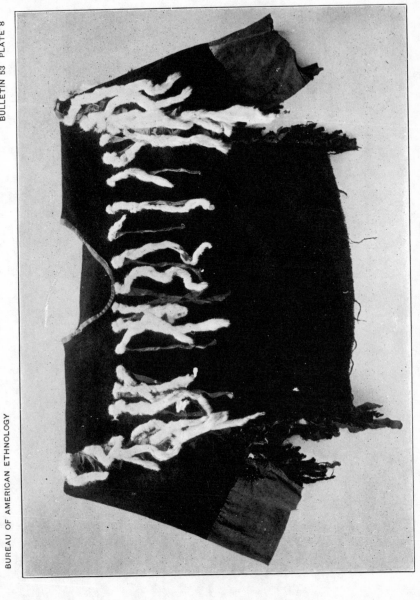

ODJĪB'WE'S WAR SHIRT

MAIÑ'GANS

bark, a method of storage generally used among the Chippewa. Several years before his songs were recorded the writer saw the old warrior wearing this shirt in a dance. The decoration is of narrow strips of weasel skin, forming a fringe. The weasel is a hunter, a wanderer, and a warrior. A well-known authority states,[1] "I can not learn of any other creature that is more thoroughly possessed of the lust for blood than are these slim-bodied little creatures."

The principal kinds of "medicine" carried by the Chippewa warriors were *bi'jĭkiwŭck'*[2] ("cattle herb medicine"), *mĭ'nĭsĭno'wŭck* ("island herb medicine"), and *wa'bŭno'wŭck* ("eastern herb medicine"). These medicines were secured by the warriors from the old men of the tribe, usually members of the Mĭde'wĭwĭn (Grand Medicine Society), who made a special study of the compounding of herbs. They were used both externally and internally and were supposed to have efficacy as charms, their mere presence serving as a protection. They were believed also to "counteract the effect of bad medicine carried by the enemy."[3]

Bi'jĭkiwŭck', a medicine which derives its name from the principal ingredient, is commonly used among the Chippewa at the present time. It is said to be taken internally as a stimulant and as a cure for fits. It is used also externally as a stimulant and to check the flow of blood from wounds.

According to Maiñ'gans[4] (pl. 9), the origin of this medicine is as follows:

There was once a Mĭde'wĭnĭ'nĭ [male member of the Mĭde'wĭwĭn] who dreamed that he saw horned animals resembling cattle, under the water. They came up from the water and talked with him, telling him how to prepare this wonderful medicine. In order to persuade them to return he composed and sang a song (No. 22). He was a young man at the time, but he sang this song until he was old. He sang it whenever he dug the roots or prepared the *bi'jĭkiwŭck'*. Others learned it from him and now it is always sung when this medicine is prepared.

It was customary for the old men when preparing this medicine to "make noises like cattle"; this was done also when the *bi'jĭkiwŭck'* songs were sung in war dances (see No. 23).

Maiñ'gans used four ingredients in compounding *bi'jĭkiwŭck'*. The number of ingredients was said to vary from two to eight, according to the judgment of the man preparing the medicine, but the principal herb, that from which the medicine took its name, was always present.

---

[1] Witmer Stone and William Gram, *American Animals*, New York, 1902, p. 237.

[2] From *bi'jĭki* and *wŭck;* the former was originally applied to the buffalo (see No. 99), but at the present time signifies "cattle," while the latter means "medicine."

[3] Cf. J. N. B. Hewitt, "Orenda and a Definition of Religion," in *American Anthropologist*, N. S., IV, no. 1, pp. 40, 41, 1902.

[4] Maiñ'gans and Odjĭb'we, treating the sick, are shown in pl. 10, Bulletin 45.

Specimens of the four herbs used by Maiñ'gans were secured and were identified by Dr. J. N. Rose, Division of Plants, United States National Museum. These herbs are as follows:

(1) *Bi'jĭkiwŭck'* ("cattle herb"), the plant from which the medicine took its name. This was said to be "a plant a few inches high which grows on the prairie toward the west and is sometimes found in sandy soil. The blossoms appear before the leaves, which are not notched but are round in shape; the root is white when dried, and is the only part used in making the medicine." The writer asked for a plant in blossom but was given a piece of dried root to which several downy white feathers were fastened (fig. 2). Maiñ'gans said that he was unable to secure a plant in bloom, and that "the cluster of white feathers was the best he could do, they having the same appearance as the blossoms, only not so white." The report of Doctor Rose is as follows:

Fig. 2. Dried root of bi'jĭkiwŭck' with feathers attached.

The root is that of *Polygala senega* L., Seneca snake-root. "The bark of the root is the most important part of the plant; the ligneous portion is comparatively inert. The root possesses various medicinal virtues. It is a stimulant, diuretic, expectorant, purgative, emetic, and a sudorific. For many years it was used by the Indians of our country as an antidote against the bite of the rattlesnake. According to their practice, it was applied externally and internally, either chewed and applied to the wound or in the form of a cataplasm. The Indians also use a decoction of this root in syphilis and in malignant sore throat. A decoction of the root has been used with marked success in cases of hydrophobia, with a view to its specific or remarkable operation on the apparent seat of this malady, the lungs, trachea, and larynx."

(2) *Bi'jĭkiwĭñ'gŭck*, a plant closely allied to the common sagebrush and identified as "*Artemisia frigida* Willd."

(3) *Bi'jĭkiwi'bŭgesa'nŭg* ("cattle plum"), identified as "*Astragalus crassicarpus* Nutt., or Ground Plum."

(4) *Bi'jĭkiwi'ginĭg'* ("cattle berry"), identified as "*Rosa arkansana* Porter, or Arkansas Rose."

The roots only are used in preparing the medicine; these are washed, scraped, and dried, and then pounded to a powder in which small shreds still remain. The principal ingredient is prepared and kept separate; the other three herbs are pounded together, equal parts of each being used. Maiñ'gans showed the writer his *bi'jĭkiwŭck'* medicine pouch (pl. 10) which he always carries with him.

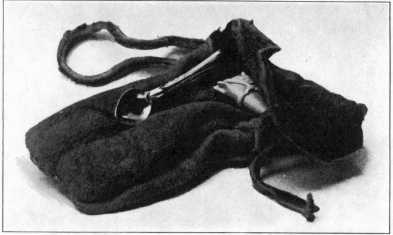

(Slightly reduced)

(Actual size)

POUCH AND MEASURE FOR BI'JIKIWÛCK'

This contained a mixture of the three ingredients and a very small tin spoon, such as is used with a child's toy tea set. Held in place by the flap of the pouch was a small tied packet of the principal ingredient. Maiñ'gans said that he frequently took a little spoonful of the powder from the pouch, and, suiting the action to the word, he took a dose of the medicine to show that it could easily be swallowed without water. On the following day, in the writer's presence, he prepared the medicine in liquid form. Taking a pail containing about a quart of hot water, he placed a little spoonful of the three mixed ingredients on the surface of the water at the eastern side of the pail, saying Wa'bûnoñg ("at the east"), then at the southern side, saying Ca'wûnoñg ("at the south"), then at the western and northern sides, saying Ningabi'anoñg ("at the west"), and Kiwe'dinoñg ("at the north"). These words were merely explanatory of his action. The surface of the water was thus dotted with four small patches of powder. He then opened the tied packet of the principal ingredient, took out one scanty spoonful of the contents, and divided it equally among the patches of powder, placing it carefully in the middle of each, beginning with the east as before but not repeating the names of the cardinal points. The ingredients soon dissolved in the hot water. According to Maiñ'gans the medicine was then ready for use, though some preferred to secure a stronger flavor by boiling it. He said that the taste was agreeable and that the medicine should be taken four times a day, the dose to be small at first and then increased, the full dose being taken in a measure (pl. 10) which he gave to the writer. This is made of birch bark and contains about a tablespoonful. The drawings on the inside are said to represent animals and to indicate that the measure was to be used for this particular medicine. Maiñ'gans swallowed a portion of the liquid after offering it to the writer.

Mĭ'nĭsĭno'wûck ("island herb medicine") also takes its name from that of its principal ingredient, which was formerly found only at a certain place on Lake Superior, but was discovered thirty years ago at Mille Lac, where it grows in fine, light sand along the shore. The medicine contains eight ingredients, said to be herbs of about the same sort. An herb called "the last ingredient" is found growing in the woods at White Earth.

Na'waji'bigo'kwe said that many years ago the Sioux were "getting too powerful for the Chippewa," and that about that time a man "dreamed of a thunderbird, who told him how to prepare and use this medicine." She related the two following incidents of her personal experience with mĭ'nĭsĭno'wûck: In the autumn of 1909 a member of her family was involved in serious and complicated difficulties. She resolved to help him by means of mĭ'nĭsĭno'wûck.

After searching many weeks in the woods she found at last one little root, not the principal ingredient but all she could find. She took this home, "sang and talked and prayed over it," wrapped it in fresh birch bark and put it into the coat pocket of the man who was to be benefited by it, telling him that it would help him out of his troubles. To the writer's personal knowledge the man was entirely freed from his difficulties a few weeks later.

Na'waji'bigo'kwe said also that two years before a man while in a drunken rage had killed his wife. His relatives hastened to Na'waji'-bigo'kwe and asked whether she had any *mĭ'nĭsĭno'wŭck*. She gave them a small piece of the root, which the man carried in his pocket. The writer is reliably informed that the man is alive and free to-day, although it is well known that he killed his wife.

Aside from its virtue .as a charm, *mĭ'nĭsĭno'wŭck* is said to be a powerful curative agent. It has the effect of checking the flow of blood from wounds, and is also used internally in many forms of sudden illness. It is a "life medicine," used for good purposes only. Four songs connected with this medicine are contained in this section (Nos. 24, 25, 26, 27).

Wa'bûno'wŭck ("eastern herb medicine") is entirely different in both nature and use from either *bi'jĭkiwûck'* or *mĭ'nĭsĭno'wŭck*. It is said to have had originally some good offices but to have had also evil uses, and as time passed the latter prevailed. Na'waji'bigo'kwe gave the following story of its origin: There was once a young man who was very anxious to join the Mĭde'wĭwĭn so that he could gain power as a hunter. His father opposed this, saying, "You are too trifling to appreciate so solemn a thing as the Mĭde'." The youth was very sad because of his father's opposition. He went away and fasted many days. At last a manido' from the east came to him and told him about this medicine, saying that it had both good and bad properties. The youth at once gathered a number of men around him and they formed a kind of alliance; these men were known as *Wa'bûnog'*.[1] They held dances and were unscrupulous in their use of the medicine. Eight men were destroyed at the first dance, given by a man who knew the secret of this medicine. This tradition was related to Na'waji'bigo'kwe by her grandfather. The medicine "would either kill or cure those who took it"; it had power also as an evil charm and the property of being able to "make things go through the air." There were said to be many songs connected with this medicine, but none have been recorded by the writer. It was said to have passed out of use among the Minnesota Chippewa except at Vermillion Lake.

---

[1] Compare Hoffman, The Midē'wiwin or "Grand Medicine Society" of the Ojibway, in *Seventh Ann. Rep. Bur. Ethn.*, pp. 156, 157.

The three medicines above described, imparting power of healing, success, and revenge, respectively, were well adapted to the use of men on the warpath.

Songs Connected with Odjïb'we's Personal Experience [1]

When Odjïb'we was a boy his paternal grandfather, two of the latter's brothers and two of his own brothers, one older and one younger than himself, were killed by the Sioux. Hatred filled his heart and he determined to hunt and kill the Sioux. Thus at an early age he chose the career of a warrior.

In preparation for this vocation he frequently fasted for several days at a time, remaining alone in the woods and hoping for a dream or vision. At length a dream came to him after a fast of four days. In this dream he saw a woman carrying several guns made of rushes. A party of Sioux approached and the woman gave a gun to each of the Sioux, telling them to shoot at him. The Sioux took the guns made of rushes and shot at him. Out of the guns came horseflies, which lit on him but could not harm him. Then the woman told him that he would be a great warrior and would always be protected. Odjïb'we said that what the woman told him came true, for he was never wounded by the Sioux. The woman also sang a song which became his "dream song." Odjïb'we stated that he "could never really sing the song until just before his first fight with the Sioux; then the dream returned to him very clearly and the song came to his lips so that he could sing it." After that he sang it freely. He placed his faith in it and often sang it before, or in the midst of, a fight. After the recording of this song on the phonograph the aged warrior bowed his head and said tremulously that he feared he would not live long, as he had given away his most sacred possession.

No. 1. Odjib'we's Dream Song   (Catalogue No. 392)

Sung by Odjïb'we

Voice ♩ = 88
Recorded without drum

na-wa-wan i - nǐ - nǐ-wa-wûn

---

[1] See also Nos. 32, 33, 34, 35, 39, 40, 41, which are included in a subsequent chapter to illustrate certain events of a typical war expedition.

WORDS

obĭc′kona′wawan′................ when they shot, they missed

inĭ′nĭwûn′[1]...................... the man

Analysis.—This song contains nine measures and is divided into four parts, the first, second, and last containing the rhythmic unit, and the third containing the words. This form suggests a definite phase of musical expression. No words occur in the rhythmic unit, the mind of the singer being concentrated on the musical idea. In the part of the song containing words the interest centers on them and the musical idea is secondary. Comparison with other songs having the same form will show in many instances a less definite rhythm in the part containing the words (see Nos. 8, 12, 13, 30, 39, 40, 81, 105). The tonality of this song is minor, but the opening interval of the first two phrases is a major third (see analysis of No. 9, also of Nos. 34, 83, 94, 120). The melody tones are those of the second five-toned scale. Two renditions of the song were recorded; these show no variation in either rhythm or melody.

In early youth Odjĭb′we took part in a dog feast. It was the custom of the tribe to hold feasts of this kind occasionally in order that the young men who aspired to become warriors might show their courage to the assembled people. An old warrior was selected to announce the feast. Walking through the village, he made the announcement in a loud voice. The next day there was a large gathering, especially of the young men. After much singing and dancing, and many speeches, the youths whose courage was to be tested were seated on the ground in a circle, in the center of which a dog was killed. The liver was then removed and cut into small pieces, one of which was given each young man on a long stick. If he chewed and swallowed the morsel without flinching, he was considered brave enough for the warpath, but if he shuddered or drew back he was deemed faint-hearted and was greeted with jeers by the assembly. Odjĭb′we said that he endured this test "without the slightest change of expression," but that for many days afterward he was unable to bear the thought of what he had done, although he never admitted this to any one.

When Odjĭb′we reached the age of 20 he felt that it was time to begin his chosen career. Accordingly he consulted his cousin Ne′bûnec′kûn ("he who walks by one side of the thing"), a young man about his own age, and they decided to go on the warpath together. They told no one of their intentions, but pretended that they were going on a hunting expedition. With heavy hearts they left the village. They thought of the friends whose deaths they were

---

[1] In order to make this word conform to the music a meaningless syllable (*wa*) is inserted. The Chippewa custom of changing the words of a song to fit the music is considered in Bulletin 45, p. 14.

to avenge, and there was probably in their minds uncertainty regarding their own fate.

Odjĭb'we said that they sang the following song every one of the four nights they camped. The words imply that there were more than two in the party, but, on being questioned concerning this seeming discrepancy, Odjĭb'we insisted that this was the song he and his cousin sang.

No. 2. Odjĭb'we's First War Song   (Catalogue No. 371)

Sung by ODJĬB'WE

* Drum-rhythm

etc.

WORDS

beba′nio′neyan .... on the fourth day
nindo′nagi′migog′ .... I am chosen by
inĭ′nĭwûg [1] .... the men

Analysis.—Four renditions of this song were recorded in August, 1909, and it was sung also on two occasions by Odjĭb'we in March, 1910, all the renditions being identical. The intonation was good throughout the renditions. The metric unit of the song is very rapid, but steadily maintained. The accents were clearly given and the transcription is divided into measures according to the accented

---

[1] This word, literally translated "men," is commonly applied to warriors (see p. 187).

tones. The rhythmic unit varies somewhat in its repetitions, but begins uniformly with a 5-8 measure. In the measure marked 3-4 the metric unit ($\flat$ = 192) is continued, but the rhythm is triple, necessitating a 3-4 instead of a 6-8 time indication. The intonation was good throughout the renditions.

Odjĭb'we's expedition was successful. On the fourth morning the party saw one Sioux and killed him. Taking his scalp, they returned to the village, where a great feast and dance were held in their honor. Odjĭb'we sang the song of that dance, but the record was not transcribed. The words, however, are of interest as showing the arrogance of the youthful warrior after his first victory.

WORDS

nisese'sĭnawa'................. I make him bite the dust
Wape'tawañ (Sioux word)[1] ... the Wapeton Sioux
wabamûg'.................... when I see him

Odjĭb'we stated that he did not sing his dream song on the expedition which has just been described, nor until first he was frightened by the Sioux, under the following circumstances: There was a Chippewa camp near the site of the present town of Little Falls, Minnesota. One day two men and their wives started from this village on a hunting expedition. While the men were away from their camp the women saw two Sioux scouts, and on their husbands' return so reported to them. All started at once to return to the main camp, arriving that evening. One of the hunters told Odjĭb'we that the women had seen the Sioux, but Odjĭb'we thought little about the matter, saying the women were probably mistaken. As Odjĭb'we was eating his breakfast the next morning a man said to him, "Let us go and see if there are really any Sioux around." Odjĭb'we consented to go, but had so little confidence in the truth of the report that he put on his brightest finery, making himself a shining mark. Odjĭb'we and his friend left the village quietly and started on a run toward the place where the women said they had seen the Sioux, the former carrying his gun on his right arm.

Two Sioux were on the watch, and when they saw Odjĭb'we and his companion approaching, they hid in bushes beside the road; one carried a spear, the other a club. Without warning they attacked the two Chippewa. The main body of Sioux warriors then appeared, some

---

[1] "The Dakota call themselves Otceti cakowiⁿ (Oćeti šakowiŋ), The Seven Fireplaces or Council-fires. This designation refers to their original gentes, the Mdewakaⁿtoⁿwaⁿ (Mdewakaŋ-toŋwaŋ), Waqpekute (Waḣpe-kute), Waqpe-toⁿwaⁿ (Waḣpetoŋwaŋ), Sisitoⁿwaⁿ (Sisitoŋwaŋ), Ihañk-toⁿwaⁿ (Ihaŋktoŋwaŋ), Ihañk-toⁿwaⁿna (Ihaŋktoŋwaŋna), and Titoⁿwaⁿ (Titoŋwaŋ). . . . The Waqpe-toⁿwaⁿ or Wahpeton [:] The name of this people signifies Village-among-the-leaves (of deciduous trees), the gens being known to the whites as Leaf Village or Wahpeton."—JAMES OWEN DORSEY, Siouan Sociology, in *Fifteenth Ann. Rep. Bur. Amer. Ethn.*, pp. 215, 216.

armed with spears and some with clubs. Odjĭb'we's companion
was killed, but he himself escaped, running a long distance before he
realized that he had a gun. Suddenly a Sioux attacked him with a
club. Odjĭb'we shot the Sioux and then hid behind a great oak tree.
According to their custom, whenever a Sioux was killed the other
Sioux suddenly disappeared. From behind the oak Odjĭb'we could
not see a single Sioux. He did not stop to scalp the man he had
killed but started for the village. On the way he met some Chippewa
and they all went back to look for the Sioux. They could not find
any living enemies, but they scalped the dead man. It was during
this skirmish that Odjĭb'we first sang his dream song (No. 1).

The following song (No. 3) was composed by Odjĭb'we after killing
a Sioux and was sung by him when carrying the scalp in the victory
dance.

A small war party was organized by Bû'gonegi'jĭg (Hole-in-the-
day), Odjĭb'we being one of the number. They went to a point on
the Minnesota River near the site of the present city of St. Paul and
took their position near the road which the Sioux would travel in going
from their village to the white settlement. Hole-in-the-day told his
men to lie in a row behind a fallen tree and gave strict orders that
they should await his signal for firing, that only one man should fire,
and that no one should shoot a woman. In silence the Chippewa lay
behind the log, waiting for an unwary Sioux to pass that way. Soon
a company of men and women came down the path, talking and laugh-
ing merrily. The warriors watched their leader but he gave no signal
and the Sioux passed on. Later a man came alone. Hole-in-the-
day gave the signal to Odjĭb'we, who fired. The Sioux staggered and
fell on his side. Odjĭb'we rushed forward and dragged the man
toward a clump of bushes, but his victim died on the way. Because he
caught the wounded Sioux by the arm Odjĭb'we was entitled to wear
thereafter a skunk-skin badge on his right arm (see pl. 6; also
p. 62). Hole-in-the-day gave the order, "Cut his throat at once."
This was done, and Odjĭb'we himself took the man's scalp. The
Chippewa then ran down to the river and, entering a canoe, started
for the opposite shore. Meantime the sound of the firing had
attracted the attention of the Sioux, who hastened from their village,
but were unable to overtake the Chippewa. Helpless the Sioux stood
on the bank and saw the Chippewa dancing on the opposite shore,
waving the fresh scalp, and taunting them. Odjĭb'we sang the
following song, which he composed at that time.

After this dance the Chippewa returned to their home, Odjĭb'we
saying that they "just killed that man to let the Sioux know they
had been around."

No. 3. "An Eagle Feather I See" (Catalogue No. 346)

Sung by ODJĬB'WE

VOICE ♩ = 100
DRUM ♩ = 104
(Drum in accented eighth notes*)

Gi-ni-wĭ-gwûn ni-wa - ba-ma *we* o - gĭ-tcĭ-da nin-de - bĭ - bi-nan

* (Drum-rhythm)

etc.

WORDS

gini'wĭgwûn'......................an eagle feather [1]
niwa'bama'.........................I see
ogĭ'tcĭda [2] ....a brave
ninde'bibina'....................I have caught

Analysis.—Triple and double measures alternate throughout this song. The first and second measures constitute a rhythmic unit, the tones being those of the major triad of A. In the third and fourth measures this unit is repeated on the minor triad of F sharp. (Compare repetitions of the rhythmic unit in No. 5.) The remainder of the song consists of three phrases, each comprising a triple and a double measure; these, however, are not repetitions of the rhythmic unit. The manner in which the rhythm of the rhythmic unit influences the rhythm of other parts of the song is worthy of observation. Four renditions of this song were recorded, the rhythm being accurately repeated.

The following song commemorates an incident unique in the annals of Indian warfare, relating to a scalp which was mislaid.

Odjĭb'we was leader of a small war party which went against the Sioux. The Chippewa were hiding in a ravine, when they saw a Sioux coming over the bluff with a gun. He did not come directly toward them, but turned toward a little lake, evidently intending to shoot ducks. He disappeared in the reeds beside the lake, and Odjĭb'we sent two men to reconnoiter, saying, "Do not kill the Sioux

---

[1] This refers to the feather worn by a warrior who took an enemy's scalp. (See p. 62.)
[2] From Sioux *aki'ćita*. Cf. pp. 76, 88, 108, 186, 190, 230.

until after he has shot the ducks." Odjĭb'we and the rest of his war party remained in concealment. Soon they heard the report of a gun, indicating that the Sioux had shot the ducks. Then they heard two shots and knew that their men had fired on the Sioux. Their aim was faulty, and the Sioux soon appeared, running toward Odjĭb'we and his warriors. Odjĭb'we stepped from his hiding place. The Sioux cried, "You can not hit me. I am a brave man." Odjĭb'we replied, "I too am brave," and struck at the Sioux with his gun. The latter dodged and attempted to strike back with his own empty gun. Finally the Sioux started to run away, and Odjĭb'we shot him in the back.

Odjĭb'we allowed Mo'kadjiwĕns' ("little hill rising up to view") to remove the scalp, and the war party started for home. The scalp was in charge of the man who removed it; when the party stopped for their noon lunch he either laid the scalp beside him or hung it on a bush and forgot it. The scalp was not missed until the party went into camp at night, many miles from the halting place at noon. It was out of the question to return and find the scalp, so they composed this song, which they sang at home in the victory dance. Mo'kadjiwĕns' was given credit for taking the scalp, but mingled with the honor was open ridicule for having left it "hanging in some marsh."

No. 4. Song of a Mislaid Scalp   (Catalogue No. 387)

Sung by Odjĭb'we

Voice ♩ = 108

Recorded without drum

Mo - ka - dji - wĕns ga - ma - mĭ - jŭñ bwan - o - sti - gwŭn gi - a -

go - de ma - na - ki - kiñ

WORDS

Mo'kadjiwĕns'..............	Mo'kadjiwĕns' (man's name)
gama'mĭjŭñ.................	took
bwan'ostigwŭn'.............	a Sioux scalp
gi'agode'...................	which is hanging
ma'nakikiñ.................	in a marsh

Analysis.—This is a particularly lively and attractive melody. It is one of the comparatively few Chippewa songs in which there is no change of time, the triple measure being steadily maintained. It contains eight measures and is divided into four parts, the first three consisting of a rhythmic unit (see Nos. 5, 19, 33, 34). In the last part it is to be noted that the dotted eighth note occurs on the second instead of on the third count of the measure. The song is harmonic in structure and minor in tonality. Six renditions were recorded; these show no variation in either rhythm or melody.

The next song concerns a war expedition which was organized by Ge′miwŭnac′ ("bird flying low through the rain"),[1] a member of the Pillager Band of Chippewa (Odjĭb′we was a member of the Mississippi Band). The Mississippi were not thinking of going to war, but a party of 20 Pillagers came to the village and wanted them to join the party. Ten Mississippi decided to go, as did seven of the Mille Lac Band. All started from Crow Wing in canoes. A few miles down the Mississippi River they made their first camp, and had their first war dance. Odjĭb′we sang the song of that dance, which, he said, was sung every evening the party was away, but the warrior was feeble that day and the record is not sufficiently clear for transcription. He told of the scene: Some of the men danced around the fire while others sat still; all sang before they went to bed. Early the next morning they broke camp and took their journey through the woods, traveling rapidly all day. When they reached the prairie, they rested in concealment by day and traveled by night. On approaching the Sioux country, they sent two scouts ahead with instructions to return at once and report if they saw signs of the enemy. At this point in his narrative Odjĭb′we assumed the attitude of a scout, one hand shading his eyes and the other signaling to those supposed to be following (see plate 11, in which his costume, as shown, is not that of the warpath).[2] These men started about dark and traveled rapidly while the others followed slowly. In a short time the scouts came running back. "What did you see?" asked the warriors. "A wide path," replied the scout. "It is a new trail. The Sioux must have passed to-day." One scout said, "There must have been a hundred;" the other was more conservative, estimating the number at forty.

It was decided to remain in a little grove until morning and then follow the Sioux trail. In the gray dawn, after cleaning and loading their guns, the Chippewa set out. Soon they came to four lodges made of green boughs where the Sioux had spent the night. Near by they saw the place where the Sioux had been dancing and where a council had been held. Forty-two stones placed in a circle indicated the number of warriors present at this council. While

---

[1] See pl. 9 of Bulletin 45 and pp. 51, 95, 114, 115 of the same Bulletin.
[2] Cf. pl. 14.

ODJIB'WE IN POSTURE OF SCOUT

looking over the camp, they heard in the distance the guns of the Sioux, who were evidently killing game on the way, and the Chippewa again sent out two scouts, with orders to go along the wooded shore of a long lake near at hand and ascertain whether the Sioux were in the open country on the opposite shore. The main body of the Chippewa followed in the same general direction. Soon they met the scouts coming back with the report that two Sioux were sitting on the other shore of the lake. When the Chippewa reached the place, the Sioux had gone. The Chippewa then very stealthily ascended a hill from which they could see the entire Sioux camp. They decided not to make an attack at that time because, owing to the distance, the Sioux could see them too soon, but to wait until night. The Sioux did not suspect the presence of Chippewa in the vicinity. From their hiding place the Chippewa watched the Sioux cook a meal and later prepare for a night march. Being reluctant to let the enemy escape, the Chippewa sent three of their number to see whether a successful attack on the camp could be made, but the Sioux had gone before they reached the camp. Odjĭb'we was one of these three. He told his two companions to stay, saying that he would creep ahead (see pl. 14). After crawling some distance, he got behind brush where he could walk upright. Later he heard the enemy. He kept very still. The Sioux were evidently making another camp in the middle of the night, for he heard them chopping wood. He ran back and found all the Chippewa at the old Sioux camp.

"Why did you not come?" he cried. "We could have killed all the Sioux." "We were waiting for you to come back and report," was the reply. Then all the Chippewa went forward and sat near the enemy's new camp. They could hear the Sioux singing and dancing. The Chippewa did not sleep, watching and waiting for the dawn. In the first light they saw the Sioux astir. Four Chippewa went ahead to watch at a spot where the Sioux would pass, and when the latter came up, shot one man. That was the beginning of a hot fight, which lasted all day and until after nightfall; it was fought in the open with no protection except the high grass. No bows and arrows were used, both Chippewa and Sioux being armed with shotguns. The fighting was particularly fierce on both sides. Odjĭb'we said that he was obliged to "dodge and look out all the time," and that in the confusion it was impossible to tell who killed each man. Toward evening No'dĭn ("wind"), the Mille Lac chief, was killed, and the Chippewa could not recover his body. Three Sioux scalps were secured by the Chippewa. After the fight they did not follow the Sioux, but returned home with these trophies.

This victory was celebrated by great dances at which the following song was sung, the words indicating that the singer would soon go on the warpath again.

No. 5. Song of an Unsatisfied Warrior (Catalogue No. 391)

Sung by ODJĬB'WE

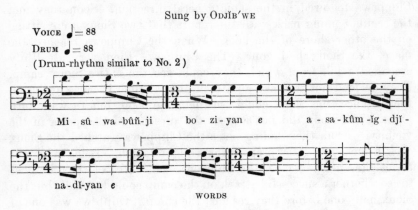

Voice ♩ = 88
Drum ♩ = 88
(Drum-rhythm similar to No. 2)

Mi - sû - wa -bûñ̄- ji - bo - zi - yan *e*　a - sa - kûm -ĭg - djĭ -

na - dĭ-yan *e*

WORDS

mi′sûwabûñjibo′ziyan′.............. to-morrow I shall start in my canoe
asa′kûmĭg′djĭna′dĭyan′............ although I have one already

Analysis.—This song comprises four parts, the first three of which contain a rhythmic unit (see Nos. 4, 19, 33, 34). It is interesting to note that the repetitions of this unit begin on the descending tones of the minor triad. Double and triple measures alternate throughout this song, the rhythmic unit consisting of a double followed by a triple measure. Reference to No. 3 will show an alternation in reverse order, the unit consisting of a triple followed by a double measure. Four renditions of this song were recorded, which are uniform in every respect.

The following five songs are connected with the last notable fight between the Sioux and the Chippewa, which occurred May 27, 1858, in the valley of the Minnesota River at the village of a Sioux chief called by the Chippewa Ca′gobĕns (Little Six). The Sioux name of this chief was Ca′kpe [1] (Six) and as his father bore the same name, the son was commonly known among both Sioux and Chippewa as Little Six. The Chippewa changed the pronunciation slightly and added the Chippewa diminutive termination ĕns,[2] so that the name became Ca′gobĕns.[3] The white men pronounced the name Shakopee, and a town of that name is now located where the Sioux village once stood. Little Six was a leading warrior and chief of a band among the Mdewakanton Sioux (see p. 70), and the writer has heard of his fame from Sioux living at Sisseton, South Dakota, and at Devils Lake, North Dakota. Both Odjĭb′we and his friend Niski′gwûn took

---

¹ Pronounced Sha′kpay.　² See pp. 186, 190, 230.　³ Pronounced Sha′gobĕns.

part in the fight and together they related its story, Niski'gwûn
also singing two of the songs.

Regarding this fight Folwell gives the following information:[1]

The lower Sioux, who late in 1853 reluctantly retired to their reservations on the
upper Minnesota, were wont to return in summer weather in straggling companies to
their old homes. . . . Shakopee and his band of 150 had early in the summer of 1858
come down and gone into camp near the town which bears his name. One of his
braves, fishing in the river (the Minnesota) at an early hour, was fired upon. Shakopee's men instantly recognized the sound as coming from a Chippeway gun. They
gathered at Murphy's Ferry and, presuming that the hostile shot came from one of
some very small party, they let their women put 30 or 40 of them across. They did
not suspect that back of the timbered bluff a mile distant there lay in hiding 150 or
more Chippeway warriors. . . . They were wary, however, and placed themselves in
ambush in a narrow space between two lakelets. The Chippeways . . . charged down
from the bluff twice or more, without dislodging the Sioux. The day was not old
when they gave up the effort and departed in haste for their homes, carrying their
wounded and perhaps some dead. Four of their corpses were left to the cruel mercies
of the Sioux. . . . Such was the so-called "Battle of Shakopee," May 27, 1858.

An account of the fight from the standpoint of the native his-
torian is given by Warren.[2] Odjĭb'we's narrative is given below in
connection with song No. 8, which concerns the death of a warrior in
the engagement.

The first song of the group has reference to the war charm worn by
the warrior, the song being sung shortly before a fight to make the
charm more effective.[3] Niski'gwûn said that he sang this song before
the battle at Ca'gobĕns' village. The last two words were sung with
the repetition of the song, the melody remaining the same. The word
"balls" was said to refer to the heads of the enemy, which the warrior
would cut off and toss about. Reference is made to No. 35, in which
war is compared to a game, the bodies of the dead being its score.
The charm usually worn by the Chippewa warrior consisted of the
skin of a bird, dried and filled with a medicine known only to the
wearer, probably an herb or other substance suggested to him in a
dream. (See No. 28.) This charm was hung around the neck of the warrior, who believed in its power to protect him. It was said that if, by
any chance, a bullet struck this charm it would kill the man. According to Ma'djigi'jĭg (see p. 84), who made a duplicate of the old war
charm (pl. 12), the bird used in preparing this charm was "the
smallest of a kind of bird that flies at evening;" it was identified by
Mr. Henry Oldys, of the Biological Survey, as the kingbird, or bee mar-
tin (*Tyrannus tyrannus*). The characteristics of this bird may explain
its use by Indian warriors in preparing a charm. "Nothing can be
more striking than the intrepidity with which one of these birds will
pounce upon and harass birds vastly larger and more powerful than

[1] W. W. Folwell, *Minnesota, the North Star State*, Boston, 1908, pp. 157-158.

[2] History of the Ojibway, in *Colls. Minn. Hist. Soc.*, vol. v, 1885, pp. 502, 503.

[3] Other songs connected with the use of "medicine" are Nos. 21, 22, 23, 24, 25, 26, 27, 28, 32, 36, 141, 142, 143.

itself. The kingbird is always prompt to perceive the approach of one of these enemies and always rushes out to meet it." [1] It does not fear to attack even hawks, owls, and eagles. The warrior's use of the skin of the weasel, the most ferocious of small animals, as a decoration has been already noted (p. 63).

If a birdskin were not available, a charm in the form of a bird (pl. 12) was made of cloth and the medicine placed between the two layers of the material.

No. 6. War Medicine Song   (Catalogue No. 384)

Sung by NISKI′GWÛN

VOICE ♩ = 138
DRUM ♩ = 108
(Drum-rhythm similar to No. 2)

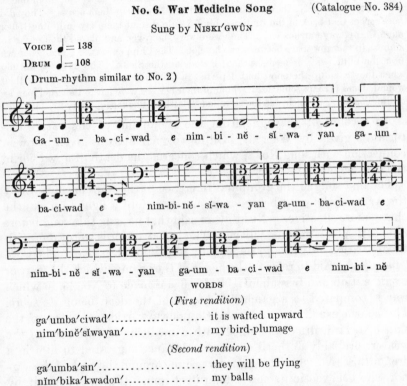

Ga - um - ba - ci - wad   e   nim - bi - ně - sĭ - wa - yan   ga - um -
ba - ci - wad   e   nim - bi - ně - sĭ - wa - yan   ga - um - ba - ci - wad   e
nim - bi - ně - sĭ - wa - yan   ga - um - ba - ci - wad   e   nim - bi - ně

WORDS

(First rendition)

ga′umba′ciwad′...................... it is wafted upward
nim′bině′sĭwayan′.................. my bird-plumage

(Second rendition)

ga′umba′sin′......................... they will be flying
nĭm′bika′kwadon′.................. my balls

Analysis.—Four renditions of this song were recorded. In two of these the close of the song was as transcribed; the other renditions were interrupted several measures earlier by shrill war cries. Indifference concerning the completion of a song has been noted in a few other instances, the singer seeming satisfied without hearing the final tone. This suggests that the relation of the tones to a keynote is not clearly felt. A strong rhythmic sense is shown by the accuracy with which the rhythmic unit is repeated. The melody tones are those of the fourth five-toned scale.

Niski′gwûn stated that before the battle he sang his dream song. This song came to him when he was a young man, after he had

---

[1] S. F. Baird, T. M. Brewer, and R. Ridgway, *North American Birds*, Boston, 1874, p. 318.

CLOTH

BIRD-SKIN

WAR CHARMS

endured a vigil of 10 days, during which time he took only enough food to sustain life. The words are obscure, a feature characteristic of dream songs, the purpose being to conceal the exact nature of the dream.

No. 7. Niski'gwûn's Dream Song   (Catalogue No. 386)

Sung by NISKI'GWÛN

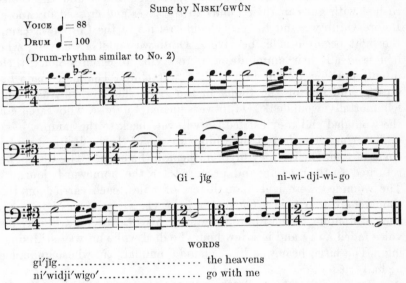

WORDS

gi'jĭg............................... the heavens
ni'widji'wigo'....................... go with me

Analysis.—This song was recorded three times; the transcription was made from the first rendition. In general character the song presents a contrast to the songs recorded by Odjĭb'we. The rhythm is less clearly marked. In it we find neither rhythmic unit nor repeated phrase; the succession of triple and double measures is irregular, and although the rhythm of the song as a whole has a certain individuality it can scarcely be said to be complete and satisfactory. The melody is based on a major triad and would be classified as harmonic except for the E flat in the first measure. This tone was sung firmly and accurately. The sixth lowered a semitone is the accidental occurring most frequently in Chippewa songs (see Table 7). This accidental is found in the following songs of the present volume: Nos. 7, 8, 19, 22, 41, 101, 156, 160.

The story of the fight at Ca'gobĕns' camp, as related by Odjĭb'we, is here given.

A war party of more than a hundred Chippewa determined to attack the encampment of Ca'gobĕns, on the southern shore of the Minnesota River. The Chippewa approached the river from the north and remained behind a bluff, from the summit of which they could see the Sioux tipis on the opposite shore. At daybreak a band of about 25 Chippewa warriors descended the bluff and hid in the bushes beside the water; among the number were Odjĭb'we and

Ga'witayac' ("whirling wind"), a very brave and handsome young man from Red Lake. Soon they saw a Sioux coming down to the shore. A woman sat on the high bank and watched him. With no suspicion of danger the Sioux entered a canoe and started to cross the river. As he neared the shore the Chippewa shot at him. In an instant the screams of the woman gave the alarm and the Sioux rushed with guns in their hands to the river and crossed in canoes. Before Odjĭb'we and his party could return to the Chippewa camp the fight began beside the river. Odjĭb'we and Ga'witayac', who had used all their ammunition, were trying to catch a Sioux, their intention being to kill him with a war club. The man made his escape, and one of the Sioux in the river shot Ga'witayac', who fell mortally wounded. Odjĭb'we signaled to those who cared for the wounded and they carried Ga'witayac' back to the camp.

The Sioux then forced the Chippewa out of the bushes and under cover of their shelter they fired on them in the open. The Chippewa returned to their camp and prepared for the homeward journey. The wounded were laid upon litters of poles, each carried on the shoulders of four men. On such a litter Ga'witayac' was borne, his friends standing around him as he sang his death song. Slowly his voice faded away and in a few hours he died while he was still singing. The large bear was his "manido' animal," in whose guidance he had trusted.

No. 8. Death Song of Ga'witayac'   (Catalogue No. 338)

Sung by ODJĬB'WE

WORDS

ki′tcĭmak′wa................. large bear
ni′waye′jimĭg′ [1].............. deceives me

Analysis.—The rhythmic unit of this song occurs eight times; it is somewhat modified in the last two measures, giving strength to the close of the song. The first two measures constitute an introduction, after which the rhythmic unit is continuously repeated except in the middle part, which contains the words. (See Nos. 1, 12, 13, 30, 39, 40, 81, 105.)

The song is major in tonality and contains the flatted sixth as an accidental. The chords of the tonic and submediant form the framework of this melody, but the accented A flat prevents the classification of the song as purely melodic in structure. It is classified therefore as "melodic with harmonic framework."

Two songs were composed concerning this fight and were sung in the dances which followed the return of the warriors. One of these songs recalls the fight beside the river and is said to have been composed during the fight. The struggle continued until past noon. Five Chippewa were killed and 10 wounded, and many Sioux were killed.

No. 9. "On the Bank of a Stream"   (Catalogue No. 339)

Sung by ODJĬB′WE

VOICE ♩ = 144
DRUM ♩ = 104
(Drum-rhythm similar to No. 2)

A - ga - mĭ - zi - bi - wi - cĕn   en -da-na - dji-mĭ-go - yan

WORDS

aga′mĭzi′biwicĕn′............ across the river
en′dana′djimĭgoyan′.......... they speak of me as being

Analysis.—The ascending interval of an octave at the opening of this song was given accurately in the four renditions. This initial interval occurs in only five other songs of the series of 340 Chippewa songs (see Nos. 170, 174 in Bulletin 45 and Nos. 31, 53, 125 in the

---

[1] One syllable of this word was omitted by the singer.

present volume). The two songs in Bulletin 45 and No. 125 in the present volume are songs of the moccasin game, No. 31 is a war song, and No. 53 the song before a boys' fight. The character of these songs suggests a correspondence between the mental state of the singer and the initial intervals of the songs. The tonality of the present song is minor, but the tonic does not appear until the ninth measure, the opening being based on the major third, which constitutes the upper part of the tonic triad. This opening is noted in five other songs of the present series (Nos. 1, 34, 83, 94, 120). Four of these are songs of war or of dances connected with war and one concerns thunderbirds. In a less marked degree it occurs in the following songs in Bulletin 45: Mĭde' songs Nos. 51, 54, 59, 69, 79, and war song No. 130.

At the close of this song we find the progression 8–7–8, which represents the descent of a whole tone to the seventh of a minor key and return to the tonic. This progression at the close of a song occurs in 9 other songs of various classes of the series of 340 (see Nos. 19, 126, 150 in Bulletin 45 and Nos. 50, 85, 100, 119, 124 of the present volume). This close of a song is frequently found in the ancient music of the white race, especially in old English Plain Song.

This melody contains no rhythmic unit, but the phrase in the 8th measure reappears in the 14th and in part of the 15th measure with a change of accent, a variation which gives character to the rhythm of the song as a whole. The metric unit was maintained with less regularity in this than in the majority of the songs.

The second song concerning this fierce fight calls to mind the grief of the Sioux. Odjĭb'we said he remembered the Sioux women following them across the river, crying, and cursing the Chippewa.

No. 10. "At Ca'gobĕns' Village"   (Catalogue No. 337)

Sung by Odjĭb'we

Voice ♩ = 100
Drum ♩ = 108
(Drum-rhythm similar to No. 3)

Ca - go - bĕns   o - do - de - nañ ma - wi - wŭg e   i - nĭ - nĭ - wŭg

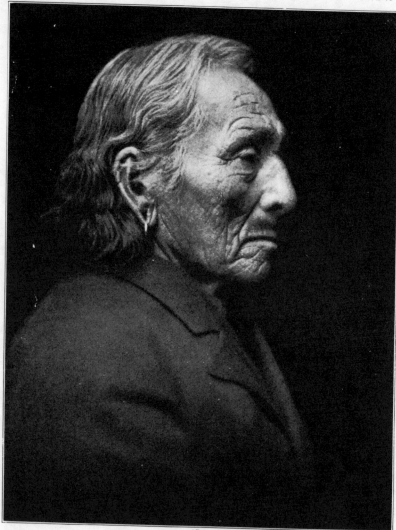

MEJA'KIGI'JĬG

WORDS

(First rendition)

Ca'gobĕns .... at Ca'gobĕns
odo'denañ'.................... village
ma'wiwûg'.................... (they) are weeping
inĭ'nĭwûg'................... the men

(Second rendition)

Ca'gobĕns .... at Ca'gobĕns
odo'denañ'.................... village
ma'wiwûg'.................... (they) are wailing
ikwe'wûg..................... the women

Analysis.—This melody is characterized by opening measures minor in tonality and by the tonic appearing in the first measure. (See analysis of No. 9.) The first five measures have a rhythm which is complete in itself and is not repeated; the last six measures also have a rhythm of their own and may be said to constitute an answering phrase. Between these sections is the part of the song containing the words. This is not strongly accented, though the note-values are the same in all the renditions. The transcription contains the first half of the words, the remainder being given with a second rendition of the song.

Eight months after this song was recorded on the phonograph it was sung again by the same singer and the renditions were found to be identical, even the slight deviations from exact time being repeated.

PERSONAL REMINISCENCES OF THREE WARRIORS

THE CHILD'S DREAM OF WAR

(BY MEJA'KIGI'JĬG)

Meja'kigi'jĭg [1] (pl. 13), chief of the White Earth Chippewa, furnished, in June, 1911, the following narrative of his childish dreams and their fulfillment. He stated at that time that he was the sole survivor of the representatives of the tribe who selected White Earth for the abode of the Chippewa under the terms of the treaty of 1867. He stated also that he was in several war parties led by Odjĭb'we, that he took part in ten campaigns against the Sioux, and was in four fights. The aged chief is honored and respected by all who know him, a man of wise counsels and kindly heart.

Speaking through his favorite interpreter, Mr. John W. Carl (see pp. 130, 303), Meja'kigi'jĭg said that when he was a little boy his father was killed by the Sioux. He well remembered trying every night to dream of something which should enable him, a boy of 7 years, to

---

[1] Rev. J. A. Gilfillan is authority for the statement that when he went to the reservation as a young man the name of the chief was explained to him by the old Indians as meaning "the sky over all the earth, coming down to the earth at the horizon."

kill a Sioux. The older people told him to "go to sleep and be good," but his young mind was filled with thoughts of war. He refused food, not going away from home to fast, after the custom of older boys, but remaining in the lodge. At length he dreamed that he shot a Sioux. Again he dreamed that his hair was gray and, pointing to his flowing locks, slightly streaked with gray, the old chief said that his dream had come true, for he was attaining the allotted age of man.

Later, without leaving home, the boy fasted five days and five nights, hoping for further dreams, but none came.

In the following spring he went away from home to fast. A few years had passed since the little boy could not "go to sleep and be good," but the purpose of his life had not changed; it had deepened and grown more serious. The birds were just beginning to come when he took his way to the "wilderness." Selecting a large tree, he built in it a "nest" for himself, in which he remained without food day after day. At last, on the fifth night of his fast, he dreamed that he held three scalps in his hand. Then he was sure of himself and of his career. With confidence he joined the warriors, and his faith in his dream remained unshaken and at last the day came when he held aloft three Sioux scalps.

Thus the boy, grown to manhood, avenged his father's death according to the custom of his people.

THE TRAINING OF YOUNG WARRIORS

(BY MA'DJIGI'JĬG)

Ma'djigi'jĭg ("great sky") was a young man when the war parties swept across the prairie. His personal reminiscences were not those of a leader, but he recalled with distinctness the trials which fell to the lot of a recruit. Later he served many times as a scout, and, as a warrior, secured three Sioux scalps. In plate 14 he is represented in the attitude of a scout on the prairie, holding a wisp of grass or bit of brush before his face, and also as telling the story of the three scalps.

According to Ma'djigi'jĭg, "the old warriors treated the beginners as though they were nothing but animals." The young warriors camped a few rods in the rear of the rest of the war party, and united with the main camp only when near the enemy. The recruits slept in little shelters, or booths, which they made of boughs, two men in each. The older warriors had plenty of food and even were allowed to eat fat meat, while the recruits were given scanty rations of wild rice, either parched or only partially cooked, and seasoned slightly with maple sugar. Sometimes they were given dried fish or tough smoked meat and occasionally lean fresh meat hardly seared before the fire.

IN POSTURE OF LOOKING FOR THE ENEMY

RECOUNTING THE TAKING OF THREE SCALPS

MA'DJIGI'JĬG

When deer or other large game were killed by the warriors it was customary to hold a "breaking-bone contest" in the camp of the recruits. This was conducted as follows: A marrow bone (usually the leg bone) was laid on the ground. The man who intended to test his skill took his place beside the bone and then walked eight paces away from it. He was then blindfolded and, hatchet in hand, walked toward the bone. When he thought himself near it, he struck at it with his hatchet. Ma'djigi'jĭg illustrated this for the writer, but age had shortened his steps and, blindfolded, he did not measure the distance correctly. In the old days the man who cracked the bone with the first blow of his hatchet hastened to carry away the spoils; after being cooked the marrow was removed by means of a stick made for the purpose. This was the only way in which a young warrior on his first expedition could secure a taste of fat. He was not given the prize unless he succeeded in actually breaking the bone, and much merriment resulted from the misdirected efforts of many of the young men.

On their first war party men were required to put mittens on both hands when they left the village and to wear them until they entered a fight with the Sioux. These mittens were tied securely at the wrist, from which a small stick was hung; this the recruit was ordered to use in scratching his head or body. Failing to do this, on reaching home he would "break out with boils on his whole body." Some recruits refused to wear mittens or to use the "scratch stick," and Ma'djigi'jĭg recalled one instance in which a man became covered with sores to so great an extent that he could scarcely reach home. The old man gave as a reason for the regulation that the recruits lacked the protective medicines carried by the warriors.

Many rules were strictly enforced in the recruits' camp. Care was taken to avoid stepping over any article belonging to another. Thus if a man stepped across another's gun he was chased and severely punished by the owner of the weapon, as such action was supposed to render it useless. It was considered a bad omen for a recruit to see a snake.

Ma'djigi'jĭg related the story of an attack on a Sioux village, which took place during his first war expedition. At dusk the leader of the party sent several experienced men to reconnoiter. Under cover of night they approached the Sioux village, counted the tipis, and estimated the number of warriors. Soon after midnight they returned and made their report. Preparations for a march were begun at once and just before daybreak the Chippewa drew near the Sioux village. The leader then called for the wind and the wind came. The Sioux heard the wind singing through the tipi poles, and the flapping of the tipi canvas, but they did not hear the soft tread of the Chippewa as the latter entered the camp. The Chippewa lowered their guns, aiming at the places where the Sioux lay asleep. When all was ready one of the warriors blew a quavering note on a tiny whistle, like the call of a waking bird. At this signal the Chippewa fired and then rushed at the tipis, tearing them down and killing as many of the wounded as possible. With a quick slash they severed the head of a Sioux from his body and ran away with it, removing the scalp afterward. Three or four scalps were sometimes cut from one head. The term "scalp lock," however, was applied to the lock situated just back of the crown. As this is the only spot at which the scalp adheres closely to the skull, the scalp lock is especially difficult to remove, but a skillful warrior could do so with one motion of his knife. He then slipped the end of the hair beneath the string which held his breechcloth, and the scalp dangled at the victor's side.

If a war party ran short of provisions the leader selected a place to camp, near a lake. He smoked his pipe, sang his dream song, and smoked again. At length he pointed in a certain direction and said, "A deer is coming there; it is sent to you." Thus the camp was supplied with meat. Ma'djigi'jĭg said he had known this to occur many times. He stated also that, before attacking a Sioux village, the leader of a war party frequently "called on the thunderbird to send rain," in order that the Sioux would remain at home, not changing their camp or wandering in the vicinity, where they might detect the approach of the Chippewa.

THE WAR BADGE

(By A'kiwĕn'zi)

A'kiwĕn'zi ("old man") wore proudly the double insignia of his success as a warrior—feathers in his headdress and skunk skins attached to his ankles (pl. 15). Even at his advanced age he was so lithe and agile in the dance that one could readily believe his statement that as a warrior he was distinguished for fleetness of foot. Two of his war-honor feathers were won at the memorable fight at Ca'gobĕns' village (see p. 79). After that fight there were many dead and wounded Sioux lying on the ground. He kicked one of the latter and thus won the right to wear a skunk skin at his ankle. Later, as a member of a war party which pushed far into the Sioux country, he killed a Sioux near the site of the present Sisseton, South Dakota, afterward kicking the body of the slain; thus he won the right to wear his third war-honor feather, and the other skunk skin at his ankle. In June, 1911, A'kiwĕn'zi was living on the White Earth Reservation. There he and his war comrades frequently joined in social dances with their old enemies, and again smoked the pipe of peace with the Sioux.

A'KIWĔN'ZI

DESCRIPTION OF CHIPPEWA WAR EXPEDITION, WITH TYPICAL SONGS

Every phase of a war expedition had its appropriate song, from the announcement of the leader's plan to the close of the victory dances.

Songs Connected with Organization of War Party

The warrior who wished to lead a war party sent an *oc'kabe'wĭs* (messenger) with tobacco to ask the warriors to join his expedition. The messenger went to each village and requested the warriors to assemble; he then explained the purpose of the expedition, filled a pipe with *apak'osigûn'* (a mixture of tobacco and the inner bark of the red willow), and, holding the bowl of the pipe, offered the stem to one warrior after another. As he did this he sang the song which follows. All who were willing to join the expedition so signified by smoking the pipe.

No. 11. Song of the War Messenger   (Catalogue No. 358)

Sung by Odjĭb'we

bĭdako′namawĭcĭn′.......... come and hold
nin′dopwa′gûn............... my pipe
no′sĭs........................ my grandchild

Analysis.—The drum-rhythm of this song is unusual; it consists of an accented stroke followed by a short unaccented stroke corresponding to the second count of a triplet. The metric unit of the drum is slightly slower than that of the voice. Four renditions of the song were secured, throughout which the rhythmic unit was maintained with great regularity, though the intonation varied perceptibly.

The tones of the melody comprise only the minor third and fourth, the principal interval being the descending minor third. The song contains a rhythmic unit, which occurs four times, constituting the entire melody.

After the smoking of the pipe the oc′kabe′wĭs returned to the man who wished to organize the expedition and reported his success in the following song.

No. 12. Return of the War Messenger (Catalogue No. 359)

Sung by ODJĬB′WE

VOICE ♩ = 192
DRUM ♩ = 100
(Drum-rhythm similar to No. 11)

O - gĭ - tci - dañ i - ji - na - gû - zi - wûg be - zi - gwi

djĭg i - nĭ - nĭ-wûg e

ogĭ′tcĭdañ .... like warriors
ijina′gûziwûg′............... they look
be′zigwi′djĭg................ who arise
inĭ′nĭwûg′.................... those men

Analysis.—This song is divided into four parts, the first, second, and last of which contain the rhythmic unit, while the words occur in the third part, which has a different rhythm. (See Nos. 1, 8, 13, 30, 39, 40, 81, 105.) The drum-rhythm is the same as in the preceding song.   The descending interval of the minor third occurs frequently, and the song is distinctly minor in tonality.

In a short time the warriors arrived and camped near the lodge of the leader.   A feast was given by the leader, at which he explained more fully the proposed expedition, asking for a final pledge from the warriors.   All who were satisfied with the plan responded with *He he he*, and the expedition was considered formally inaugurated. The leader then said, "We will have the first dance to-night, and we will dance every night until we reach the enemy." According to Odjĭb'we the following song was usually sung by the Mississippi Band of Chippewa at this initial dance (see also No. 81).

No. 13. "I Feel no Fear"   (Catalogue No. 328)

Sung by ODJĬB'WE

VOICE ♩ = 160
DRUM ♩ = 104
(Drum-rhythm similar to No. 3)

Ka - wĭn   nin - ca - gwe - nĭ - mu - si   ka - wĭn   nin - ca -
gwe - nĭ - mu - si   ka - wĭn nin - ca - gwe - nĭ - mu - si   kĭ - tci -
zi - bi - wi - nĭ - nĭ   ni - bo - ĭn   wa - ya - win - dĭ - gĭn   e   ka -
wĭn nin - ca - gwe - nĭ - mu - si   ka - wĭn nin - ca - gwe - nĭ - mu - si   ka -
wĭn nin - ca - gwe - nĭ - mu - si   ka - wĭn nin - ca - gwe - nĭ - mu - si

WORDS

kawĭn' .... nincagwe'nĭmusi'	I feel no fear
Kĭtcizi'biwinĭ'nĭ	when the Great River man [1]
nibo'ĭn	death
waya'windûñ [2]	speaks of

[1] The "Great River" was the Mississippi, and the term "Great River man" referred to a member of the Mississippi Band of Chippewa.
[2] The last syllable is divided and also changed, to fit the music.

Analysis.—This is the first song recorded by Odjĭb'we. Four renditions were secured and found to be uniform. The first two were without the drum; these were followed by a pause, during which it was explained to the singer that the drum was desired; he then resumed his singing with the accompaniment of that instrument. On comparison it is found that the pitch and metric unit of the two parts of the record are identical. This ability to resume his song in the same tempo is the more interesting when we note the discrepancy between the metric units of voice and drum.

The rhythmic unit occurs six times and is interrupted only by the change of words. (See Nos. 1, 8, 12, 30, 39, 40, 81, 105.) In this part of the song there is no decided accent and the enunciation of the words resembles rapid speech. The excitement of the song centers in these words, given on a high tone, descending in the next phrase to the flatted sixth, the accidental most frequently found in Chippewa songs. The flatted seventh also occurs, which strengthens the phrase. The song is grim in its suggestion, yet it is major in tonality and cheerful in its rhythm.

The following song was sung at the dances preceding a war expedition. It contains the name of a man who once stayed at home, and was intended to shame all who, without proper excuse, failed to join the warriors.

No. 14. "The Man who Stayed at Home" (Catalogue No. 388)

Sung by ODJĬB'WE

VOICE ♩ = 152
Recorded without drum

Mi-nodj Jĭñ-gwa-be   *mi no* i - nĭ - niñ gi-ne - ni-mud *e*   wi -

wûn go - cû o-don-da - me-ni-man

WORDS

mi'nodj	although
Jĭñgwa'be	Jĭñgwa'be (man's name; meaning, "man of the spruce tree")
inĭ'niñ [1]	a man
ine'nimud'	considers himself
wi'wûn	his wife
gocû'	certainly
odon'dame'niman'	takes all his attention

---

[1] The initial *g* of the fourth word in the music is carried over from the ñ, the final letter of the preceding word—an example of elision by Chippewa singers.

CHIPPEWA WAR BANNER

Analysis.—Four renditions of this song were recorded with a short interval between the second and third. The rhythm was accurately repeated, even the slight variations in time being duplicated. It is a taunting, mocking melody, different from any other war song and admirably expressing the idea contained in the words. Compare No. 38, which is also a song of derision.

The leader appointed four men to act as his aids during the entire expedition. These men, like the messenger sent with the tobacco, were called *oc'kabe'wĭs.* They attended to all the preparations for the expedition and made the arrangements for the dances held before leaving the village. One of them carried the leader's pipe and the other carried the drum when the war party was on the march. They also arranged for the camps on the expedition. A war party always carried a generous supply of "medicine," also materials necessary for making and mending moccasins. Part of the equipment was provided by the leader, who also borrowed the "banner" or "flag" borne by the war party. This was made of eagle feathers sewed on a strip of cloth about 4 feet long, which was fastened lengthwise to a pole. Odjĭb'we stated that in the old days he knew of only one such banner among the Mississippi Band of Chippewa, made by a man named Gaga'gĭwĭgwûn' ("raven feather") and loaned to the war parties. It was considered the common property of the warriors, but this man was its custodian in time of peace, and it was preserved in his family after hostilities ceased. At the present time (1912) there is one war flag preserved at White Earth, but this is believed not to be the one made by Gaga'gĭwĭgwûn'. It was carried in the wars against the Sioux by Mi'gĭsĭns' (Little Eagle), and is now in the possession of his daughter. In plate 16 this banner is shown, held by the daughter of Mi'gĭsĭns', though a woman would not have carried such a banner in actual warfare. Mi'gĭsĭns' was so distinguished a warrior that a song in his honor is still sung at White Earth (No. 126, Bulletin 45). A similar banner, used at Waba'cĭñg, is shown in plates 44 and 45.

The final event before the departure of the war party from the village was the dog feast. The head alone was eaten and only the men who were going with the expedition partook of it. Participation in this feast was considered equivalent to a pledge that the warriors were prepared to meet the full fortune of war, whether death or worse, at the hands of the enemy.

No. 15. Pledge Song   (Catalogue No. 360)

Sung by ODJĬB'WE

Drum-rhythm

WORDS

nin'dacamĭgog'............... they feed me
ogĭ'tcĭdag'.................... the braves
nin'dacamĭgog'............... feed me

Analysis.—The second and third measures of this song constitute the rhythmic unit. Five renditions of the song were recorded. The opening measure was uniformly given, but in two instances the last measure was omitted, the corresponding quarter notes an octave higher taking its place.

The written music appears to consist of seven two-measure phrases with an introductory measure, but the Indian's rendition divides the song into two parts, the first containing eight and the second seven measures, a strong accent being given the first note of the ninth measure.

At the conclusion of the dog feast all the warriors danced, guns in hand, and sang the following song, which contains no words. All the final preparations had been made and they were ready to start on their journey.

No. 16. Dance of the Dog Feast   (Catalogue No. 361)

Sung by ODJĬB'WE

VOICE ♩ = 92
DRUM ♩ = 92
(Drum-rhythm similar to No. 15)

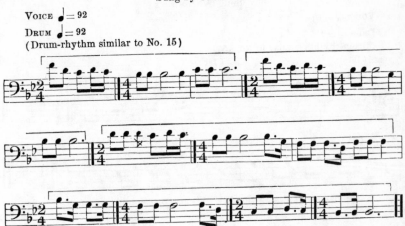

Analysis.—This song contains a rhythmic unit which is slightly varied in repetition. No variation in either melody or rhythm appears in the four renditions of the song except that in the second of each group of two renditions the singer avoided the first high note and began with the last note of the second measure. The tempo is slow and the drum and voice are in consonance. In general character the song is dignified, yet vigorous, as befitted the song of those who were equipped and ready for the warpath.

At the conclusion of the dog feast and dance the leader of the party began the "song of departure" and his warriors took up the melody. Dancing, not marching, they left the scene of the feast, and followed their leader toward the land of the enemy. Only one woman, usually the wife of the leader, was allowed to go with the war party. Four women escorted the warriors as they left the village, walking back and forth in front of them and joining in their song. These women had their faces whitened with clay. At last they divided, two standing on each side of the path, and the warriors passed between them. There were no farewells and the song did not cease. With eyes turned toward the enemy's country the warriors went forth to meet their uncertain fate.

No. 17. Song of Departure [1]   (Catalogue No. 362)

Sung by ODJĬB'WE

VOICE ♩ = 108
DRUM ♩ = 108
(Drum-rhythm similar to No. 15)

Bi-ma-cĭ-wûg ni-mi-gwûn-ûg *e*   bi - ma-cĭ-wûg ni-mi-gwûn-ûg *e*   *he*

WORDS

bima'cĭwûg'.................. they are sailing on the breeze
nimi'gwûnûg'................ my feathers

Analysis.—The words of this song probably refer to the birdskin charm worn by the warrior (see pp. 77, 78). The song contains two rhythmic units, similar in the division of the last three counts but differing in the division of the first two. Each unit occurs twice, its repetition being followed by a triple measure. Thus the first unit followed by a triple measure constitutes the first part of the song, and the second unit, steadier and stronger in rhythm and followed by a triple measure, constitutes the second part. The melody is harmonic in structure and is based on the tonic chord.

SONGS OF THE WARPATH

At evening the oc'kabe'wĭs selected a suitable place for the camp. According to Odjĭb'we, every evening the warriors seated themselves in a row facing the enemy's country; the four oc'kabe'wĭs sat in front of them, and in advance of all sat the leader with his drum. The leader sang alone, and the warriors did not respond with the shrill cries which punctuated many of the war songs. He placed two crotched sticks upright in the ground, with a crossbar between them, on which rested the stem of his lighted pipe, with the bowl on the ground. As he sang the leader shook his rattle of deer hoofs or laid it beside the pipe and looked away toward the enemy's country, while his silent warriors waited on his divination.[2]

---

[1] See No. 150, Bulletin 45.
[2] Cf. George Earl Church, *Aborigines of South America*, London, 1912, p. 284: [Among the Pampas Indians the wizards] "used the *maracá* [rattle], which they said told them many secrets and made all they said oracular."

The following song was said to have been sung by the leader every night while on an expedition.

No. 18. Song of the Leader   (Catalogue No. 343)

Sung by ODJĬB′WE

VOICE ♩ = 104
DRUM ♩ = 104
(Drum-rhythm similar to No. 15)

A-ni de-ba-bûn-da-man a-ki *we* a-ni de - ba-bûn-da-

man a - ki *we* *na* ga-kĭ ĕn - i - go-kwag ga-kĭ-

na a - ni de - ba-bûn-da-man a - ki *we* a - ni de-

ba-bûn-da-man a-ki *we* a-ni de-ba- bûn-da-man a - ki *we*

WORDS

ani′............................ as
deba′bûndaman′............. I see
aki′.......................... the earth
gakĭ′na.....................⎫
                           ⎬ the whole compass of it
ĕn′igokwag′.................⎭

Analysis.—The transcription of this song is from the first of four renditions, which differ only in the intonation of the tones marked. These tones are given with what might be termed a "toss" of the voice. Thus the third tone of the song is sung in one instance almost as high as G flat. There is an evident intention to lower slightly the next to the last tone of the rhythmic unit, but the interval is not definite. The close of the last phrase is given with more accuracy than the preceding, although the low pitch of the tone makes it more difficult to sing.

The rhythmic unit occurs six times, its repetitions comprising the entire song. An additional quarter note is inserted after the second and fifth repetitions; this is found in all the renditions and adds interest to the rhythm of the song as a whole. The metric unit of voice and drum is the same, the voice slightly preceding the drum.

The following song was sometimes sung by a leader and was also used by oc'kabe'wĭs and by scouts (see No. 82). This is a dream song and was always sung by men who were alone, never at the dances.

No. 19. "I will go to the South"   (Catalogue No. 333)

Sung by ODJĬB'WE

VOICE ♩ = 112
DRUM ♩ = 112
(See drum-rhythm below)

Nin-ga - dĭ - ja   ca - wûn - oñg ning-a - dĭ - ja   ca - wûn-

oñg *a*   nin-ga - dĭ - ja   ca - wûn - oñg ning-a - dĭ -

ja   ca - wûn-oñg *a*   nin-ga-bi - don ca-wûn - i - no - dĭn

e   nin-ga-dĭ - ja   ca-wûn-oñg ning-ga - dĭ   ca - wûn-oñg *e*

Drum-rhythm

etc.

WORDS

nin'gadĭja'..................... I will go
ca'wûnoñg'.................. to the south
nin'gabidon'................ I will bring
ca'wûnino'dĭn.............. the south wind

Analysis.—This song was recorded twice, an interval of two weeks elapsing between the making of the two records. On the first occasion the singer sang the song twice, and, after pausing to explain the words, again sang it twice. On the second occasion also he sang the song twice. Thus six renditions were secured, in groups of two. On comparison it is found that these renditions vary in intonation, but that the note-values and accents are the same, with some slight exceptions in the tones which connect the phrases. In all the songs it seems allowable to divide or prolong these connecting tones at the will of the singer. The song contains a rhythmic unit, which occurs six times and is slightly varied near the close of the song. Each group of two rhythmic units forms a melodic phrase. The song is melodic in structure according to the present basis of classification because an accent is placed on an accidental tone, but the remainder of the accented tones follow the intervals of the tonic chord. The accidental is the sixth lowered a semitone. In form the melody resembles Nos. 4, 5, 33, 34.

Many songs were used in the dances at the nightly camps, the warriors frequently singing of their former victories. The following two songs are characteristic of this class.

No. 20. "A War Bird" (Catalogue No. 332)

Sung by ODJĬB'WE

VOICE ♩ = 112
DRUM ♩ = 116
(Drum-rhythm similar to No. 19)

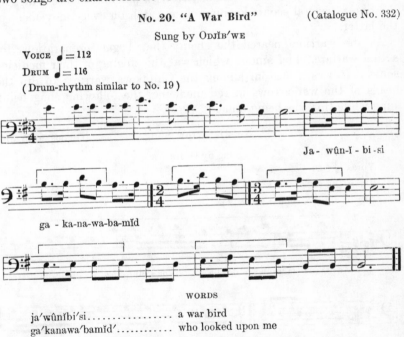

Ja - wûn-Ĭ - bi -si

ga - ka-na-wa-ba-mĭd

WORDS

ja′wûnĭbi′si.................. a war bird
ga′kanawa′bamĭd′............ who looked upon me

Analysis.—In the number and manner of renditions this song is similar to No. 19, two sets of records being made at an interval of a fortnight. As in the preceding instance, the rhythm remains identical throughout the renditions, but several unimportant note-values are altered. The rhythmic unit is short and occurs in both double and triple measures; the song as a whole has an interesting completeness or unity of rhythm. The melody is clearly in the key of G, although the tonic does not appear until the eighth measure.

By midday the warriors were on their journey. Odjĭb'we said that before starting the leader frequently filled and lighted a pipe, after which he took a puff and held the stem toward the enemy's country, saying, "Every Sioux who puffs this pipe will soon be a dead man." He then passed the pipe to all the warriors, each of whom took a puff. The leader then spoke to the drum in a low muttering tone, "Be faithful, my drum," or "Be faithful, be true."

When this ceremony was finished the drum gave the signal and the warriors took up their journey, with the pipe-bearer leading the way, and the leader walking last, carrying his rattle of deer hoofs. After the party was well underway the drum ceased beating and the war party walked in silence except for the occasional sound of the leader's rattle. A Chippewa war party frequently traveled 25 miles in a day, stopping at intervals to rest and smoke. According to Odjĭb'we they made a camp and "had a good rest," if possible, before attacking the Sioux, several scouts keeping close watch on every movement of the latter.

As the warriors neared the enemy they began preparations for actual warfare, chief among which was the singing of their medicine songs. It was a custom among the Chippewa warriors to dip the heads of the war arrows in red medicine, the following song being sung while this was being done.

No. 21. Arrow Song   (Catalogue No. 370)

Sung by ODJĬB'WE

VOICE ♩ = 60
DRUM ♩ = 84
(Drum-rhythm similar to No. 2)

WORDS

o'namûnûn'........................ scarlet
de'bwan............................ is its head

Analysis.—The rhythmic unit of this song is short and vigorous. The melody is inspiring in character and well fitted to increase a warrior's confidence in his success. The ending is peculiar but was given uniformly, the five renditions of the song being identical in every respect.

The principal war medicine carried by the Chippewa was the bi'jĭkiwŭck' ("cattle herb medicine"), which was said to "make men strong," and to be a powerful healing medicine (see p. 63). It was the warrior's custom to chew this medicine and spray it from his lips upon his body and his equipment. The following song was sung while preparing the medicine.

No. 22. Origin of the Bi'jĭkiwŭck'   (Catalogue No. 372)

Sung by ODJĬB'WE

VOICE ♩ = 100
DRUM ♩ = 100
(Drum-rhythm similar to No. 2)

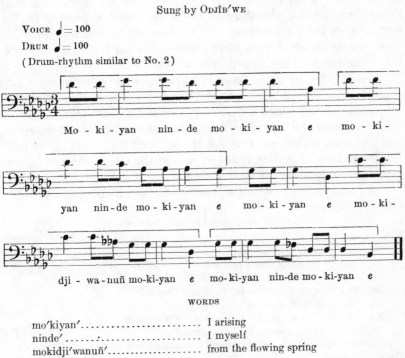

WORDS

mo'kiyan'.......................... I arising
ninde'............................ I myself
mokidji'wanuñ'..................... from the flowing spring

Analysis.—This is the first of a large number of songs based on the interval of a fourth or in which that interval is especially prominent. This group includes 11 songs in Bulletin 45 and 25 songs in the present volume, a total of 36, or 11 per cent of the entire collection. The interval of the fourth is usually (in its first occurrence) a descending interval and, except at the close of a song, is rarely if ever followed by the interval of a third, completing the chord of the sixth. It occurs in three ways, which form a basis for a closer observation of the group: First, two continuously descending fourths form the framework of the melody; thus Nos. 6 and 9 in Bulletin 45 are based on the descending intervals D–A, A–E, ending with the descending tonic triad D–B–G in the closing measures. No. 3 in Bulletin 45 and No. 82 in the present volume are based on the intervals C sharp–G sharp, F sharp–C sharp. Second, the melody is based on two descending intervals of a fourth, the second interval being only one tone below the first. No. 28 in the present volume is based on the intervals E flat–B flat, D flat–A flat. (See also No. 23.) Third, the interval of the fourth is especially prominent but this interval is, as it were, inclosed in the interval of the fifth; thus in the present instance (No. 22) the intervals which form the framework of the first four measures are the fifths E flat–A flat, D flat–G flat, but the principal intervals are the fourths D flat–A flat, C flat–G flat. The next four measures are characterized by descending fourths, the third of the tonic chord appearing for the first time in the final measure. The close of the song suggests that there should be another measure ending on G flat but that G flat was below the range of the singer's voice.

Since 11 per cent of the series of 340 songs have a common melodic characteristic, we note with interest that they have also a common subject, all being songs concerning motion (20) or animals (15), in some instances the two ideas being combined. The single exception is a love song which contains the words "I sit here thinking of her." While the idea of motion is not expressed therein, it can not be considered entirely absent from the mind of the singer.

The numbers and titles (or words) of this group of songs are as follows:

(a) SONGS CONCERNING MOTION

Bulletin 45:

No.   6. "I am raising my pipe"
No.   9. "A bubbling spring comes from the hard ground"
No.   10. "You are going around the Mĭde′ lodge"
No.   63. "The shell goes toward them and they fall"
No.   86. "The flame goes up to my body"
No.   91. "To the spirit land I am going, I am walking"
No. 109. "The big bear, to his lodge I go often"
No. 132. "The women are enjoying it [the dance] with us"

Present volume:

No.   22. "I arise from the flowing spring"
No.   32. "The prairie land whence I arise"
No.   34. "The Sioux women gather up their wounded"
No.   39. "Odjĭb′we brings back our brother"
No. 105. "Go with me"
No. 106. "Now I go"
No. 110. "I go around weeping"
No. 111. "Come, let us sing"
No. 121. Ca′wûno′ga dance
No. 162. "The sound of his approaching footsteps"
No. 170. "Work steadily, I am afraid they will take you away from me"
No. 174. "You shall depart"

(b) SONGS CONCERNING ANIMALS (USUALLY REPRESENTED AS IN MOTION)

Bulletin 45:
    No.   3. "In form like a bird it appears"
    No. 121. "I am afraid of the owl"
    No. 196. "Round-hoofed had pity on me"
Present volume:
    No. 23. "Strike ye our land with curved horns"
    No. 28. "My bird-skin charm is my trust"
    No. 64. "The ravens are singing"
    No. 82. "Riding on my horse"
    No. 85. "I am walking in the sky, a bird I accompany"
    No. 95. Song of the deer (a)
    No. 96. Song of the deer (b)
    No. 97. Song of the deer dancing
    No. 103. Moccasin game song taught by a manido' in the form of a bear (a)
    No. 104. Moccasin game song taught by a manido' in the form of a bear (b)
    No. 147. "One bird, I am going with him"
    No. 180. "The crawfish cringes"

    Songs in praise of bi'jĭkiwûck' were sung in the war dances. When singing these songs the warriors imitated the action of wild cattle, holding their arms above their heads to simulate horns and pretending to paw the ground; they imitated also the calls of various wild animals, these being calls which they intended to use in decoying the Sioux.

No. 23. Dancing Song of the Bi'jĭkiwûck' (Catalogue No. 382)

Sung by MAIÑ'GANS ("LITTLE WOLF")

VOICE ♩= 96
Recorded without drum

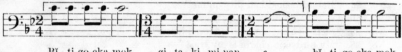

Bĭ - ti-go-cka-mok   gi - ta - ki - mi-nan   *e*   bĭ - ti - go - cka-mok

gi - ta-ki-mi - nan   *e*   bĭ - ti-go-cka-mok   gi - ta - ki - mi-nan   *e*

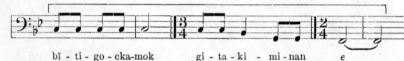

bĭ - ti - go - cka-mok   gi - ta - ki - mi - nan   *e*

we-wa - gi - wĭ - nĭ   bĭ - ti - go-cka-mok gi - ta - ki - mi - nan   *e*

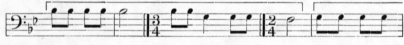

bĭ - ti-go-cka-mok   gi - ta-ki - mi - nan   *e*   we - wa - gi - wĭ -

nĭ   bĭ - ti - go - cka-mok   gi - ta - ki - mi - nan   *e*

WORDS

bĭ'tigo'ckamok'..................... strike ye
gi'takiminan'........................ our land
wewa'giwĭnĭ'........................ with curved horns

Analysis.—The descending interval of the fourth is especially
prominent in this melody (see analysis of No. 22). The first five
measures comprise the rhythmic unit, which is well adapted to the
expression of the words. This rhythm, combined with the peculiar
melodic outline, causes the song to produce an effect of rugged
strength.

During the preparation of mĭ'nĭsĭno'wûck ("island herb medicine")
and also before a battle the following four songs were sung by the

warriors to make the medicine effectual as a charm. This group of songs was rendered by Na′waji′bigo′kwe ("woman dwelling in the midst of the rocks").

No. 24. First Song of the Mǐ′nǐsǐno′wûck

Sung by Na′waji′bigo′kwe

(Catalogue No. 373)

Voice ♩= 69

Drum ♩= 108

(Drum-rhythm similar to No. 2)

Ka - ga - gi - wi - wan nin - dau ba - on - dji - o - non - ge -

wi - *hi*- yan ka - ga - gi - wi - **wan** nin-dau ba-on - dji - o-non-ge - *wi* - yan

WORDS

[Free translation]

kaga′giwiwan′...................... ⎫

nindan............................. ⎬ light as a raven's feather

ba′ondji′onongeyan′............... ⎭ is my flight

Analysis.—This melody was sung very slowly with a rapid drumbeat. The song is harmonic in structure and contains the tones of the fourth five-toned scale. The rhythmic unit does not vary in the four renditions of the song, but there is a slight variation in unimportant melody progressions. Attention is directed to the register of the woman's voice. Several other phonographic records made by Chippewa women show the same register.

All the songs of this series close with the ejaculations *We ho ho ho*, which characterize also the Mǐde′ songs.

No. 25. Second Song of the Mĭ′nĭsĭno′wûck

Sung by NA′WAJI′BIGO′KWE

(Catalogue No. 374)

VOICE ♩= 152
DRUM ♩= 92
(Drum-rhythm similar to No. 2)

WORDS

gi′jĭg......................... the heavens
ĕ′yoyan′ [1] .... I use

Analysis.—The words imply that the heavens are secured as a defense by the singer. In all the renditions of this song the drum is struck after the melody tone is sung. This gives an effect of great irregularity to the performance and also shows the independence of vocal and instrumental expression. The rhythmic unit, which is accurately repeated, occurs 11 times. The double measures vary in length and apparently serve as resting places for the voice.

---

[1] See footnote 2, p. 89.

No. 26. Third Song of the Mĭ´nĭsĭno´wŭck

Sung by NA´WAJI´BIGO´KWE

(Catalogue No. 375)

WORDS

ga´mĭnogi´wepû´yane´........ I will return to my home in safety

Analysis.—This melody contains no tones except those comprised in the rhythmic unit, which was steadily maintained throughout the six renditions. Owing to the rapid tempo, the measure is a more convenient metric unit than the individual count in the measure; thus the metronome indication is for a dotted half instead of a quarter note. The song is harmonic in structure and contains the tones of the fourth five-toned scale; it was recorded without the drum.

No. 27. Fourth Song of the Mǐ'nǐsǐno'wûck

Sung by NA'WAJI'BIGO'KWE

(Catalogue No. 376)

VOICE ♩ = 168
Recorded without drum

Na-mûndj-ge - do-gwĕn ĕ ba - ön - dji - o - nan - ge- yan   ĕ

na-mûndj-ge - do- gwĕn ba - ön - dji - o - nan - ge - yan   ĕ

na-mûndj-ge - do-gwĕn ĕ ba - ön - dji - o - nan - ge - yan   ĕ

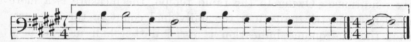

na-mûndj-ge - do- gwĕn bû - ön - djǐ - bû - si - gwi - yan   ĕ

na-mûndj -ge - do- gwĕn bû - ön - djǐ - bû - si - gwi- yan   ĕ

WORDS

namûndj'gedogwĕn'.......... it is uncertain what will happen
baöndjǐ'onan'geyan'.......... to the one from whom I fly
namûndj'gedogwĕn'.......... it is uncertain what will happen
bûöndjǐ'bûsigwiyan'.......... to the one from whom I rise

Analysis.—This melody is unusually irregular in form. The principal measures are in 7–4 time; the rhythmic unit contains three measures and occurs five times. Four renditions were secured; these are identical except that after the first rendition the singer omitted part of the last phrase, closing with the calls *We ho ho ho.* Apparently this was done to avoid the very low tone at the close, which was sung with difficulty. The song is freely melodic in structure and contains all the tones of the octave except the seventh.

If a great fight were expected, the Chippewa made preparations for the care of the wounded. Litters were constructed of poles, these being especially required, as the Sioux always pursued the Chippewa in an effort to capture the wounded. Every war party included an old man whose duty it was to carry an extra supply of medicine and of water; he did not fight but held himself in readiness to attend those in need of assistance. The feather flag (see p. 91) was carried by one of the bravest warriors, who ran to and fro with it during the fight. This man was a target for the Sioux and defended the flag with his life. The drum was beaten during the contest by one of the warriors, who also sang to inspire the men. This duty likewise required special courage. Before entering a fight the leaders arrayed themselves in brilliant trappings. Each wore a band around the head in which were bright feathers; this rendered them conspicuous and showed their fearlessness. The neck was usually encircled by a charm consisting of the dried skin of a bird, which contained a medicine known only to the wearer (see p. 77). This charm was wrapped in birch bark but before a battle the warrior tore off the cover, exposing the bird skin, and also sang the song which should make the charm effectual. The following song was used for this purpose.

No. 28. Song of a War Charm (Catalogue No. 369)

Sung by Odjïb'we

Voice $\quad\downarrow = 80$
Drum $\quad\downarrow = 92$
(Drum-rhythm similar to No. 2)

We-go-nĕn - i - wi - nĕ - hĕ - hĕ - ne e - pĕ - ni - mo -

ya - ha-han e we-go-nĕn - i - wi - nĕ - hĕ-hĕ - ne e-pĕ - ni - mo -

ya - ha-han nin-bĭ-nĕs-i-wa-yan e he he e e - pĕ-ni-mo -

ya - ha-han e we-go-nĕn-i-wi-nĕ - hĕ-hĕ-ne e-pĕ-ni-mo-yan e

WORDS

wegonĕn'iwinĕn'[1] .... in what
epĕ'nimoyan' .... is my trust?
ninbĭnĕs'iwayan' .... my bird-skin charm
epĕ'nimoyan' .... is my trust

[1] See footnote 2, p. 89.

Analysis.—This song is transcribed in the key of D flat, though the third of that key does not appear in the melody (see analysis of No. 53). In broad outline the framework of the melody may be said to be the descending interval of the fourth—E flat–B flat, and D flat–A flat (see analysis of No. 22). The song is regular in form, the rhythmic unit occurring four times; the first two occurrences contain the words of the question while the last two contain the answer.

According to Odjĭb'we the Chippewa always sang, if possible, before attacking the enemy. If the attack were to be made at daybreak, the Chippewa crept stealthily to an ambush near the village, the drum was beaten very softly, and the following song was sung in subdued tones. Then came a piercing yell as the warriors dashed on the sleeping enemy. In open fight the war cry of the Chippewa was *Bwan, Bwan,*[1] the word by which they designated a Sioux. Odjĭb'we stated that the leader started the drum song. The title is not fully explained, but may have been suggested by the muffled throb of the drum, which impressed itself indelibly on the mind.

No. 29. Drum Song   (Catalogue No. 341)

Sung by ODJĬB'WE

Voice ♩ = 96
Drum ♩ = 96
(Drum-rhythm similar to No. 15)

Ga - ki - na - ni - ni - mi - äg o - gĭ - tcĭ-dag 'e en - da - cĭ - wad e

ya e   ga - ki - na - ni - ni - mi - äg o - gĭ - tcĭ - dag   e   en - da - cĭ -

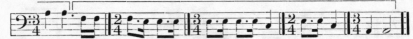

wad e ga-ki - na-ni-ni-mi - äg o - gĭ-tcĭ-dag en-da-cĭ - wad e

WORDS

gakina'ninimiäg'	I make them dance
ogĭ'tcĭdag'[2]	those brave men
en'dacĭwad'	every one of them

Analysis.—This melody is grouped about the tones of the chord of A minor, but begins on the tone above the fifth of that chord, a similar approach to the harmonic tone being found in the fourth and fifth measures from the close of the song (see analysis of No. 53).

[1] The full form of this word is *Abwan'*, plural *Abwan'âg* ("Roasters"), but the contraction is the form in common use. (See Warren's History of the Ojibways, in *Colls. Minn. Hist. Soc.*, vol. v, 1885, p. 36.)
[2] From Sioux *aki'čita* + *g* (*ug*), Chippewa plural ending. See also pp. 76, 186, 190, 230.

The tone material comprises only the first, second, third, fifth, and sixth tones of the minor scale, the second being lowered in one measure. Although the song is minor in tonality it is found that 8 of the 17 intervals (47 per cent) are major thirds. (See Nos. 83, 99.) The reverse of this, namely, prominence of minor thirds in songs of major tonality, is considered in the analyses of Nos. 140, 141, 151, 161, 163. The rhythmic unit is repeated once accurately but is slightly changed at the close of the song, this change relieving the monotony and giving character to the rhythm of the song as a whole. The metric unit of voice and drum is the same, the voice slightly preceding the drumbeat.

Three renditions of the song were recorded; these are identical in every respect. After a lapse of eight months the song was again recorded, the repetition of the melody being exact but the words being slightly different.

When the Chippewa met the Sioux in open fight one of their number might inspire the others to bravery by making himself a target. Throwing aside his weapons and divesting himself of all clothing, he rushed toward the enemy. If the Sioux failed to kill him at the first shot, it was permissible for him to attempt to escape. It is said that a man named Ogĭma′wûdjiwĕb′ ("chief of the mountains") had an experience of this kind and made his escape.

No. 30. Song of a Man Who Rushed Toward the Enemy

Sung by ODJĬB′WE   (Catalogue No. 329)

VOICE ♩ = 76
DRUM ♩ = 88
(Drum-rhythm similar to No. 2)

Ni - dji - ki-wĕ - i-dog e ge -go   ji - mo-ke - gun

nin zon-gi - de-ë

WORDS

nidjiki′wĕidog′	my friends
ge′go	do not
o′jimoke′gun [1]	flee
nin	I
zon′gideë′	am strong-hearted

[1] The first syllable of this word was omitted because the previous word ends with the same vowel. See footnote, p. 90.

Analysis.—The rhythmic unit of this song is short but interesting. It occurs three times and comprises the entire song except that part which contains the words. (See Nos. 1, 8, 12, 13, 39, 40, 81, 105.) The song was recorded four times, the renditions being uniform except that in the fourth from the last measure the progressions vary slightly. It is worthy of note that this is the only measure whose principal tones are not those of the chord of F minor. The melody is strongly harmonic in feeling, although classified as melodic because of the accented B flat.

The difference in intonation between the first and second E flat in measures 1 and 3 is interesting, as it appears in all the renditions. The song contains ten measures and is divided into four parts. The metric unit is slower than in most Chippewa songs. A slow metric unit is found in other songs of self-control under excitement (see songs Nos. 51, 52, 103, 161). As a rhythmic whole this song is particularly complete and satisfactory.

During a fight a man frequently sang his dream song or a song which he had composed concerning a former victory. Odjĭb'we stated that in time of great excitement a man would sing louder but probably no faster than was his usual custom. It is said that the following song was composed and sung on a field of battle by a woman named Omĭskwa'wegi'jĭgo'kwe ("woman of the red sky"), the wife of the leader, who went with him into the fight singing, dancing, and urging him on. At last she saw him kill a Sioux. Full of the fire of battle, she longed to play a man's part and scalp the slain. Custom forbade that Chippewa women use the scalping knife, although they carried the scalps in the victory dance.

No. 31. If I Had Been a Man (Catalogue No. 349)

Sung by ODJĬB'WE

VOICE ♩ = 76
DRUM ♩ = 92
(Drum-rhythm similar to No. 2)

A - pi - dûc i - nĭ - nĭ-yan - ban ke - gĕt i - nĭ-nĭ nin - da -

gi - ta - bi - bi - na

WORDS

api′dûc	at that time
inĭnĭ′wiyanban [1]	if I had been a man
kegĕt′	truly
inĭ′nĭ	a man
nindagi′tabibina′	I would have seized

Analysis.—The first progression of an ascending octave, followed by a descent along the tones of the tonic chord, characterizes this melody (see analysis of No. 9). The harmonic feeling is strong throughout the song, the accented C in the sixth measure being the only departure from the tonic and submediant chords. There is no rhythmic unit, but the rhythm of the song as a whole is complete and satisfactory.

Three renditions of the song were recorded. In each the tempo was more rapid and less regular in the four measures following the words, returning in the last two measures to the metric unit of the beginning. This unit is slow, as in other songs of self-control. The more rapid and free rhythm of the middle part is the more interesting if considered in connection with the words and origin of the song. Other songs composed by women are Nos. 39, 40, 112, 127, 151, 177, 178.

When a Chippewa shot a Sioux he shouted, "I have killed a Sioux," and others took up the call, adding the victor's name. Thus other warriors were nerved to renewed endeavor. After the fight the

---

[1] A syllable is omitted to make the words conform to the music.

names were remembered, and the warriors were given proper credit. In the old days each warrior marked his arrows, hence it could usually be determined by whose hands the slain fell; but after the introduction of guns it would have been impossible to ascertain who had killed the Sioux unless the call above mentioned were given during the engagement.

It was not unusual for a warrior to sink exhausted during a fight. This misfortune once befell Odjĭb'we, and the incident was related by his friend Niski'gwŭn, who was present on one occasion when Odjĭb'we was recording songs on the phonograph. Niski'gwŭn was with Odjĭb'we in many of the contests with the Sioux. Niski'gwŭn stated that on one occasion Odjĭb'we went into a fight without his "medicine." The fight had scarcely begun when Odjĭb'we appeared to be almost paralyzed. He was not able to strike a blow in his own defense and would have fallen an easy prey to the Sioux had not Niski'gwŭn rushed to him and given him medicine from his own bag, mixing it with water. Niski'gwŭn also sprayed the medicine on Odjĭb'we's feet and limbs with a wisp of brush. This revived him and enabled him to rise. Soon he was entirely himself and the fight was won, the Sioux village being captured.

Niski'gwŭn stated that he sang the following song when he applied the medicine.

No. 32. Song of Help in the Fight   (Catalogue No. 385)

Sung by Niski'gwŭn

Voice ♩= 144
Drum ♩= 108
(Drum-rhythm similar to No. 2)

Mûc-ko - de   a - kiñ   we-yan-e - ba-si-gwi-yan   e

mûc-ko - de   a - kiñ   we-yan-e - ba-si-gwi-yan   e

mûc-ko - de   a - kiñ   we-yan-e - ba-si-gwi-yan   e

WORDS

mûckode'...................... the prairie
akiñ'........................ land
weyan'eba'sigweyan'......... whence I arise

Analysis.—Four renditions of this song were recorded, in all of which
the final word was mispronounced, this license being allowed in Chippewa songs. On the octave and fifth the intonation is fairly correct,
and these tones were sung firmly; the other tones are variable in
pitch, and the transcription should be understood as approximate.
The signature is that of the key of D, as both F sharp and C sharp
occur in the melody, but the "sense of key" is not clear. It seems
probable that the singer's recollection of the song was not quite distinct. The rhythmic unit contains seven measures, and its repetitions comprise the entire song. The framework of the melody is the
descending interval of the fourth, a peculiarity which is fully considered in the analysis of No. 22. While this is not an inspiring melody, there is something in it deeper and stronger than enthusiasm;
there are steadiness and control. Strongest of all is the idea of the
words—the picture of the prairie, calm in its consciousness of power.

The following three songs relate to one of Odjĭb'we's war expeditions and illustrate the singing of a death song and the composing of
songs concerning a notable victory.

These songs are connected with an expedition against a Sioux
village called Gaye'dawima'miwŭñ ("lake in the valley"), which was
located on the upper waters of the Minnesota River; its chief was
known among the Chippewa as Manda'mĭnĕs (Little Corn). A war
party of more than a hundred Chippewa attacked this village and
the first man killed was the Sioux chief. During the fight the Sioux
women rushed out and dragged back the wounded men that they
might not be scalped. Although seven of their number were killed
the Chippewa would have been victorious had not a large party of
Sioux come on the field from a distance. Finding themselves out-
numbered, the Chippewa began to retreat. The Sioux used poisoned
arrows. One of the Chippewa warriors was wounded in the foot by a
barbed, poisoned arrow, but his friends were able to carry him away.
The Sioux followed the Chippewa a long distance and many of the
former were killed in this running fight. Name'binĕs' (Little Carp),
a leading warrior of the Chippewa, was terribly wounded in the
abdomen. His retreating comrades tried to take him with them but
after a time, realizing that the attempt was useless, at his own
request he was laid in a clump of bushes. There his friends left him
with his gun, saying, "Defend yourself as best you can." Soon the
Sioux came in hot pursuit of the Chippewa and from his hiding place
Name'binĕs' shot a man. With ebbing strength he gave his last war
whoop and his friends heard him cry, "Men, I have killed a Sioux."

When Name'binĕs' was laid in the bushes he sang his death song,
which he is said to have composed at that time. Looking into the
faces of his comrades he said, "When you reach home sing this for
the women to dance by and tell them how I died."

No. 33. Death Song of Name′bĭnĕs′ (Catalogue No. 335)

Sung by ODJĬB′WE

VOICE ♩ = 104
DRUM ♩ = 104
(Drum-rhythm similar to No. 2)

Ni - ma - ji-man-dĭs   ni - ma - ji-man-dĭs   nim - bi - dji-man-dĭs   nim -

bi-dji-man-dĭs   nim - bi-dji-man-dĭs   ĕ - na - su-mi - ka-yan e

WORDS

nima′jiman′dĭs...................... the odor of death
nimbi′djiman′dĭs................... I discern the odor of death
ĕna′sumi′kayan′................... in the front of my body

Analysis.—Ten renditions of this song are on the phonograph
cylinder, the transcription being from the eighth rendition. The
words vary in the several renditions, sometimes only one word being
used or meaningless syllables sung. The principal variation in intonation is on the tone A in the second measure. The intonation of the
last three measures is uniform and the rhythm of the entire song shows
no variation. The song contains a short rhythmic unit, which occurs
five times without interruption. The last three measures are in a
different rhythm. (Compare Nos. 4, 5, 19, 34.) In these measures
the length of the tones is unusually regular and the voice and drum
exactly coincide. The structure of this song is interesting. The
accented tones follow the intervals of the triad of A minor and the
unaccented tones in the fourth and sixth measures introduce the
chord of C major, the song being in the major key. Thus the first
two measures are on the chord of A minor and the next two measures
on that of C major; then follows a measure in A minor (without the
third), giving way again to C major in the last three measures. This
alternation of minor and major is worthy of special note in connection
with the origin of the song. (See No. 128.)

At the first camp after this fight the Chippewa composed a song,
the words of which refer to the Sioux women who came from the
village to drag back the wounded men.

No. 34. "The Sioux Women Gather Up their Wounded"

Sung by Odjĭb′we

(Catalogue No. 336)

Voice ♩ = 100
Drum ♩ = 108
(Drum-rhythm similar to No. 3)

O -ma-mi-kweg *o ya ne* pa-ba - ma-de - mo-wûg   *e*   o - na - dji -

da - ba - ma -   wûn *e* o - di - ni - ni - mi - wûn *e* a - ni - mû-

de - mû - wûg *e*

WORDS

Oma′mikweg′......................	the Sioux women
paba′made′mowûg′.................	pass to and fro wailing
ona′djida′bamawûn′................	as they gather up
o′dinini′miwûn...................	their wounded men
ani′mûde′mûwûg′.................	the voice of their weeping comes back to us

Analysis.—Six renditions of this song were recorded, the transcription being from the third rendition. The rhythm and the melody tones are the same in all the renditions but the words vary slightly, affecting the length of the tones; for instance, the word meaning "village" is used in one rendition and the order of the words is sometimes changed. The tonality is minor but, as in many similar songs, the tonic does not appear in the opening measures. (See analysis of No. 9, also of Nos. 1, 83, 94, 120.) This song contains a short rhythmic unit which is repeated without variation except for the addition of a quarter note after the second occurrence of the unit. The closing measures are in a different rhythm (see Nos. 4, 5, 19, 33) and the rhythm of the song has a well-defined individuality. The interval of the fourth is especially prominent. (See analysis of No. 22.)

On their homeward journey the Chippewa composed another song. Remembering the tread of the pursuing enemy, they sang of war as a game with the bodies of the dead as its score.

No. 35. "They are Playing a Game" (Catalogue No. 342)

Sung by ODJĬB'WE

VOICE ♩ = 104
DRUM ♩ = 104
(Drum-rhythm similar to No. 15)

Ga - bi - mi - bi - di - kweg   mûc - ko - deñg   bi - mi - ä - ta -

di - wûg e   i - nĭ - nĭ - wûg e   ga - bi - mi - bi - di - kweg mûc - ko -

deñg bi - mi - ä - ta - di - wûg e   i - nĭ - nĭ - wûg e   ga - bi - mi - bi - di -

kweg mûc - ko - deñg bi - mi - ä - ta - di - wûg e   i - nĭ - nĭ - wûg e

WORDS

gabimi'bidikweg'.................... the noise of passing feet
mûc'kodeñg'........................ on the prairie
bimi'atadiwûg'..................... they are playing a game as they come
inĭ'nĭwûg'......................... those men

Analysis.—This melody is based on the tones of the minor triad, the sixth being used as a passing tone and occurring only once. The song contains a rhythmic unit eight measures in length, which occurs three times, is accurately repeated, and comprises the entire song. It is worthy of note that the song contains only one upward progression; this occurs between the second and third sections of the song. The compass of the song is unusual, as it begins on the tenth above the tonic and ends on the fifth in the octave below the tonic. Four renditions of the melody were recorded; the intonation of the tones marked − is uniform in the several renditions.

Odjĭb'we stated that on one occasion a warrior sank exhausted as the war party was returning home. The other warriors, reluctant to leave him a prey to some wandering enemy, stayed with him. It seemed impossible for him to rise. However, he used his medicine, and after a time sprang to his feet, singing this song, which he composed at the time. The war party resumed its journey, and he accompanied them, still singing his new song.

No. 36. Song of the Exhausted Warrior

Sung by ODJĬB'WE

(Catalogue No. 367)

VOICE ♩ = 84

DRUM ♩ = 104

(Drum-rhythm similar to No. 2)

Ba - ba - pi - nĭ - si - wa - gûn   ge - non - de - ci - naı

i   e   ba-   ba - pi - nĭ - si - wa - gûn   ge - non - de - ci - nan

i   e   nin - ga - ä - da - woñ- gĕ - yĕn   ge - ön - dji - da - go -

ci - nan   e   ge-ön- dji - da - go   -   ci - nan   e

WORDS [1]

baba'pinĭ'siwa'gûn............ alas
genon'decinan'................ I can not travel
ningä'ada'woñgĕn'[2]........... but I will borrow that
geöndji'dago'cinan'........... by means of which I can arrive

Analysis.—Three renditions of this song were recorded; these are uniform in every respect. This uniformity is of interest, as the rhythmic unit is long and irregular; it occurs three times without variation. The remainder of the song contains fragments of the unit, but no complete repetition. The song is minor in tonality and is characterized by the sharped seventh, which is found but rarely in the minor songs under analysis. By this accidental the song is more fully identified with what is commonly termed the minor scale. The relation of the rhythm to the content of the song is worthy of note, the effect of perturbation in the first part of the song being contrasted with the more regular rhythm of the latter part.

---

[1] Where no words appear in the music above, meaningless syllables were sung.
[2] A syllable is added to this word to make it conform to the music.

Songs on the Return of a Victorious War Party

On returning, a victorious war party sent runners in advance to carry the news of their approach, and preparations for a suitable reception were begun at once. Meantime the warriors made their last camp before reaching home; here they rehearsed the songs concerning the victory and arrayed themselves in their finest apparel. Then began the final stage of the journey. As they approached the village they fired guns as a signal and the women came out to meet them. One woman led the party, to whom were given the scalps taken by the warriors. Each scalp was dried, and fastened inside a hoop at the end of a pole. Occasionally several were fastened in the same hoop (see pl. 17, showing five scalps in a decorated hoop). Frequently a man gave his wife the Sioux scalp he had taken. The women took the warriors' blankets, beadwork, and tobacco bags, and even their guns, none of which were they required to return. Then the women led the procession, the scalp bearers in advance, waving the scalps and singing. After the party reached the village preparations for the victory dance were begun. A suitable place was selected, to which was carried a large quantity of food—dried meat, wild rice, and maple sugar. The poles bearing the Sioux scalps were stuck in the ground beside the pile of food, and the feast was called "feasting the Sioux." There was no song connected with this feast. After the feast a simple ceremony in praise of the warriors took place. The victors were seated in a row and their friends brought gifts, which were laid before them. Often the following song was sung at this time. The words of this song require explanation. According to Odjĭb'we, defeated warriors were treated with scorn and derision when they returned. This is the song of victorious Gull Lake warriors, who were being honored at some other village, the inference intended to be drawn from the words being the exact opposite of their direct translation. Odjĭb'we stated that the words of the song *meant* "at Gull Lake [our home] they will be proud of us," but the correct translation is as given. This song was recorded three times, a period of several weeks elapsing between the renditions. The words varied somewhat, but Odjĭb'we stated that all have the same general meaning and that it was allowable to change the words of a song provided the "tune" and the meaning of the words remained the same.

BULLETIN 53 PLATE 17

FRONT   BACK

SCALPS ATTACHED TO HOOP

No. 37. Gift Song   (Catalogue No. 389)

Sung by ODJĬB'WE

VOICE ♩ = 116

Recorded without drum

WORDS

ga'gayac'gonsĭkag'............ at Gull Lake
manoga'yana'wenimĭgo'min.. let them speak lightly of us

Analysis.—This song was transcribed from the first of three renditions. The melody consists of four parts. The rhythmic unit was accurately repeated except for a slight change in the note-values of the last measure. The other renditions were only partial and were similar to the latter half of the transcription. When different words were used the note-values differed accordingly, but the trend of the melody remained the same. The song is harmonic in structure and contains only the tones of the major triad and sixth.

In response to this song the warriors rose and danced, singing of what they had done on the warpath. These songs were composed on the way home (see No. 35). The following is an example of this class of songs.

Odjĭb'we stated that this song was composed by his brother and sung in the victory dance. His brother had been on a war party with his father and Hole-in-the-day and had cut off a Sioux woman's head, bringing home the scalp.

No. 38. Scalp Song   (Catalogue No. 366)

Sung by Odjĭb′we

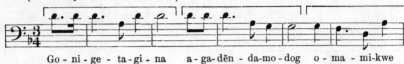

VOICE ♩ = 160
DRUM ♩ = 104
(Drum-rhythm similar to No. 2)

Go - ni - ge - ta - gi - na   a - ga - děn - da - mo - dog   o - ma - mi-kwe

we   gi - kic - ki-gwe - jûg

WORDS

gonige′tagina′................. I wonder
agaděn′damodog′............. if she is humiliated
Oma′mikwe′.................. the Sioux woman
gikic′kigwejûg′.............. that I cut off her head

Analysis.—This is a song of derision, and in that respect it resembles No. 14; comparison of the two songs is therefore of interest. Both are minor in tonality, begin on the octave, and, as is unusual, have the descending fourth as their first progression. Both end on the fifth, the compass being from the dominant below the tonic to the octave above it; a more common range is from the tonic to the twelfth above it. Both songs are melodic in structure and neither contains an accidental. With these features the resemblance ends. No. 14 is in double time with two triple measures, begins on the accented part of the measure, and contains no rhythmic unit; while the song under analysis is in triple time throughout, begins on the unaccented part of the measure, and contains a short rhythmic unit continuously repeated. These points of difference show the individuality of the two songs. The derision in No. 14 is subtle and tantalizing and the rhythmic swing is long, without a clearly defined unit; while in the present instance the derisive idea is more direct, the taunting more keen, finding expression in a short, crisp rhythm. Five renditions of the song were recorded, the rhythm showing no variation.

Gifts were distributed to all the people by members of the warrior's clan; for instance, Odjĭb′we's *do′dem* (clan animal) was the bear. When he returned bringing a scalp, all the men and women belonging to the Bear Clan danced around him with their arms full of presents, after which they distributed the presents throughout the village in his honor.

The next event was the victory dance, which often continued until daylight, by the light of torches and bonfires. At this dance the Sioux scalps were carried and songs were sung in honor of the warriors. (See Nos. 80, 83, 165.) This is illustrated by the following two songs, which were composed, respectively, by the wife and the mother-in-law of Odjĭb'we and sung in recognition of his prowess. Odjĭb'we recorded the first song ǐn August, 1909, and sang it again in March, 1910, the renditions and the accounts of the incident being identical.

Odjĭb'we stated that his wife's brother was killed by the Sioux and that he organized a war party in return. The purpose of this expedition was to attack a certain Sioux village located on an island in Sauk River, but before reaching this village the Chippewa met a war party of Sioux, which they pursued, killing one man. There were nine Chippewa in Odjĭb'we's party; not one was killed. They returned home at once and Odjĭb'we presented the Sioux scalp to his wife De'kûm ("across"), who held it aloft in the victory dance as she sang the following song.

No. 39. The Song of De'kûm   (Catalogue No. 348)

Sung by Odjĭb'we

VOICE ♩ = 168
DRUM ♩ = 108
(Drum-rhythm similar to No. 2)

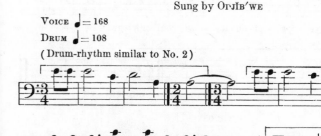

O - djĭb-we   gi - sai - ye-nañ   o - bi - nan

WORDS

Odjĭb'we.....................	Odjĭb'we
gisai'yenañ...................	our brother
obi'nan......................	brings back

Analysis.—The five renditions of this song recorded are uniform in all important respects. The rhythmic unit is interesting; this occurs three times, comprising all the song except the part in which the words occur. (See Nos. 1, 8, 12, 13, 30, 40, 81, 105.) The minor tonality is well established and the approach to the tonic by the descending interval of a fourth is somewhat unusual. (See analysis of No. 22.) Other songs composed by women are Nos. 31, 40, 112, 127, 151, 177, and 178.

When De′kûm had finished the song, her mother, Djiñgwa′kûmigo′-kwe ("rumbling-earth woman"), arose, and, taking the scalp, danced while singing the following song, which she composed in honor of Odjĭb′we.

No. 40. Song of Rejoicing   (Catalogue No. 365)

Sung by ODJĬB′WE

VOICE ♩= 168
DRUM ♩= 104

(Drum-rhythm similar to No. 2)

Mĭ - sû - na   dji-mĭn - wĕn - da-man niñ-gwĭ - zĭs   *a*

mĭ- sû - na   dji-mĭn - wĕn-da-man niñ - gwĭ - zĭs   *a*

gi - sai - ye   gi - pi-da-ma - wi - yan niñ - gwĭ - zĭs   *e*

mĭ - sû - na   dji - mĭn-wĕn - da-man   niñ - gwĭ - zĭs   *a   ye*

WORDS

mĭ′sûna′	it shall be
djimĭnwĕn′daman′	that I rejoice
niñgwĭ′zĭs	O, my son
gisai′ye	your elder brother
gipi′damawiyan′	you have brought back
niñgwĭ′zĭs	O, my son
mĭ′sûna′	it shall be
djimĭnwĕn′daman′	that I rejoice
niñgwĭ′zĭs	O, my son

Analysis.—The rhythmic unit of this song, which occurs 3 times, is particularly interesting and inspiring. The song is divided into four parts, the words changing in the third section. (See Nos. 1, 8, 12, 13, 30, 39, 81, 105.) The melody is major in tonality and moves freely along the fourth five-toned scale. In songs based on the fourth five-toned scale the second and sixth frequently occur only as passing tones. The sixth is accented in one measure and the song is therefore classified as "melodic with harmonic framework" instead of purely

harmonic in structure. The four renditions of the song recorded
are identical in every respect. Other songs composed by women are
Nos. 31, 39, 112, 127, 151, 177, 178.

Odjĭb'we stated that he took part in a severe fight with a band of
Sioux led by the famous chief Gaga'gins (Little Crow). The circumstances were as follows: Little Crow's band was in camp on the west
side of the Minnesota River a few miles below the site of the present
St. Paul. The blind warrior accurately described a level tract of land
west of the first bend in the river. A large war party of Chippewa
prepared to attack the Sioux village and sent two scouts in advance,
who killed and scalped a Sioux woman coming out of a tipi. Thinking that the scouts were unprotected, the Sioux warriors pursued
them and soon met the entire force of the Chippewa. A terrible fight
followed in which the Chippewa were victorious. The following song,
which relates to this victory, was composed by Hole-in-the-day,
leader of the expedition. (See p. 61.)

No. 41. Victory Song   (Catalogue No. 345)

Sung by ODJĬB'WE

VOICE ♩ = 92
DRUM ♩ = 104
(Drum-rhythm similar to No. 2)

WORDS [1]

aci'doka'ma.......................... surely
gewa'winigoyan'.................. I will have great praise

Analysis.—Seven renditions of this song were recorded, the transcription being from the sixth, which is the only one in which the
words occur twice. The rhythm of the first part is uniform in the several renditions recorded, while that of the latter part varies with the
presence or omission of words. The melody moves freely along the

---

[1] Where no words appear in the music above, meaningless syllables were sung.

intervals of the fourth five-toned scale. The first three measures constitute an interesting rhythmic phrase but it is not repeated and the song as a whole lacks rhythmic unity; it is, however, inspiring and joyful in general character. Attention is directed to the discrepancy between the metric units of voice and drum.

The following incident illustrates the use of a dream song, which the warrior sang while on the warpath, to secure supernatural aid, and afterward in the victory dance to commemorate the triumph and the means by which he believed it had been attained.

Odjĭb′we stated that long ago a party of Chippewa attacked the Sioux, killing several and securing the scalps. Then they started for home with the Sioux in hot pursuit. The leader of the party was the singer of this song. In his youthful vision he saw a protecting cloud, and when the Sioux pressed close he sang his dream song. Suddenly a dark cloud came across the sky, the rain fell in torrents, and through the storm the Chippewa made their escape. After reaching home the leader sang this song at the victory dance. (Compare Nos. 63, 64, 66, 85, 87, 94, 140, 141, 145, 147, 148, 150, 151, 152, 153.)

No. 42. "A Cloud"   (Catalogue No. 330)

Sung by Odjĭb′we

VOICE ♩ = 96
DRUM ♩ = 96
(Drum-rhythm similar to No. 3)

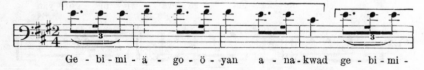

Ge - bi - mi - ä - go - ö - yan   a - na - kwad   ge - bi - mi -

ä - go - ö - yan   e   ya   ge - bi - mi - ä - go - ö -

yan   a - na - kwad   ge - bi - mi - ä - go - ö - yan   ge - bi - mi -

ä - go - ö - yan   a - na - kwad   ge - bi - mi - ä - go - ö - yan

WORDS

ge′bimiä′goöyan′.................... circling above me
a′nakwad′......................... a cloud

Analysis.—This song contains three accidentals—the second, third, and sixth lowered a semitone. The F natural was imperfectly given at the opening of the song but accurately sung in the latter part. Three renditions of the song were recorded and the accidentals were uniformly given though the intonation varied on several other intervals. The rhythmic unit occurs six times, the prolonged tones between the second and third occurrences of the unit being uniform in the renditions.

The following is the dream song of a forgotten warrior.

No. 43. "I am Called"   (Catalogue No. 331)

Sung by Odjïb′we

VOICE ♩ = 104
DRUM ♩ = 116
(Drum-rhythm similar to No. 2)
(1st phrase)

(2d phrase)

Na - na - wa - gam kĭ - tci - gam - ĭñg   e   nin - on - do - mig

(3d phrase)

ma - ni - do   e

WORDS

nana′wagam′	from the middle
kĭ′tcigam′iñg′	of the great water
ninon′domig′	I am called
manido′	by the spirit

Analysis.—Four renditions of this song were given, with a pause between the second and third. Two weeks later the song was recorded twice. The six records are identical except that in the last two the tone E (last count, fifth measure from the close) was sung F natural. In one or two of the first set of renditions this tone was raised slightly, less than a semitone. The ascending progression on the last count of the first measure was given with a sliding of the voice which can not be accurately transcribed.

It will be noted that the first five measures of the song constitute a rhythmic phrase, marked "1st phrase"; instead of repeating this, however, the song introduces another phrase of 7 measures, marked "2d phrase," followed by still another of 5 measures, marked "3d phrase." Thus the song contains 17 measures, divided into three parts, each part making "rhythmic sense," the three forming a rhythmic whole.

The tones of the song are grouped about the chord of E minor, the tone A in the ninth measure being the only accented tone not belonging to that chord. The presence of this tone, however, makes it necessary to classify the song as melodic rather than harmonic in structure. The song contains all the tones of the octave, also one accidental—the sixth raised a semitone.

The principal drum-rhythm is that of accented eighth notes, but in the latter part of the first record the accent is intensified and the unaccented beat shortened until the drum-rhythm consists of triplets, the accented beat representing the first note, and the unaccented beat the third note, of the triplet, an eighth rest occurring between the two. This change of drum-rhythm in a record is unusual.

At the conclusion of these dances [1] the scalps were carefully wrapped and kept until the next dance. When one village was tired of dancing with the scalps they were sent to another village, where similar dances were held. Mrs. English (the writer's interpreter) stated that she remembered when Sioux scalps were sent from the Minnesota villages to those on the shore of Lake Superior, a distance of more than a hundred miles. The scalps were carried by the same oc'kabe'wĭs who bore the war message and tobacco before the organization of the war party. On this occasion also he carried tobacco and was prepared to sing the songs connected with the taking of the scalps.

When all the villages had finished dancing the scalps were brought back to the first village, where speeches were made and the poles were set in a grave. This was frequently the grave of the man whose death was avenged by the war party. There the poles bearing the scalps remained undisturbed until wind and weather completed the conquest of the Sioux.

Songs of the Peace Pact

Interspersed through the troubled years of strife there were periods of peace between the Chippewa and the Sioux. Odjĭb'we stated that the tribe desiring peace sent messengers to the other tribe asking for a cessation of hostilities. According to him, the Sioux were usually the tribe who sought peace. If the Chippewa were willing to join in a peace pact, the messenger returned to the enemy with a favorable reply. The Sioux then brought their families and camped near the Chippewa while each tribe made preparations for the formal proceedings. The meeting was attended with much

[1] Other songs of the war dances are Nos. 83–93.

pomp and ceremony. The warriors arrayed themselves in their gayest attire. In each camp was the sound of singing and of shrill war cries, excitement was in the air, and it seemed that an encounter instead of a truce was in preparation. Amid shouting the opposing forces made ready to advance. The Chippewa were led by an oc'kabe'wĭs bearing the pipe, followed by four women; next came the leaders of the war party, while behind them were the warriors. The Sioux followed in similar array. As the two tribes approached each other the excitement subsided. One of the greatest scenes in the drama of Indian warfare was to be enacted. To and fro in front of the warriors walked the women. Often it was only their presence that prevented violence, the fire of battle bursting forth afresh as the warriors drew near their recent enemies. All sang as they came forward. The melody was the same in both tribes but the Chippewa sang the names of the Sioux leaders and the Sioux the names of the Chippewa leaders, each praising the valor of the other. Odjĭb'we recorded the song, first as it was sung by the Chippewa, the transcription being from the first rendition which contained the name of Ga'gagins' (Little Crow), who is mentioned in connection with song No. 41. Without a pause he continued the song, introducing the names of the following Sioux leaders in the successive renditions: Ca'gobĕns (Little Six), Bĭ'nĭcŏns', and Wa'-bacŏns'. He then stated that he wished to record the song as it was sung by the Sioux. The melody was the same but the following names of Chippewa leaders were introduced: Bû'goṅegi'jĭg (Hole-in-the-day), Wa'bejic' ("marten"), and Zon'gakûm'ĭg ("strong earth").

No. 44. Song of the Peace Pact   (Catalogue No. 352)

Sung by Odjĭb'we

Voice ♩ = 126
Drum ♩ = 76
(Drum-rhythm similar to No. 2)

E huñ - ga   e   huñ - ga   Ga - ga - gins

o - gi - ma e huñ - ga e huñ - ga e huñ - ga

WORDS

huñ'ga [1] .... leader
Ga'gagins' .... Little Crow
o'gima .... chief

---

[1] From Sioux *huṅka'*. See S. R. Riggs, Grammar and Dictionary of the Dakota Language, *Smithson. Contrs.*, vol. IV, Washington, 1852.

Analysis.—This melody is characterized by directness and simplicity. It begins on the tonic, an unusual beginning in minor songs, and the minor tonality is fully established in the first two measures. The song contains 12 measures and consists of three parts, the rhythmic unit occurring in the first and last parts and the names in the middle part. The slow metric unit was maintained in the renditions with both Sioux and Chippewa names, suggesting that this was the tempo in which the song was actually sung, a tempo which gives dignity to the song, appropriate to the occasion of its use.

The Sioux fired their guns into the air and did not reload them. The Chippewa did likewise. Nearer they came, the singing women walking to and fro, brave as the wives of warriors should be. Then the tribe which had asked for peace sent forward its pipe bearer. Holding the pipe in his hands, he offered the stem in turn to the opposing leaders, each of whom puffed the pipe. Then the other tribe sent forward its pipe bearer in the same manner.

The following song was sung by the Chippewa pipe bearer when offering the peace pipe to the Sioux.

No. 45. Song when Offering the Peace Pipe

(Catalogue No. 390)

Sung by ODJĬB'WE

VOICE ♩ = 72
Recorded without drum

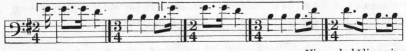

Nin - do-kĭdj *an* nin-

do - kĭdj *an*   nin-do - kĭdj *an*

WORDS

nindo′kĭdj.......................... my pipestem

Analysis.—This song is in the key of G, yet the tonic appears only once (in the seventh measure) as an accented tone. Harmonic tones are frequently approached from the tone above. (See analysis of No. 53.) The rhythmic unit occurs only twice, the latter part of the song containing a division of the count similar to one which occurs in the unit but not containing a repetition of the unit. The rhythm of the song as a whole is particularly interesting and produces an effect of dignified action well suited to the occasion of its use. The melody tones are those of the fourth five-toned scale. The four renditions recorded are uniform in every respect.

When the smoking of the peace pipe was finished, the opposing warriors shook hands, and the Sioux were offered the hospitality of the Chippewa camp.

After the forming of a peace pact the two tribes camped near each other for some time and social dances were held every night; these were called ca'wûno'ga (southern dance). Odjĭb'we stated that only ca'wûno'ga songs were sung at the peace dances and that these songs were sung at no other time. Presents were sometimes given, but the exchange of gifts did not form an essential feature, as in the woman's dance (see p. 38). A woman sometimes beckoned to a gayly arrayed young man, threw her blanket over his head, and took some of his finery as they danced together. It is said that the ca'wûno'ga songs were particularly pleasing and that the people were so carried away with the excitement that the dance often lasted all night.

The origin of the ca'wûno'ga was thus described by Na'waji'-bigo'kwe:

> The ca'wûno'ga is a very old dance and was first a dance for healing. It was not to cure people who were very ill, for that was done by the Mĭde', but it was for people who were not in good health. The South Manido' taught this dance to a very good young man whose relatives were ill. It is called ca'wûno'ga because it came from the South Manido', and the people who first used it were people living south of the Chippewa country. The young man got up the dance as he was instructed by the South Manido' and his relatives recovered. Afterward the dance was used as a social dance, and the songs are particularly pleasing.

No. 46. Ca'wûno'ga Song (a)   (Catalogue No. 354)

Sung by ODJĬB'WE

VOICE ♩ = 88
DRUM ♩ = 104
(Drum-rhythm similar to No. 2)

Analysis.—This song should be regarded as one of those fugitive melodies in which the signature indicates the pitch of the tones rather

than an established key. The six renditions of the song recorded
are identical. In every instance the close was as transcribed, and
the return to the first measure was without a pause. The first two
measures are in an ordinary rhythm, and around them, in the repetitions of the song, there circles a succession of measures so irregular
in rhythm as to fascinate and hold the attention. One can readily
imagine that to such rhythms the excitable Indians might have danced
all night.

No. 47. Ca′wûno′ga Song (b)　　(Catalogue No. 355)

Sung by ODJĬB′WE

VOICE ♩ = 168
DRUM ♩ = 108
(Drum-rhythm similar to No. 2)

WORDS

ca′wûno′....................... south
ga′yan........................ dancing

Analysis.—The four renditions of this curious song show no variation. The general effect of the song is jerky, yet the rhythm has an
element of indefinite continuity; it is a rhythm which fascinates and
could be kept up for a long time. The principal rhythmic unit occurs
four times at the opening of the song, and is followed by a shorter
rhythmic unit, which likewise occurs four times and contains the
same syncopations as the first. These syncopations were uniformly
given and are the principal characteristic of the song. (See No. 88
of present work and Nos. 123, 147, 152, in Bulletin 45.)

WAR SONGS CONCERNING WOMEN

The incident concerning the first of this group of songs was narrated
to the writer by Mr. John W. Carl (see pp. 83, 303). Mr. Carl, who is a

grandson of Bĭca′ganab, said that in his childhood he often heard the following story:

There was once a Hudson's Bay trader who came to the Chippewa country, loved a Chippewa maiden, and wooed her according to the custom of her people. He gave a great feast, invited her father, and asked his consent to the marriage. Three daughters were born to them, one being the mother of Bĭca′ganab. Years passed and Bĭca′ganab, granddaughter of the Hudson's Bay trader, grew to womanhood. One day as she was lighting her breakfast fire she heard the cry, "The Sioux are upon us!" This was followed by the report of guns. Immediately the camp became a scene of confusion, the men trying to repulse the Sioux and the women hastening to put their household goods into canoes. The father of Bĭca′ganab went into the fight; he was wounded five times but contrived to get near the water and was helped into a canoe. It was supposed that Bĭca′ganab had been killed, but when the escaping party were far from shore they saw a woman fighting the Sioux with a club. The Sioux drove her into the water and she swam toward a canoe. The Sioux followed, trying to strike her on the head with a club, but she actually broke and tore their canoe with her hands. It was said that she was like a great bear in her ferocity. The Sioux were forced into the water and she pounded them with a paddle as they made for the shore. Instead of following the retreating Chippewa she went upstream, hiding in the bushes, returning later to the battlefield by a circuitous path. There she found only the dead Sioux, covered with their blankets; beside them lay their guns and much beautiful beadwork. Bĭca′ganab scalped the Sioux, put on a Sioux war bonnet, and made a great pack of blankets, guns, and beadwork; then she painted her face and went to the Chippewa camp with her trophies.

Bĭca′ganab, one of the bravest of Chippewa women, died in 1892.

No. 48. Song Concerning a Brave Woman

Sung by ODJĬB′WE

(Catalogue No. 351)

VOICE ♩ = 160
DRUM ♩ = 160
(Drum-rhythm similar to No. 15)

Ĕ - ni - wĕk *we* win ja - wa - so   win gi - ja - wa - so   mĭn - di -

mo-yan *we*   ja-wa-so - no-da-go-nan *ya*   e   *ya*   e   *we*   a   *he*

WORDS

ĕ′niwĕk′	greatly
win	she
gija′waso	defending her children
mĭn′dimoyan′	the old woman
gigijawa′sonoda′gonan[1]	fought for us all

[1] The first two syllables of this word, and in one instance the first syllable of the third word, are omitted to make the words conform to the music.

Analysis.—This melody presents an interesting study of rhythm. It contains 19 measures and is divided into three parts, the first containing 5 measures, the second 4, and the third 10. It has no rhythmic unit, yet there is a melodic phrase which occurs three times—in the second and third, and in the sixth and seventh, measures. It occurs also in the tenth and eleventh measures, but in the latter instances the first measure is a triple one, strongly accented on a tone not found at the opening of the song. If the first tone of the song were unaccented it might be regarded as the second count of a triple measure, but it is strongly and unmistakably accented. Five renditions of the song were recorded, all identical. The metric unit of voice and drum is the same, but in rendition the voice slightly preceded the drum.

The following two songs were composed about a war expedition which occurred when Odjĭb'we was a young man. The fight took place on the prairie, a few miles north of the site of the present St. Cloud, Minnesota. It was a hard-fought engagement and 20 Chippewa were killed. One of the Sioux women seized an ax and attempted to repulse the Chippewa who attacked her, but she and all her children were killed. The father of Odjĭb'we composed this song concerning the incident.

No. 49. "The Sioux Woman Defends Her Children"

Sung by Odjĭb'we

(Catalogue No. 364)

Voice ♩ = 92
Drum ♩ = 92
(Drum-rhythm similar to No. 2)

Ne - ta - gi - ca - wa - so - sĭg   Wa-pe-toñ bi - ä - pi - sĭ - ka - dug go-

ca-win bi-gi - ca-wa-sud

WORDS

neta'gica'wasosĭg'	once careless of her children
Wape'toñ [1] (Sioux word)	she of the Wapeton Sioux
biäpi'sĭka'dug	now comes in haste
go'cawin'	surely
bigica'wasud'	to their defense

Analysis.—The five renditions of this song recorded are singularly uniform. Not only is the rhythm identical, but slight variations in

---

[1] See footnote, p. 70.

tempo are duplicated. The melody is based on the major triad and would be classified as harmonic in structure except for the accented E in the fourth measure.

Among those taken captive in this fight was a Sioux woman. It was decided to kill her and she was led forth to be shot. After the preparations for her execution were complete she was allowed to sing. We do not know what the song may have been, but it moved the elder brother of Odjĭb'we so strongly that he rushed forward and rescued her. The war party soon started on its homeward way. At the first camp a dance was held. During this dance the captive woman arose, shook hands with the warriors and kissed them to show gratitude for her deliverance; she also sang the following song, which she composed at that time.

No. 50. Song of the Captive Sioux Woman

(Catalogue No. 334)

Sung by Odjĭb'we

VOICE ♩ = 80
DRUM ♩ = 100
(Drum-rhythm similar to No. 3)

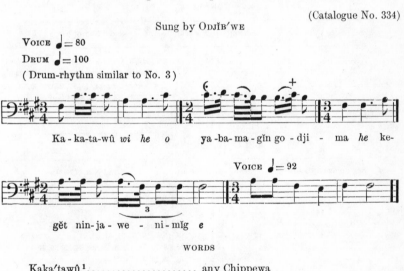

Ka - ka-ta-wû *wi he o* ya -ba- ma - gĭn go - dji - ma *he* ke-

VOICE ♩ = 92

gĕt nin-ja- we - ni-mĭg *e*

WORDS

Kaka'tawû [1]	any Chippewa
waya'bamagĭn' [2]	whenever I see
nin'gaödji'ma	I will greet with a kiss
kegĕt'	truly
nin'jawe'nimĭg'	he pities me

Analysis.—Five renditions of this song were recorded. The metric unit varies slightly in these renditions, the metronome indication being from the fourth rendition. The same rhythmic pecularities appear in all the renditions, the first count in the second measure receiving more than the regular time and the last two measures being sung more rapidly than the preceding part of the song. The upward progressions in the second measure are uncertain in intona-

---

[1] Word used by the Sioux in designating the Chippewa.

[2] The first syllable of this word is omitted and the following word is changed in order to adapt the words to the music.

tion, the upper tones not being clearly sung but rendered with what might be termed a "toss" of the voice. The song contains no rhythmic unit, yet the melody as a whole has a complete and satisfactory rhythm. Attention is directed to the interval of a whole tone between the seventh and eighth of the scale, near the close of the song. This interval was firmly given. It is an unusual progression in recorded Chippewa songs although found also in songs Nos. 9, 85, 100, 119, 124.

After an interval of eight months three renditions of this song were recorded by the same singer; these were identical with the first record in both melody and rhythm but differed slightly in the words.

War Songs—White Earth Reservation

MELODIC ANALYSIS

TONALITY

	Numbers	Per cent.	Serial Nos. of songs
Major	27	54	2, 3, 5, 6, 7, 8, 13, 16, 18, 19, 20, 21, 22, 23, 25, 26, 27, 28, 31, 32, 33, 37, 40, 41, 42, 47, 49
Minor	23	46	1, 4, 9, 10, 11, 12, 14, 15, 17, 24, 29, 30, 34, 35, 36, 38, 39, 43, 44, 45, 46, 48, 50
Total	50	....	

BEGINNINGS OF SONGS

Beginning on the—	Numbers	Per cent.	Serial Nos. of songs
Thirteenth	3	6	19, 20, 29
Sixth	1	2	45
Twelfth	11	22	1, 2, 3, 7, 12, 16, 22, 27, 40, 41, 42
Fifth	8	16	5, 9, 15, 18, 24, 31, 39, 47
Tenth	11	22	8, 10, 11, 17, 21, 26, 33, 34, 35, 36, 49
Ninth	5	10	6, 13, 23, 25, 28
Octave	10	20	4, 14, 30, 32, 37, 38, 43, 44, 48, 50
Fourth	1	2	46
Total	50	....	

ENDINGS OF SONGS

Ending on the—	Numbers	Per cent.	Serial Nos. of songs
Tonic	31	62	1, 2, 3, 4, 6, 7, 8, 9, 10, 11, 12, 16, 19, 24, 25, 26, 27, 29, 30, 31, 32, 33, 34, 36, 37, 40, 41, 42, 47, 49, 50
Fifth	14	28	5, 13, 14, 15, 17, 21, 23, 28, 35, 38, 43, 44, 46, 48
Third	5	10	18, 20, 22, 39, 45
Total	50	....	

MELODIC ANALYSIS—continued

TONE MATERIAL

	Numbers	Per cent.	Serial Nos. of songs
Second five-toned scale...............	6	12	1, 17, 24, 30, 34, 44
Fourth five-toned scale................	16	32	3, 6, 8, 16, 18, 19, 21, 22, 23, 26, 31, 40, 41, 42, 45, 47
Major triad and sixth..................	2	4	33, 37
Major triad and second................	1	2	49
Minor triad and seventh...............	1	2	36
Minor triad and sixth.................	2	4	29, 35
Minor triad and fourth................	2	4	10, 12
Minor third and fourth................	1	2	11
Octave complete......................	1	2	43
Octave complete except seventh........	5	10	2, 7, 25, 27, 32
Octave complete except seventh and sixth	1	2	38
Octave complete except seventh and second	2	4	14, 15
Octave complete except sixth..........	3	6	9, 39, 46
Octave complete except fourth.........	3	6	13, 20, 48
Octave complete except fourth and third	1	2	28
Octave complete except fourth and second	1	2	5
Octave complete except second.........	2	4	4, 50
Total.............................	50	....	

ACCIDENTALS

Songs containing—	Numbers	Per cent.	Serial Nos. of songs
No accidentals.........................	38	76	1, 2, 3, 4, 5, 6, 9, 10, 11, 12, 13, 14, 15, 16, 17, 18, 20, 21, 23, 24, 25, 26, 27, 28, 31, 33, 34, 35, 37, 38, 39, 40, 44, 45, 47, 48, 49, 50
Seventh raised a semitone..............	1	2	36
Sixth raised a semitone................	1	2	43
Sixth lowered a semitone...............	5	10	7, 8, 19, 22, 41
Fourth lowered a semitone.............	1	2	30
Second lowered a semitone.............	2	4	29, 46
Second, third, and sixth lowered a semitone	1	2	42
Second lowered a semitone and fourth raised a semitone	1	2	32
Total.............................	50	....	

STRUCTURE

	Numbers	Per cent.	Serial Nos. of songs
Harmonic..............................	11	22	3, 4, 5, 10, 17, 24, 26, 33, 35, 37, 50
Purely melodic........................	25	50	1, 2, 6, 7, 9, 13, 15, 16, 20, 21, 22, 23, 25, 27, 28, 29, 32, 34, 36, 38, 39, 42, 43, 46, 48
Melodic with harmonic framework......	14	28	8, 11, 12, 14, 18, 19, 30, 31, 40, 41, 44, 45, 47, 49
Total.............................	50	....	

MELODIC ANALYSIS—continued

FIRST PROGRESSIONS

	Numbers	Per cent.	Serial Nos. of songs
Downward..........................	30	60	1, 2, 3, 4, 5, 6, 8, 12, 14, 15, 17, 19, 21, 22, 23, 24, 27, 28, 29, 30, 33, 35, 36, 38, 39, 40, 41, 45, 47, 49
Upward............................	20	40	7, 9, 10, 11, 13, 16, 18, 20, 25, 26, 31, 32, 34, 37, 42, 43, 44, 46, 48, 50
Total...........................	50	....	

RHYTHMIC ANALYSIS

PART OF MEASURE ON WHICH SONG BEGINS

	Numbers	Per cent.	Serial Nos. of songs
On accented part......................	24	48	2, 3, 5, 6, 8, 14, 15, 16, 17, 20, 23, 25, 26, 27, 31, 32, 37, 38, 40, 43, 44, 46, 48, 49
On unaccented part....................	26	52	1, 4, 7, 9, 10, 11, 12, 13, 18, 19, 21, 22, 24, 28, 29, 30, 33, 34, 35, 36, 39, 41, 42, 45, 47, 50
Total............................	50	....	

RHYTHM OF FIRST MEASURE

Beginning in—	Numbers	Per cent.	Serial Nos. of songs
2–4 time..............................	26	52	5, 6, 9, 11, 13, 14, 16, 18, 21, 23, 24, 29, 30, 31, 32, 33, 34, 35, 37, 40, 41, 42, 45, 46, 48, 49
3–4 time..............................	19	38	1, 3, 4, 7, 8, 10, 12, 15, 19, 20, 22, 28, 36, 38, 39, 43, 44, 47, 50
7–4 time..............................	1	2	27
5–4 time..............................	3	6	17, 25, 26
5–8 time..............................	1	2	2
Total............................	50	....	

CHANGE OF TIME

Songs containing—	Numbers	Per cent.	Serial Nos. of songs
Change of time..........................	38	76	1, 2, 3, 5, 6, 7, 8, 9, 11, 12, 13, 14, 15, 17, 18, 19, 20, 23, 24, 25, 27, 29, 30, 31, 32, 34, 35, 36, 39, 40, 41, 42, 43, 45, 46, 48, 49, 50
No change of time.....................	12	24	4, 16, 21, 22, 26, 28, 33, 35, 37, 38, 44, 47
Total............................	50	....	

RHYTHMIC ANALYSIS—continued

RHYTHMIC UNIT

Songs containing—	Numbers	Per cent.	Serial Nos. of songs
A rhythmic unit......................	38	*76*	1, 2, 3, 4, 5, 6, 8, 11, 12, 13, 15, 16, 18, 19, 20, 21, 22, 23, 24, 25, 26, 27, 28, 29, 30, 32, 33, 34, 35, 36, 37, 38, 39, 40, 42, 44, 45, 46
Two rhythmic units...................	2	*4*	17, 47
No rhythmic unit.....................	10	*20*	7, 9, 10, 14, 31, 41, 43, 48, 49, 50
Total.............................	50	....	

COMPARISON OF METRIC UNIT OF VOICE AND DRUM [1]

	Numbers	Per cent.	Serial Nos. of songs
Unit the same.........................	12	*24*	5, 15, 16, 17, 18, 19, 22, 29, 33, 42, 48, 49
Unit different.........................	29	*58*	2, 3, 6, 7, 8, 9, 10, 11, 12, 13, 20, 21, 24, 25, 28, 30, 31, 32, 34, 36, 38, 39, 40, 41, 43, 44, 46, 47, 50
Recorded without drum................	9	*18*	1, 4, 14, 23, 26, 27, 35, 37, 45
Total.............................	50	....	

[1] For more detailed analysis see Table 20, p. 30.

CHILDREN'S GAMES OF WAR

The children as well as the older members of the tribe formed new acquaintances while the Chippewa and the Sioux camped near together. Games were arranged in which the children of the two tribes contended with each other. War was the chief interest and even found its way into the play of the children.

Odjĭb'we stated that he remembered an instance which happened when he was a little boy. The Chippewa and the Sioux were camped near each other and the small boys had a sham battle, with the men and women of each tribe as spectators, cheering on their young warriors. Rushes, sharpened at one end and notched at the other so that they could be shot from bows, were used as arrows. The sting inflicted by these was painful, as the boys wore no clothing, but no one who entered the contest was allowed to run away. The rules of the game forbade shooting at the heads of the opponents, as otherwise serious injury might have resulted, but the fight was waged right lustily and blood flowed freely.

No. 51. War Song of Odjĭb'we's Childhood [1]

(Catalogue No. 278)

Sung by ODJĬB'WE

VOICE ♩ = 80
DRUM ♩ = 80
(Drum-rhythm similar to No. 19)

Nin - do-kĭdj a nin-

do-kĭdj a nin-do-kĭdj a

WORDS

nindo'kĭdj......................... my pipestem

Analysis.—This song contains the tones of the fifth five-toned scale according to Helmholtz (see p. 4), a scale which comprises the tones of the diatonic octave, with the exception of the second and fifth. The song is in the key of D minor and the tones E and A do not appear. No. 52 is based on the same scale. This song is characterized by the approach to an harmonic tone by means of the tone above. (See No. 53.) The three renditions recorded are uniform in every respect. The metric unit is very slow, a characteristic of many songs of self-control. (See Nos. 30, 52, 103, 161).

The following song was used as a preliminary to a sham battle between Chippewa and Sioux boys. The combatants, divested of clothing, were ranged in facing lines. The men of each tribe stood behind the boys and sang the song with them. When the song was finished the men shouted, "Now start to fight," and thereupon the little warriors flung themselves into the scrimmage. The rules of this battle were different from those referred to in connection with the preceding song. In this contest the boys tried to kick one another down, not being allowed to use their hands. If a Sioux boy succeeded in felling a Chippewa, the war whoop arose from the whole band of Sioux. Perhaps this exultation was still at its height when a Sioux boy fell before the sturdy kicks of the Chippewa, and a whoop arose from the Chippewa ranks. The battle was well fought and in it many a boy received his first training for the sterner game of tribal warfare.

---

[1] This and the two songs next following are included in the tabulated analysis of White Earth songs, p. 306.

No. 52. Song Before the Boys' Fight (Catalogue No. 279)

Sung by ODJĬB'WE

VOICE ♩ = 63
Recorded without drum

Analysis.—This melody, like the preceding, is based on the fifth five-toned scale with D as the tonic. The song is minor in tonality and very slow in tempo. The subdominant triad (G–B flat–D) is prominent in the middle section while the minor third on the tonic (D–F) characterizes the first and last sections. A slow metric unit in songs of controlled excitement is noted also in Nos. 30, 51, 103, 161.

No. 53. Little Girls' War Song (Catalogue No. 280)

Sung by ODJĬB'WE

VOICE ♩ = 96
Recorded without drum

Nin-a-bem   ga-mo-kwa-na-wĭnd

WORDS

nina'bem.......................... my husband
gamo'kwanawĭnd'.................. who was wounded

While the boys held their sham battles the little girls mimicked the woman's share in war. The aged warrior remembered well the boys' contests and also the song which the little girls sang, giving several uniform renditions of it, but in his description of the girls' play there lingered a trace of the boy's condescension. Odjĭb'we said merely that "the little girls were dancing and jumping around."

Analysis.—This melody contains three peculiarities which rarely occur in Chippewa songs. First, it begins and ends on the same tone. This feature is found in only 11 songs (3 per cent) of the entire series of 340. The examples found in Bulletin 45 are Nos. 132, 142, 149,

150, 170, 174, 197; those in the present volume are Nos. 53, 112, 125, and 127, the last being another version of No. 149 in Bulletin 45. Of this number 4 are moccasin game songs, 2 are war songs, 1 is a love song, and 3 (including the present example) are songs for the entertainment of children. Second, it begins with the upward progression of an octave, a characteristic of only 5 other songs of the entire series; possible connection of this with the content of the song is noted in the analysis of No. 9. The other examples are Nos. 170 and 174 in Bulletin 45, and Nos. 9, 31, and 125 in the present volume. Third, this song does not contain the third tone of the scale. Only 12 songs (3.5 per cent) of the series of 340 show this peculiarity, the song here considered being the first of the group in this volume. The serial numbers of the entire group are 45, 49, 60, 91 in Bulletin 45, and 28, 53, 112, 113, 116, 121, 178, 180 in the present work. We note that three of these songs were sung by women or by little girls and that 3 concern women, the 6 constituting half the group. Three of the remainder are songs of the Mĭde′wĭwĭn, to which women as well as men belonged, 1 is a begging dance song, 1 a war song, and 1 a song for the entertainment of children. The present song (No. 53) is the only one which contains only the first, second, fourth, and fifth of the scale. No. 121 contains only the first, second, and fifth; No. 113, the octave complete except the third; No. 60 (Bulletin 45), the octave complete except the seventh and third; No. 28 (herein), the octave complete except the fourth and third; and No. 116, the sequence of tones designated by Helmholtz as the first five-toned scale (see p. 4); and we find only the first, second, fifth, and sixth tones in Nos. 45, 49, 91 of Bulletin 45, and in Nos. 112, 178, 180 of the present volume. With the exception of No. 45 in Bulletin 45, and No. 180 herein, these songs are major in tonality. A brief analysis of them for comparison is given herewith.

Bulletin 45

No. 45.—"I can tame the shell;" Mĭde′ song; key of B minor; tones comprised in melody, 1, 2, 5, 6; trend of melody, 2–1, 6–5.

No. 49.—"Do not speak ill of a woman;" Mĭde′ song; key of A flat major; tones comprised in melody, 1, 2, 5, 6; trend of melody, 2–1. 6–5.

No. 60.—"Weasel, thou art calling me;" Mĭde′ song; key of G flat major; octave complete except seventh and third; progression 2–1 occurring frequently in the melody.

No. 91.—"I am walking to the spirit land;" Mĭde′ song; key of B major; melody tones, 1, 2, 5, 6; trend of melody, 2–1, 6–5.

Present work

No. 28.—Song of a war charm; key of D flat major; octave complete except third and fourth; trend of melody, 2–1, 6–5.

No. 53.—Little girls' war song; key of F major; melody tones, 1, 2, 4, 5; trend of melody, 5–4, 2–1.

No. 112.—Song of an ambitious mother; love song; key of E flat major; melody tones, 1, 2, 5, 6; a free melody with the progressions 6–5 and 2–1 occurring frequently.

No. 113.—Love song; key of E flat major; octave complete except third; the progressions 6–5, 2–1 emphasized in melody.

No. 116.—Begging dance song; key of G major; melody tones, 1, 2, 4, 5, 6; progressions 6–5 and 2–1 prominent in melody.

No. 121.—Song of ca'wûno'ga dance; key of A flat major; melody tones, 5, 2, 1; trend of melody, 5–2–1.

No. 178.—"He is going away;" love song; key of F major; melody tones, 1, 2, 5, 6; progressions 6–5 and 2–1 prominent in melody.

No. 180.—Song of the crawfish story; key of C sharp major; melody tones, 1, 2, 5, 6; trend of melody, 6–5, 2–1.

In examining these outline analyses we note that 2 and 6 occur as tones of approach to 1 and 5. This characteristic allies the group under analysis with another group in which the harmonic tone is frequently approached by the tone above, this group consisting of Nos. 29, 45, 51, 53, 65, 137, 139, 141. It will be noted further that the tones 1, 2, 5, 6 (in a song of major tonality) are the tones of the fourth five-toned scale lacking the third; another form of the incomplete fourth five-toned scale consists of the tones 8, 6, 5, 3, 1 occurring as given in descending order. This is the major tonic triad and sixth, which constitutes the tone material of 42 per cent of the 340 Chippewa songs under analysis. (See Table 6.) It has been noted that in songs containing this tone material the sixth is usually a preparatory tone to the fifth; the present group, however, may be considered the more primitive as both tonic and dominant are approached from the tone above and the intermediate third is absent. The emphasis of the fifth suggests a particularly strong feeling for that interval. The fifth is absent from only 2 (Nos. 51, 52) of the 340 Chippewa songs. The prominence of the octave and twelfth (or fifth) in the beginning, as well as in the range, of these songs is shown in Tables 2–5. In this connection it is interesting to note that these are the principal "overtones" (see p. 4) of a fundamental tone.

DRUM-PRESENTATION CEREMONY

In October, 1910, the writer witnessed the ceremony accompanying the presentation of two drums by the Lac du Flambeau Band of Chippewa in Wisconsin to the Menominee Indians in the same State. Part of this ceremony was enacted on the Lac du Flambeau Reservation and part on the Menominee Reservation. It is called by the Lac du Flambeau Chippewa *Dewe'igûn omï'giwen'* ("a drum is given away") or the Drum-presentation Ceremony and is described by Barrett under the title of the Dream Dance.[1]

During four days before their departure the Chippewa danced on their own reservation, the Menominee dancing the same length of time before their arrival. There were also four days of dancing on the Menominee Reservation when the drums were presented and four days of dancing together after the ceremony.

So great is the veneration in which the drum and its ceremonies are held that there has sprung up what is called the "drum religion." This does not supplant the Mïde' (Grand Medicine), but introduces a new element. The Mïde'[2] has regard chiefly for the individual; its aim is to secure health and long life for him, and its instructions concern his own character. Its precepts regarding the relation of man to his neighbor (so far as observed) are connected with the cure of illness and general rectitude of conduct. The "religion of the drum" inculcates a developed and broadened sense of responsibility and concerns peace between peoples who have been at enmity. The ceremonies of the Mïde' are not marked by extreme ritual exactness and some latitude is allowed the leaders in the choice of songs as well as in the text of their discourses, but in the ceremonies connected with the drum certain songs and no others must be sung, and dancing once begun must be continued the prescribed length of time regardless of conditions. The central idea of the "drum religion" is that of peace, yet mingled with this idea is law, rigorous and inflexible. The Chippewa say that the drum and its "religion" came to them from the Sioux many years ago, but it came to them also through development of character, as a step in the progress from the childhood toward the manhood of a race.

---

[1] S. A. Barrett, Dream Dance of the Chippewa and Menominee Indians of Northern Wisconsin, in *Bulletin of the Public Museum of the City of Milwaukee*, vol. 1, art. 4, 1911, pp. 251–371. Cf. also section entitled "The Dreamers," in The Menomini Indians, by Walter James Hoffman, M. D. (*Fourteenth Ann. Rep. Bur. Ethn.*, pt. 1, pp. 157–161.

[2] See Bulletin 45, p. 13.

No attempt has been made herein to analyze this "drum religion," but the attitude of the Indians toward it is indicated by the following statement of Wĭs'kĭno ("bird"), the Menominee chief to whom one of the Chippewa drums was given. Referring to his position as owner of a drum, Wĭs'kĭno said:[1]

I will keep this drum in my house. There will always be tobacco beside it and the drum pipe will always be filled. When I smoke at home I will use the pipe that belongs to the drum. My friends will come to my house to visit the drum. Sometimes my wife and I will have a little feast of our own beside the drum, and we will ask the drum to strengthen us in our faith and resolution to live justly and to wrong no one. When my wife and I do this alone there will be no songs. Only special men may sing the songs of the drum, and my part is that of speaker.

When asked how often his friends came for this purpose, he said:

We visit the drum about every fourth night and sing a few songs. Any persons who desire may come and each brings a gift of tobacco. The owner of the drum is the only speaker at these small gatherings. He speaks as representative of those who come, and presents the tobacco to the drum, after which it is given to the singers who sit at the drum.

It is said that many generations ago the Sioux gave to the Chippewa a large drum similar to the one used at the present time in the ceremony here considered, taught them the "songs belonging to the drum," and related to them the tradition concerning its origin. It is believed that permanent peace between the two tribes was a result of this presentation of the drum. Following this presentation, in accordance with the instructions which accompanied it, the Chippewa made similar drums, which they afterward gave away, with the proper songs. In presenting a drum it is customary for the giver to relate his individual dream to the recipient, thus adding to the value of the gift and strengthening the bond between the two men.

The tradition concerning the origin of the drum was a subject of inquiry among the Lac du Flambeau Chippewa, the Bad River Chippewa on the La Pointe Reservation in northern Wisconsin, and also among the Menominee. Ten or twelve informants agreed on the principal features of the account, all stating that a woman was the means used by the manido'[2] in giving this type of drum to the

---

[1] This and other speeches by Wĭs'kĭno were interpreted by Mr. Frank Gokay, a prominent member of the Menominee tribe.

[2] The word *manido'* (spelled also *manito*) is defined by Baraga as "spirit, ghost." The following explanation of the word in some of its compounds was given by Rev. J. A. Gilfillan: *Ki'jĭe' manido'*, literally, "he who has his origin from no one but himself, the Uncreated God"; *Mĕn'ido wenda'g wŭk*, that which is so astonishing as to be considered superhuman; *Manido' wab*, the name of a man, meaning, "he looks through the thing as God does, or with superhuman insight"; *Man'idoka'zo*, he tries to make people believe he has superhuman power, but he is an impostor. The same authority states that a small wild animal is called *man'idowĕns'*, meaning "a poor, miserable little spirit," the explanation being that the little animal is not a clod of earth, as is shown by its running around, but has life, or "spirit."

Na'waji'bigo'kwe, a member of the Mĭde'wĭwĭn, said that the Chippewa believe in many manido', or spirits (see Bulletin 45, p. 21), the highest of all being called Ki'jĭĕ' manido', and that there are four manido' connected with the Mĭde', each being regarded as dwelling at a cardinal point of the compass. Four Mĭde' manido' are mentioned in songs Nos. 16 and 24, Bulletin 45, as "living in the four layers of the earth." The word is applied to animals in the Mĭde' (songs Nos. 34 and 41, Bulletin 45), and a man who sees an animal in his youthful vision calls that animal his manido' and wears some part of the animal on his person as part of his "medicine."

Indians, thus securing peace between the Sioux and the Chippewa. They agreed also in the statement that the woman hid in the water four days, her face being concealed by a broad lily pad. In minor details the accounts differ somewhat. The first part of the following account was given by a Lac du Flambeau Chippewa and the remainder by one of the Bad River Band living at Odanah, Wisconsin. These two narratives were the clearest and most authoritative secured by the writer, and they are given, combined, as nearly as possible in the words of the interpreters.

When the Sioux were fighting the white men a party of them were closely pursued, and one woman, unable to keep up with the warriors, hid in a pond of water. There she stayed four days, submerged in the shallow water at the edge of the pond, with a lily leaf over her face. At the end of four days she heard a voice say, "The people who have been killing your friends are about to eat; come and share their food." The woman was afraid to leave her hiding place. Soon she heard the voice again, saying, "Come; I am calling you to come." At last she believed the voice and came from the water. The voice said, "Keep right on this path and I will see you after a while." The next the woman knew she was among soldiers and eating with them. She could see them, but they could not see her. After eating she started in the direction her people had taken. Then she saw the person whose voice she had heard. He was a manido′ and appeared in the form of a white man. He gave her directions for making the drum, taught her the songs which should be sung with it, and told her that by means of it the Sioux would make friends with all their enemies. He told her that the women could sing with the drum, but that only the men could dance around it; he also told her that when the first drum was finished he would come down to it and that two men must be offered to him in return for his gift of the drum.

The woman told the men how to make the drum. When it was finished and the singers had learned the songs they all gathered around it. The instant that the drummers struck the drum for the first time [1] the manido′ appeared again and the two men who had made the drum fell dead beside it.

It is said that the drums now given by one tribe or band to another are similar to the one made at the direction of the manido′, and that the same songs are still sung. Thus the songs used at all important points of the Drum-presentation Ceremony witnessed by the writer were Sioux songs and were credited to the Sioux. When a drum is transferred the proper songs are carefully taught to the members of the new drum party by the leading singers of the party presenting the drum.

During the dancing which precedes and follows the presentation each tribe sings its own songs, the Chippewa using certain of their war songs on these occasions. In accordance with this custom, typical Chippewa songs are interspersed with the Sioux ceremonial songs in the following narrative, but the songs of the two tribes are considered separately in the tabulated analyses.

Drums of two types may be given in this ceremony. These differ slightly in size and in elaborateness of decoration. The larger is

---

[1] A certain formality attends the first stroke on the drum made by the person to whom the drum is given (see p. 171).—F. D.

DRUM AND STAKES USED IN DRUM-PRESENTATION CEREMONY

DRUM AND ITS CUSTODIANS

called *o'gima dewe'igûn* (chief drum) and the smaller *ogi'tcĭda dewe'igûn* (warrior drum). The chief drum, as the name implies, is usually given by one chief or leader to another and the warrior drum is presented by one member of the tribe to another. The word "chief" as used in this connection refers to the leading man of a village or settlement and throughout the description of the ceremony the word "warrior" refers to any of the men of the assembly.

At the ceremony witnessed by the writer the chief drum was presented to Wĭs'kĭno, chief or "speaker" of the West Branch Settlement of the Menominee tribe, by Bi'jĭkĕns [1] ("small óx"), a prominent member of the Lac du Flambeau Band of Chippewa, and the warrior drum was presented to a Menominee from another part of the reservation by a Lac du Flambeau Chippewa.

The chief drum (pl. 18) presented on this occasion was seen by the writer in the house of Bi'jĭkĕns. It was placed on a low box in one corner of the room; the box and the floor around it were covered with a clean white quilt. Beside the drum were the various articles belonging to it, the pipe filled and ready for use, and the drumsticks in neat cloth cases. The drum and all that pertained to it were treated with greatest respect by Bi'jĭkĕns and his family. After some hesitation he gave his consent to the photographing of the drum and it was carried to the dancing circle by his son and his son-in-law (pl. 19), two of the men officially intrusted with its care.

The curved stakes supporting the drum were more than 3 feet in height and when in position were about 6 feet in span (pl. 18). The drum was 27 inches in diameter and about 12 inches in thickness. It had two heads of untanned hide decorated alike—one half painted blue and the other half red, with a band of yellow near the edge of the blue segment. The sides of the drum were concealed by a strip of red flannel edged with blue, which hung below the rim; this was decorated with pierced silver disks. Around the upper rim was a band of otter fur 2 inches wide, with four loops of fur which served as handles for lifting the drum and also as a means of suspending it from the stakes when in use. Below the band of fur was a broad band of beadwork edged with a deep fringe of beads terminating in tassels and metal thimbles. Four ornaments of heavy beadwork decorated the sides of the drum. The stakes supporting the drum were completely covered with beadwork and bands of otter fur. In a socket on the top of each were placed two large feathers, and each stake was tipped with the tufted end of a cow's tail and several ribbon streamers, blue on the stakes at the west and north and red on those at

---

[1] This name is composed of two words, "*bi'jĭki*," meaning originally "buffalo" and later applied to "cattle" (see pp. 63, 203), and "*ĕns*," a diminutive termination. The meaning of the name was given as "small ox," this being the more common translation of *bi'jĭki*.

the east and south. Beside the drum were the four drumsticks used by the leading drummers, each covered with soft brown deerskin and decorated with a band of otter fur and long ribbon streamers. There was also a longer stick used only by the owner of the drum in a particular part of the ceremony (see p. 171). This stick was more than 3 feet long. Over the curved end was slipped the skin from the neck of a loon, its glossy black feathers dotted with white. The pipe belonging to the drum had a flat stem decorated with geometric drawings, with a tuft of red woodpecker feathers sunk in the wood (fig. 3). (The second pipe belonging to the drum, known as the warrior pipe, is not shown in the illustration, as it had been sent to Wĭs'kĭno in anticipation of the ceremony.) Beside the pipe are seen also a turtle shell, which contained *apak'osigûn'* (tobacco mixed with the inner bark of the red willow) and a wooden box having three compartments; those at the ends contained, respectively, tobacco and red willow and the middle one contained matches. In a similar box are kept the feathers which decorate the stakes of the drum. There are also 8 or 10 ordinary drumsticks used by the drummers.

Four years ago this drum was given to Bi'jĭkĕns by a leader of the Bad River Chippewa. Although he has parted with it, Bi'jĭkĕns retains the right to make duplicates and to give them away at any time. In connection with this right the following incident came to the writer's notice: A few weeks before the presentation of the drums to the Menominee a drum was given by Mec'kawiga'bau to a Chippewa at a neighboring settlement. Mec'kawiga'bau stated that he intended to make a duplicate of the drum during the coming winter and to give it away the next summer. According to him there are no songs or ceremonies connected with the making of a drum, but the songs used in connection with the new one must be those he received with the original drum. He did not receive the drum in the usual manner. It had been

FIG. 3. Stem of the drum pipe.

given to Me'dweya'sûñ (see p. 249), the chief of the Lac du Flambeau Chippewa, whose advanced age rendered him unable to discharge the obligations associated with it. A few months before his death, therefore, he gave a dance at which he made a speech saying that he was very feeble and wanted the drum to be in safe keeping, but that he was not strong enough to visit some other settlement in order to present it to the people. As he did not want to impose that duty on his children in the event of his death, he publicly transferred the drum to Mec'kawiga'bau, who was willing to assume the responsibility.

Drums of similar design have been seen by the writer on the White Earth, Leech Lake, and Red Lake Reservations in Minnesota. These, which were said to have been received from the Sioux, were used in the social dances. At Waba'cĭñg settlement, on the Red Lake Reservation, the drum was suspended from crotched sticks (see p. 252); in all other instances it rested on the ground. No decorated drumsticks were used, there was no pipe belonging to the drum, and its significance as a peace symbol seemed to have been lost. It is reported, however, that occasional ceremonies of drum-presentation are still held in remote parts of the Minnesota reservations. The Chippewa of Minnesota are in frequent contact with the Sioux, the two tribes advancing side by side in civilization. In Wisconsin the contact is less recent and more of a glamor is thrown around the past, the old men telling how in former days the war canoes of the Sioux came up the Chippewa River from the Mississippi.

A drum party originally consisted of 29 persons and it was not customary for a person to "belong" to more than one drum. At the present time, however, it is necessary for each of the good singers to belong to more than one and even for the same person to hold more than one office in a drum party. The complete personnel of such party is as follows: The chief of the settlement; the owner of the drum; the speaker; the aid (oc'kabe'wĭs); the manager of the dancing hall or circle; five men who take care of the drum; the man who takes care of the drum pipe (used by the drummers); the man who takes care of the warrior's pipe (used by the dancers); the chief drummer and singer; four leading drummers and singers (one being seated at each "leg" of the drum); four leading women singers (seated behind the leading drummers); four assistant women singers (seated between the leading women singers); four leading dancers (said to be "one for each 'leg' of the drum"). There are also other singers and drummers.

During a ceremony the chief drummer is usually seated at the western side of the drum and at his right hand are placed the drum pipe, the turtle shell filled with *apak'osigûn* (tobacco mixed with red willow bark), and the other articles belonging to the drum. He it is who starts the songs and leads the singing. The leading drummers are seated by the four stakes, or "legs" supporting the drum, and between them are the singers and drummers of less importance, who have no permanent seats. The women form a large outer circle, sitting with bowed heads, their mouths covered by their hands or shawls. The singing of the women, which is entirely through the nose, gives the melody with clear intonation, an octave above the voices of the men. The octave appears to be a natural interval between the voices of men and women when singing together. It is possible that the perception of the octave as a pleasing musical interval may have come to the Indians from this source. The prominence of the octave in Chippewa melodies is noted on page 4.

The chief of the band, owner of the drum, speaker, and the four leading dancers sit on the long seat which surrounds the dancing hall or circle. The aid sits alone at a little distance, ready to act as messenger. Those who take care of the drum and the pipes have no official duties during a ceremony and are usually seated with the drummers.

As the gift of a drum involves the return of gifts supposed to equal in value the drum and the presents bestowed by the original drum party, it is customary for the man presenting the drum to ascertain from the one to whom he wishes to present it whether the latter desires to assume the obligations associated with its acceptance. This is done several months before the drum is to be given. It is the duty of the recipient to see that a suitable quantity of gifts is presented to the drum party at the ceremony, that one or more feasts are provided for the guests, and that their camp is supplied with food during their entire stay. At some later date he must return a full equivalent of gifts to the donor of the drum. A year or two may elapse before he is prepared to do this. When he is ready he sends a messenger to the donor, and shortly afterward visits him with a large party carrying the gifts.

About 10 days before the presentation of the drums by the Lac du Flambeau Chippewa to the Menominee two messengers were sent with the warrior pipes belonging to the two drums. Before they left Lac du Flambeau a dance was held, the final song being the Sioux song of departure sung at the close of all the gatherings connected with the Drum-presentation Ceremony.

All the ceremonial songs given in connection with the following narrative were sung by Mec'kawiga'bau (pl. 20), one of the prominent singers of the tribe. As he was the leading singer of the drum presented by Bi'jĭkĕns, these songs represent those of a chief drum; the songs used during the presentation ceremony of the warrior drum were different, although they have the same general characteristics.

MEC'KAWIGA'BAU

No. 54. Song of Departure   (Catalogue No. S. 1)[1]

Sung by Me′ckawiga′bau

VOICE ♩ = 76
DRUM ♩ = 76
(Drum-rhythm similar to No. 2)

Analysis.—The three renditions of this song recorded are uniform throughout. The time is not rigidly maintained, but varies in corresponding measures in the several renditions. The intonation of the D flat in the opening measures was faulty in the first two renditions, but practically correct in the third rendition (compare Nos. 129, 133, 146, 164). A faulty intonation on the interval of a second occurs also in Nos. 55, 61, 64, 145, 166.[2] It is noted that the rhythmic unit occurs in both double and triple measures.

The two messengers smoked the pipes with the two Menominee who were to receive the drums, and said that they would return with their people after a certain number of days and smoke the pipes again. This number of days was supposed to allow adequate time for the messengers to return and the people to make the journey.

When the messengers reached Lac du Flambeau, active preparations for departure were begun. It was the custom for each tribe to dance four days on its own reservation, and during this period the Chippewa held a ceremony called the Restoring of Mourners, and, if occasion required, a Ceremony of Divorce.

---

[1] Catalogue numbers preceded by S. refer to phonograph records of Sioux songs.
[2] As this concerns manner of rendition and not structure of melody, the reference includes both Sioux and Chippewa songs.

At the presentation of the drum the tribes dance together for four days, and on the fourth day a Dog Feast may be held for the further cementing of the peace bond. This feast was not held on the Menominee Reservation, but the writer witnessed it on the Leech Lake Reservation in Minnesota during the celebration of July Fourth, 1910 (see p. 173). A Dog Feast may be held independent of a Drum-presentation and is of somewhat frequent occurrence on the Wisconsin Reservation.

On the first day of dancing on their own reservation the Chippewa sang a series of five songs, called, respectively, the Song of the Chief, Song of the Speaker, Song of the Owner of the Drum, Song of the Warriors, and the Song of Giving Away the Drum. These were also sung at the opening of the ceremony on the Menominee Reservation, and if the final four days of dancing had been held at Lac du Flambeau these songs would have been repeated at the beginning of that period of the ceremony.

No. 55. Song of the Chief   (Catalogue No. S. 2)

Sung by MEC′KAWIGA′BAU

VOICE ♩ = 88
DRUM ♩ = 96
(Drum-rhythm similar to No. 2)

Analysis.—All the renditions of this song show faulty intonation on the interval of a second in the opening measures, in some instances the upper tone being flatted and in others the lower tone being sharped. This uncertainty suggests that it may be difficult for the singer to adapt his voice to so small an interval (see Nos. 54, 61, 64, 100, 145, 166). The interval of the eleventh was sung with reasonable accuracy in beginning the repetitions of the song. In the first two measures the harmonic tone is approached by the tone above, which is accented; this characteristic leads to the classification as melodic with harmonic framework of a song which otherwise would be classified as harmonic in structure. The song contains only the tones of the minor triad and fourth.

No. 56. Song of the Speaker
(Catalogue No. S. 3)

Sung by Mec′kawiga′bau

Voice ♩ = 184

Drum ♩ = 80

(Drum-rhythm similar to No. 3)

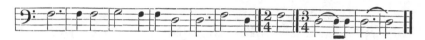

Analysis.—This song is transcribed as it was sung in three renditions. The first part of the song is distinctly major and the last part minor in tonality; therefore it is transcribed in the keys of D major and D minor. The F in the opening measures is clearly sung F sharp, and the F in the latter part is as clearly sung F natural; the C in the twelfth measure is sung C sharp in the first two renditions, C natural in the third, and between the two tones in the last. The rhythm does not vary in the several renditions. A half note followed by a quarter note occurs frequently but can scarcely be said to constitute a rhythmic unit. The metric unit of the voice (indicated by ♩=184) is very rapid. If each drumbeat were regarded as a quarter note the tempo of the drum might be indicated as ♩=160, but the drumbeats are in groups of two; it is more convenient therefore to regard each drumbeat as an eighth note and indicate the tempo as ♩=80.

No. 57. Song of the Owner of the Drum

Sung by Mec′kawiga′bau

(Catalogue No. S. 4)

Voice ♩ = 80

Drum ♩ = 92

(Drum-rhythm similar to No. 2)

Analysis.—This is an instance in which the sharps at the beginning of the transcription should be regarded as indicating the pitch of certain tones rather than as implying an established key. Thus the song is transcribed as in the key of E major although the third of that key does not appear. The principal chords of the key of E accompany the melody in a satisfactory manner and the tones F sharp, C sharp, and D sharp are found in the melody.

No. 58. Song of the Warriors   (Catalogue No. S. 5)

Sung by MEC′KAWIGA′BAU

VOICE ♩ = 108
DRUM ♩ = 116
(Drum-rhythm similar to No. 15)

Analysis.—This song is characterized by the approach to an harmonic tone by means of the tone above it. The melody tones are those of the fourth five-toned scale and the trend of the song is an almost unbroken descent. Four renditions were recorded, which are uniform in every respect.

No. 59. Song of Giving Away the Drum (Catalogue No. S. 6)

Sung by MEC′KAWIGA′BAU

VOICE ♩ = 80
DRUM ♩ = 80
(Drum-rhythm similar to No. 2)

Analysis.—The intonation of the opening measures of this song was faulty in all the renditions. The melodic tones are those of the fourth five-toned scale and the trend of the melody is steadily downward. Although strongly rhythmic in character, the song contains no unit of rhythm.

Ceremony of Restoring the Mourners

The ceremony called Restoring the Mourners, usually held during the preliminary days of dancing, begins on the first day, if possible, in order that those whose period of mourning is formally ended may join their friends in the remainder of the dance.

This ceremony was witnessed by the writer at Lac du Flambeau October 16, 1911. It was held in the dancing inclosure of the Lac du Flambeau Chippewa, which is situated on a knoll overlooking the Indian village; this inclosure is surrounded by a high board fence (see pl. 19). Four drums were placed at intervals around the circle and beside them were seated their respective drummers and singers. Ĕ′niwûb′e ("sits farther along"), leader at one of the drums, had painted the lower half of his face black, as a token of mourning.

At this ceremony the period of mourning of four persons—a man who had lost his wife, two young women who had lost children, and an aged woman who had lost her husband—came to an end. All these deaths had occurred since a similar gathering of the tribe, the period of mourning usually lasting from six months to a year. During that time a mother who has lost her child carries a cup tied in a cloth around her waist. This she frequently fills with berries or some other delicacy and places beside her "for the child." After a little while she gives the food to some needy person and replaces the cup in the cloth.

The mourners were seated in the center of the circle. The women were newly arrayed in bright dresses and gay shawls. The man wore a bright blue shirt with beaded sash. Even the aged woman was dressed in bright colors and her hair was tied with a gay ribbon. These brilliant colors contrasted sharply with the evident sadness of the mourners, who sat with downcast eyes. At intervals some one stepped forward and hung a bead chain around the neck of one of them or laid a bright garment or shawl at his side, but the gifts were received without response.

It was a strange scene. Looking beyond the inclosure one saw the towering pines, majestic in outline but wondrous in soft shadows; to the right lay the scattered cabins of the Indians grouped on the shore of the lake, and at a little distance was another hillside on which were the smaller cabins of the dead. Above all was the bluest of October skies. Some said the ceremony was pagan, yet in it was mingled all that is deepest and most tender in human life.

The leader of the ceremony was White Feather, who is highly respected by both Indians and white men. On being asked his "Indian name" he gave, not the Chippewa equivalent of White Feather (Wa'bĭckigwûn'), but Odja'nimwe 'wegijĭgons'.[1]

At the opening of the ceremony a woman brought water and soap, which she placed before the man who had lost his wife. He washed his hands, drying them on a towel which she offered for the purpose. A man then parted his hair and combed it very smooth, while the following song was sung at one of the drums.

No. 60. Song of Restoring the Mourners

(Catalogue No. S. 7)

Sung by MEC'KAWIGA'BAU

VOICE ♪= 176
DRUM ♩= 88
(Drum-rhythm similar to No. 2)

Analysis.—This song is characterized by a very rapid tempo and by measures containing five counts. A few measures in quadruple time break the monotony. It is worthy of note that the interval of an octave and a fourth is compassed in three measures.

After a short time a woman brought water and offered it to one of the women who had lost a child, this being done also for each of the women while the same song was sung at one of the drums.

When this was finished White Feather rose and said:[2]

---

[1] The meanings of the component parts of this word are as follows: *odja'nim* signifies a disturbance; *wewe* is a root implying a swaying motion (see footnote 2, p. 241); and *gi'jig* in proper names is usually translated "sky." The last-mentioned part of the word is found also on p. 249, with the prefix *ki'tci*, "large." Hence the name as analyzed thus far may be translated " sky in commotion." The termination *ons* in some cases indicates that the bearer of the name was small in stature, but more often that his father bore the same name. (Cf. pp. 76, 145.)

[2] This and other speeches made by White Feather were given the writer at a later date by White Feather himself and are transcribed in the words of the interpreter.

A person who believes in the drum and has lost friends can not go to a dance unless he is invited, but I asked that these mourners be invited.   I came myself and spread my own blanket on the ground for them, and I asked the warriors that they be invited and their mourning ended.   When I did this I knew how this ceremony should be conducted.   I thank my people and Manido´ that the warriors are so generous as to bring these mourners here to share our happiness.

A woman then stepped forward and painted a row of dark blue dots below the eyes of the man who had lost his wife.   Before the painting of the two younger women White Feather made another speech somewhat similar to those which are here recorded.   There is no prescribed pattern for the painting.   The younger women were painted with a horizontal red line below the eyes, and on one the parting line of the hair was painted red.   It was said, "Red means blood (life), and the red paint is for long life."   While the faces were being painted the following song was sung.

No. 61. Song of Painting the Faces   (Catalogue No. S. 8)

Sung by Mec´kawiga´bau

Voice ♩ = 92
Drum ♩ = 96
(Drum-rhythm similar to No. 15)

Analysis.—This melody contains a peculiar grace and charm.   The E in the opening measures was sung slightly below pitch (see Nos. 54, 55, 100, 145, 166).   After the opening measures the song flows smoothly along the intervals of the second five-toned scale, with special emphasis and feeling of repose on the tonic.   There is no unit of rhythm, yet the rhythm of the song as a whole is pleasing and well defined.   The metric unit of the drum is slightly more rapid than that of the voice and seems constantly urging the voice forward.   Four renditions were recorded, which are uniform in every respect.

The eldest woman among the mourners was White Feather's mother, who mourned the death of his father; for this reason it was deemed not fitting that he should make the speech which preceded the painting of her face, so he asked that one of the old men speak in his stead.

An old man arose and, leaning on his staff, said that he had fought in the Civil War. He told of his bravery as a soldier and said that he would give to this mourning woman the strength and power which upheld him on the field of battle. He then handed paint to a woman, who, kneeling before the aged mourner, traced scarlet lines on her thin face.

It is said that a man who has distinguished himself in war may give the full result of his prowess to a friend in this ceremony, and yet by so doing not lose it himself. If he is entitled to wear a feather, he may give his friend the right to wear a similar feather, and even to point to it saying, "*I* was as brave as that." Sometimes the right thus generously shared was won at the risk of the man's life.

The following song was sung during the ceremony.

No. 62. Mourners' Song   (Catalogue No. S. 9)

Sung by Mec'kawiga'bau

Voice ♩ = 84
Drum ♩ = 84
(Drum-rhythm similar to No. 2)

Analysis.—The metric unit of this song is unusually slow and was not maintained with absolute regularity. The three renditions recorded show no variation. The rhythm is less interesting than in many songs of the present series, but was clearly marked and accurately repeated. The song is minor in tonality and has a range of 12 tones.

When the painting of the faces was finished, White Feather thus addressed all the mourners:

Lift up your eyes. Look at your friends sitting around you so gaily arrayed. If you still look down your sorrow will not leave you. Do not think so much about your sorrow and that you, too, will soon die. It is true that we all must die, but we shall meet afterward. You must not cling to your sorrow nor hold an unkind feeling toward anyone. Have faith in yourselves and people will think more of you and Manido′ will help you. There are no enemies around you. Think only of what is good.

The mourners were then led to their respective seats, those who belonged to one of the drum parties being seated at the drum and the others being placed with friends at the edge of the circle. From time to time additional gifts were silently laid beside them, but they made no response, sitting with downcast eyes or sadly touching the gay little trinkets.

On the evening of the day following the ceremony of Restoring the Mourners the writer went again to the Lac du Flambeau village. The Indian village is about 4 miles from the Government school, but the drum could be heard distinctly and, as there was a full moon, it was thought possible that the Indians were dancing outdoors. On arriving at the village, however, the bright light in Ĕ′niwûb′e's window and the sound of the drum indicated where the Indians were gathered. The house is small and in beating the drum the Indians make little difference whether they are beneath a roof or the dome of the sky. The four or five drummers, seated around the warrior drum which would be presented to the Menominee, played and sang right heartily. A drum of similar type was on a table, the decorations of the two instruments forming spots of vivid color. A few women were seated on the floor behind the drummers, with heads bowed and their shawls held over their mouths as they sang in a weird, high falsetto. From time to time the men sitting in the room rose, and danced in their places with a bending of the knees and a rhythmic shifting of their weight from one foot to the other. There were soft brown tints of unpainted wood, dull colors of weatherworn garments, and a bit of brilliant green where Ĕ′niwûb′e's familiar blanket hung against the wall. The dark faces were grave with the import of the dance and the lamplight cast strange shadows. It was a scene long to be remembered. Chippewa war songs were sung during these dances. It was stated that all war songs could not be used, but that the following three songs were frequently sung at the dances preceding or following the presentation of a drum.

No. 63. "The Sound Comes Pleasingly"

(Catalogue No. 423)

Sung by Ĕ′NIWÛB′E

VOICE ♩ = 100
DRUM ♩ = 112
(Drum-rhythm similar to No. 19)

Ge - bi - o - dja- mĭn - we - we   gi - jĭg e   ge - bi - moc

ki - ne - ä - ci - yan   gi - jĭg e

WORDS

gebi′ odja′ mĭnewewe′............ the sound comes pleasingly
gi′ jĭg............................ across the sky
gebi′ mockine′ äciyan′.......... filling the air

Analysis.—This is the dream song of a man who had a vision of the thunderbird. On hearing thunder he took tobacco in his hand, and, holding it toward the sky, said to the storm, "Go around that way," tossing the tobacco in the direction he wished the storm to go and singing this song. The three renditions recorded show no variation. The melody contains the tones of the fourth five-toned scale and is melodic in structure.

No. 64. "The Ravens are Singing"   (Catalogue No. 424)

Sung by Ĕ'NIWÛB'E

VOICE ♩ = 120
DRUM ♩ = 120
(Drum-rhythm similar to No. 19)

Ka-ga - gi-wûg   e   ka-ga - gi-wûg   e   na-gûm - o-wûg   gi -

jĭg- uñg

WORDS

kaga'giwûg.................... the ravens
na'gûmo'wûg................. are singing
gi'jĭguñg'.................... in the sky

Analysis.—The rhythmic unit of this song is short, interesting, and repeated frequently. In the five renditions recorded the only difference was that in one rendition the tone G in the sixth measure was sung as a quarter instead of as a half note. This exact repetition of the rhythm is interesting because the intonation in the first part of the song was very uncertain. It appeared difficult for this singer to keep correct intonation on small intervals (see Nos. 54, 55, 61, 100, 145, 166). The song is minor in tonality, melodic in structure, and contains all the tones of the octave except the seventh. The interval of the fourth is prominent in the structure of the melody (see No. 22).

No. 65. War Song   (Catalogue No. 425)

Sung by Ĕ′NIWÛB′E

VOICE ♩ = 116
DRUM ♩ = 126
(Drum-rhythm similar to No. 19)

Analysis.—In structure this song is classified as melodic with harmonic framework. It begins on the twelfth and ends on the tonic, the descending intervals of the tonic chord being varied by a frequent occurrence of the tone above the harmonic tone, which is accented and forms an important part of the melody (see No. 53). The rhythmic unit is long and occurs only twice. Five renditions of the song were recorded.

No. 66. "I am Small"   (Catalogue No. 432)

Sung by Mec′kawiga′bau

VOICE ♩ = 88
DRUM ♩ = 112

(Drum-rhythm similar to No. 19)

Wen-dji - ä - ga - ci - ya - an   wen - dji - ä - ga - ci - ya - an   *wa* ca-wûn-o-nañg   don-dji-ba   *a*   wen-dji - ä-ga -ci - ya - an

WORDS

wendjiä′gaciyan′............ I am small
ca′wûnonañg′............... from the south
don′djiba′.................. I come

Analysis.—This melody, which contains seven sections, is based on a rhythmic unit, although that unit does not appear at either the beginning or the end of the song. The opening phrase has a rhythm of its own, and the closing measures were slightly hurried in tempo, as though the singer were in haste to reach the final tone. The song is major in tonality and comprises the tones of the fourth five-toned scale. In structure it is melodic with harmonic framework.

After listening to a number of songs in the house of Ě′niwûb′e the writer passed into the open air. The lake was white and glistening in the moonlight and the pines were outlined darkly against the sky. A party of Indians, carrying a drum, were coming down the road, and in the distance a light shone from Bi′jĭkĕns's window. On inquiry it was learned that the party belonging to the chief drum had been dancing at Bi′jĭkĕns's house and that they were bringing that drum to Ě′niwûb′e's, where they would sing with both drums.

Remembering the sound of the lesser drum in the house of Ĕ'niwûb'e, one did not wish to return and hear the chief drum. Far on the road through the pine forest the throb of the drum was heard, and one knew that in Ĕ'niwûb'e's lamplight the dark figures were dancing as the Indians danced before ever a white man came to their shores.

CEREMONY OF DIVORCE

A Ceremony of Divorce is sometimes held on the last day of one of the periods of dancing. There are four songs for this ceremony; these are similar in character, and only two are recorded. The ceremony is said to be very simple, the man or woman desiring the divorce merely going through the motions of throwing something outside the dancing circle as these songs are sung.

No. 67. Divorce Song   (Catalogue No. 428)

Sung by MEC'KAWIGA'BAU

VOICE ♩ = 88
DRUM ♩ = 80
(Drum-rhythm similar to No. 2)

Analysis.—This melody consists of four parts, two of which are major and two minor in tonality. The song opens with a particularly bright and happy strain in which the rhythmic unit occurs twice; a few measures later this unit is used (without the tied notes) in the minor tonality. It does not appear with the return to the major tonality, the rhythm of these measures being direct and somewhat emphatic, but is used in the recurring minor passage and is suggested in the triple measure near the close of the song, as though sung in a lingering fashion. (Other instances of a change in tonality are Nos. 189, 192, in Bulletin 45.) It is of interest to compare this melodic form with the content of the song. The rhythm was clearly given and the important tones of the song were accurate in intonation. The three renditions recorded are uniform in every respect.

No. 68. Divorce Song   (Catalogue No. 429)

Sung by Mec′kawiga′bau

VOICE ♩ = 84
DRUM ♩ = 80
(Drum-rhythm similar to No. 2)

Analysis.—The rhythmic unit of this song resembles that of the preceding, but is in triple instead of double time. This unit occurs five times, comprising practically the entire song. The interval of the fourth is emphatic at the close of the song, but can not be said to characterize it as a whole. In this connection the frequent use of the fourth in songs concerning motion (see No. 22) should be noted. The six renditions of this song recorded show no variation.

————

There was a controversy regarding the day for leaving Lac du Flambeau, some maintaining that if they started on the day after the dancing they would reach the Menominee Reservation before they were expected. A certain number of days were to elapse between the presentation of the pipe to the Menominee chief and the arrival of the Chippewa drum party, but it was uncertain whether the day on which the pipe had been given should be included in the count. It was finally decided that the start should be deferred a day. As a result the Menominee awaited their arrival with some anxiety.

The Chippewa village is about 7 miles from the railroad station at Lac du Flambeau. Thither the Indians drove their shaggy ponies and then turned them loose to forage. On Tuesday morning, October 18, 1910, a party of about 70 Chippewa took the train, carrying the two drums, tents and camp equipment, rolls of blankets and matting, and huge packs containing the gifts intended for the

Menominee. The distance to the Menominee settlement by rail, the route taken by the writer, was about 150 miles. The Indians, however, left the train at Antigo, a station about half that distance from Lac du Flambeau, and walked eastward 20 miles across the country. This part of the trip was carefully planned—they would walk 12 miles the first day, camp at night, finish the journey the second day, and, after camping overnight, would be ready for the ceremony.

From the car window at Antigo they were seen starting gaily on their way, strange figures on the streets of a prosperous little city. They walked in groups of two or three. The packs did not seem heavy nor the clutter of small articles a burden. The bearer of the large drum walked alone, not forgetting his dignity, with the drum fastened on his back. From within the shawl on many a woman's back there peered a grave little face with blinking eyes. The older children trudged sturdily along and the women jested together. The road was hard and firm beneath the feet and the sweetness of the autumn was in the air. Surely it was good to go to the country of the Menominee.

After a circuitous journey, the writer arrived the following day at Neopit, a town on the Menominee Reservation. The place of the ceremony was reached by driving westward about 5 miles through the pine forest. There the Menominee were found dancing. They had completed the four days of preliminary dancing and, while awaiting the Chippewa, they spent part of each day in their dancing circle (pl. 21). The place selected was near a vacant Government day school, the house intended for the teacher and two or three cabins occupied by Indians completing the settlement. An open area of several acres afforded ample space for a camp. The Menominee who came to attend the gathering did not use this ground but left it for the Chippewa. The dancing circle was about 30 feet in diameter and was outlined by a bank of earth which served as a seat for the dancers. The bare earth within the circle was pounded hard, but the seat for the dancers was turfed. There were three openings in the circle, located approximately at the east, south, and west, but only the one nearest the east was used; the others were narrower and had been closed by logs. An American flag on a tall pole was placed near the eastern opening, where the man was seated who took the toll of tobacco, each person who entered the inclosure giving him a small piece. Two drums were at the right of the entrance, resting on rush matting similar to that made by the Chippewa.

Wĭs′kĭno ("bird"), the chief of the West Branch Settlement of the Menominee, received the writer with courtesy and said, through an interpreter, that the Chippewa were reported as on the way and greatly wearied with their long journey. He had requested his people to go to meet them and to bring the women and children in their wagons. Some had already gone and he was hourly expecting their return. Several miles westward the first Chippewa were found resting by the roadside, while in the distance others appeared, toiling and staggering beneath their packs. Could these be the same men who had set forth so bravely the day before? Footsore, dusty, tired, and bedraggled, they had reached the country of the Menominee.

The next morning the Chippewa were much refreshed. A temporary camp had been established about a quarter of a mile from the dancing circle. The tents, which were close together, shone white beneath the pine trees; camp fires burned brightly, kettles were steaming, and a pleasant, cheery atmosphere pervaded the scene.

Meantime the Menominee assembled in the dancing circle and danced at intervals for about two hours. Shortly before 12 o'clock on the 20th of October Wĭs′kĭno summoned his messenger and said:[1] "We are now ready to receive our visitors. You will go to them and tell them to proceed to this place. They will inform you what we are to do."

Wĭs′kĭno's messenger was a tall, finely built Indian. His headdress was of stiff moose hair and erect feathers and his garments were bright with beads and scarlet trimmings. He was a picturesque figure as he ran down the winding road in the direction of the Chippewa camp. In a short time he returned and said, "They have accepted your invitation and are on the way."

Wĭs′kĭno then directed the messenger to take up the American flag and carry it before him. Preceded by the flag, Wĭs′kĭno left the dancing circle, the members of the tribe following him in single file, and took his position about 50 feet from the entrance of the circle, with the flag bearer beside him. The men of the tribe formed a line which extended almost to the circle; behind this were two lines of women and children, a space of about 6 feet being left between the lines. Thus the Menominee stood ready to receive their guests.

Soon a wagon was seen at the turn of the road, heaped to its highest capacity with the camp equipage of the Chippewa. Beside the swaying load walked Na′ganac′ (Head Flier), who might be termed the "man of affairs" among the Chippewa. At a short distance followed the drum parties, each consisting of a flag bearer, a pipe bearer, the owner of the drum, an aid, a man carrying the drum, and others carrying the supports and drumsticks; these were followed by the singers and drummers, while other members of the tribe, with the women and children, brought up the rear of the procession. All were arrayed in their brightest garments and gayest decorations.

The Chippewa paused a short distance from the Menominee and planted their flags in the ground. White Feather then advanced,

---

[1] This and all the other speeches of Wĭs′kĭno were given the writer by him a few days later and were interpreted by Mr. Frank Gokay.

followed by the pipe bearer of the chief drum (pl. 21). When about midway between the two tribes, White Feather made the following speech (see footnote 2, p. 154):

This is the day which the warriors named for our meeting. Manido′ commanded us to meet here to-day. We meet in order to have a happy time together. Manido′ gave us this happy time that we might be at peace with each other. We will use a pipe as we meet before Manido′. After we smoke we will all shake hands and enjoy ourselves in the sight of Manido′.

In response to this speech the Menominee aid stepped forward, shook hands with White Feather, and returned to his place. The Chippewa pipe bearer then advanced and made a somewhat similar speech. A Menominee pipe bearer then came toward him, the two presented their pipes four times to the circle of the sky, and lit them; the pipes were then crossed, each man puffing the other's pipe. The Chippewa pipe bearer then approached Wĭs′kĭno and offered him the pipe, Wĭs′kĭno puffing it as he held the bowl. The pipe bearer then passed down the lines, offering the pipe to each member of the tribe.

Meanwhile the company of Chippewa approached Wĭs′kĭno. First to shake hands with him was Bi′jĭkĕns, from whom he would soon receive the chief drum. Others followed rapidly and greetings were exchanged. Wĭs′kĭno had an especially cordial welcome for many whom he had met at previous gatherings (pl. 22). After shaking hands with Wĭs′kĭno the Chippewa passed down the three lines, each member of the Chippewa party shaking hands with each of the Menominee.

When this was finished Wĭs′kĭno led the way to the dancing circle, preceded by the flag of the Menominee, which was returned to its former place, the two flags belonging to the Chippewa being set in the ground outside the circle at the left of the entrance. The two drums brought by the Chippewa were placed within the circle, the chief drum at the left of the entrance and the warrior drum next to it. The drummers seated themselves in their proper places and the drum pipe was laid at the right of the leading drummer, with the tobacco pouch, the turtle shell, and the other articles belonging to the drum (see p. 147).

Wĭs′kĭno then made a speech of welcome in Chippewa:

My relatives, the Chippewa. I thank Ki′jië′ Manido′ [see footnote 2, p. 143] that we join in peace where we were once at war. We leave all differences behind us as we shake hands. Ki′jië′ Manido′ has seen us shake hands. Let us remain in peace as we are now. My relatives, the Chippewa, when the Indians of one tribe present a drum to those of another tribe they perform that ceremony in the sight of Ki′jië′ Manido′. To-day Ki′jië′ Manido′ sees all that we do. I thank you all. Now I shall wait to see how you will proceed. I hope that you will proceed at once and that we may finish this ceremony by to-morrow. I have work undone. The product of my farm is not gathered, but I prefer to serve Ki′jië′ Manido′ before I finish gathering my harvest. Then I shall return to my work with good spirit. Of course I may expect success by serving Ki′jië′ Manido′ before I finish my harvest.

MENOMINEE AWAITING APPROACH OF CHIPPEWA

APPROACH OF CHIPPEWA

PARTICIPANTS IN DRUM-PRESENTATION CEREMONY

CHIPPEWA SHAKING HANDS WITH MENOMINEE

MENOMINEE LISTENING TO SINGING OF CHIPPEWA

PARTICIPANTS IN DRUM-PRESENTATION CEREMONY

The Menominee beat their drums and sang and danced around them, the Chippewa then sang the songs used at the opening of the four days of dancing at Lac du Flambeau, the series containing the special songs of the various officials of the drum party (see p. 150). The Menominee listened as the Chippewa sang, the women sitting with heads bowed, in a position similar to that assumed when they were singing (pl. 22).

At the conclusion Wĭs'kĭno rose again and said, "My relatives, the Chippewa, you must be tired and hungry after your journey.[1] We will set before you whatever cooked food we have. I will send some of my men to my own house and to the houses of my people and they will bring the food here to you."

Wĭs'kĭno asked the Chippewa aid where the food should be placed and he directed that it be put at the left of the entrance. Soon both men and women appeared with kettles and pails containing wild rice, white rice, squash, and tea, while others brought pans heaped with fried bread. Each Chippewa took out his cup or pan and spoon and the Chippewa aid superintended the distribution of the food. Thus the Chippewa enjoyed the hospitality of the Menominee, none of whom partook of the feast. When the feast was finished the kettles, pails, and pans were placed outside the entrance where, a few hours later, the Menominee women were seen identifying their own by familiar dents or by colored strings on the handles.

During the remainder of the day the two tribes danced together. Meantime Na'ganac' had piloted the swaying load of equipage to the place assigned for the camp, the white tents had sprung up, and that night the camp of the Chippewa was fully established.

The next morning a cold, dismal rain was falling. The water was deep in the little hollows of the dancing circle. At the Chippewa camp a few fires were smoldering and most of the tents were tightly closed. It was evidently impossible to proceed with the ceremony and that day was not counted as one of the four days of dancing. It was stated that this was permissible because the actual presentation of the drums had not taken place.

With the sudden changes of weather which characterize the autumn season the next morning dawned bright and clear. Preparations were begun at once for the presentation of the chief drum. Every one was in good spirits. Gala trappings were brought out, faces were carefully painted, and long braids rearranged. The men in charge of the drums cut branches of pine trees and laid them in the dancing circle, spreading them thick where the drum was to rest and the drummers and singers were to sit. These circles of fresh green added effectiveness to the picture, setting off the bright shawls of the women and the beadwork worn by the men.

---

[1] The Chippewa were supposed just to have arrived after a continuous journey from their own reservation.

By about half-past 10 in the morning all the Chippewa and Menominee were in the dancing circle. Wĭs'kĭno, his aid, and his leading dancers were seated on the farther side, opposite the entrance. On the right of the circle were two Menominee drums; at the left, next to the entrance, was the chief drum, which was to be given away that day, and next to it was the warrior drum to be given away the following day, while nearest Wĭs'kĭno was a Menominee drum. Thus there were five drums in the circle. Only a few persons were seated around the Menominee drums, but the full quota were around the two Chippewa drums, where most of the singing was to be done. The aid of the chief drum sat on a low seat at the entrance and received a toll of tobacco from all who entered the circle. He was elaborately attired and as a badge of his office wore a garment received from the Sioux, called by them *wami'hina'ka*. The writer has seen a similar garment worn by the Teton Sioux in their social dances and also by the Chippewa at Leech Lake, Minnesota, July 4, 1910, who said they received it many years ago from the Sioux. This garment consists of a piece of cloth about 18 inches wide and 40 inches long, on which large feathers are closely sewed, being lightly fastened by the quills, so that they move with every motion of the wearer. The garment, which is attached to a belt, hangs behind the wearer, reaching to his ankles (pl. 23). In order that it may not be injured, it is customary among the Chippewa and the Menominee for the wearer to spread a blanket over the box on which he sits, allowing the garment to rest on the ground behind him. As he sits down he spreads the feather garment carefully on this blanket, so that it may not be injured. The four leading Menominee dancers wore these feather garments, resembling a row of brilliant birds.

The officials of the chief drum sat at the side of the circle, on the left of the entrance. Their faces were painted, and they wore ornaments of beadwork and many streamers of bright-colored ribbon.

PRESENTATION OF THE DRUM

Bi'jĭkĕns opened the ceremony with a formal speech, after which the tobacco which had been placed before him was distributed to the entire assembly. As chief of the band, he gave what might be termed an "invocation," standing with right hand extended toward the drum and speaking with dignity, and then repeated it as owner of the drum, dancing three times around the drum with right hand extended over it and pausing after completing each circuit (pl. 23).

The leading drummer then started the Song of the Pipe, and the pipe bearers of both drums rose in their places and, after presenting the pipes to the circle of the sky, lighted them and offered them first to the drummers in order of importance, then to the entire company,

AID

OWNER OF DRUM (DANCING)

PROMINENT CHIPPEWA ACTORS IN DRUM-PRESENTATION CEREMONY

the Song of the Pipe being sung continuously. In presenting the pipe to the sky the drummer stood facing the east, holding the pipe almost horizontal and turning it four times in a circle above his head.

This was done four times during the day, at intervals as nearly equal as possible, the last offering of the pipe being near the close of the day. By reason of its frequent repetition this song became particularly familiar to those attending the ceremony.

No. 69. Song of the Pipe (Catalogue No. S. 10)

Sung by Mec′kawiga′bau

Voice ♩ = 84
Drum ♩ = 92
(Drum-rhythm similar to No. 2)

Analysis.—This song consists of two distinct parts, each of which is characterized by a rhythmic unit. These units are somewhat similar in divisions of the count and form answering phrases. It should be noted that the melodic feeling of the song seems to require a break between the first and second measures of the repetition of the second rhythmic unit, a feature showing the extreme freedom of native musical expression. The effect of the triple measures is interesting, as they add character and effect to the rhythm of the song as a whole. The song is minor in tonality and contains the interval of a whole tone between the seventh and tonic. (See No. 9.) The accidental was uniformly given in the several renditions.

There were many speeches, and the ceremony, so briefly described, lasted many hours. At noon a feast was held similar to that of the preceding day. Certain delicacies had been "presented to the drum"; these were placed beside the drum until the time of the feast, when they were divided among the singers and drummers.

It sometimes happens that the untanned head of the drum becomes loosened during a ceremony. When this occurs, the Song of the

Drum is started by one of the drummers.   At this signal the five men who have charge of the drum rise and dance around it.   When their special dancing is finished, they take the drum from the inclosure and hold it near a fire until the desired resonance is restored.   The fastening of a drumhead is rarely disturbed, tightening being accomplished by exposing it to the heat of a fire or of the sun.

No. 70. Song of the Drum   (Catalogue No. S. 11)

Sung by MEC′KAWIGA′BAU

VOICE ♩ = 84
DRUM ♩ = 92
(Drum-rhythm similar to No. 2)

Analysis.—This melody is major in tonality and contains the tones of the fourth five-toned scale.   The rhythmic unit, which is short, is found in both double and triple measures.   The song is somewhat awkward in both phrasing and progressions.

The actual presentation of the drum began about 3 o'clock in the afternoon.   Bi′jĭkĕns crossed the dancing circle, and, taking Wĭs′kĭno by the hand, led him to a seat beside the officers of the chief drum. Standing before him, Bi′jĭkĕns then made the presentation speech, asking him to select those among his people whom he intended to intrust with the care of the drum.   Removing all his beadwork, Bi′-jĭkĕns hung it around the neck of Wĭs′kĭno, even bestowing on him his coat and vest.   A blanket was then spread on the ground before Wĭs′kĭno, and the Chippewa proceeded to heap gifts upon it.   Among other articles women brought strips of cloth or garments they had made and shawls and quilts, while the men brought blankets and shirts.   There seemed no end to the variety of gifts, some new and some well worn.   More than one woman, taking the shawl from her shoulders, laid it on the pile and walked away with no protection from the chilly autumn wind.   Even little children added their gifts to the constantly growing store.

When the pile of gifts was considered complete, the drum was lifted from its supports and allowed to rest on the matting, the supports were taken down and laid beside the drum, the singers and drummers retired, and the singing was done by the party at the other Chippewa drum. Only Bi'jĭkĕns and the pipe bearer remained near the chief drum.

Wĭs'kĭno then crossed the circle, and taking a young man by the hand, led him to a seat on the matting beside the drum. This was the man whom Wĭs'kĭno had selected to have charge of the pipe belonging to the drum. It would be his duty to see that the pipe was always filled and also to be present whenever the drum was taken from Wĭs'kĭno's house for use in a general assembly. The pipe belonging to the drum was then presented to Wĭs'kĭno by the Chippewa pipe bearer.

The drum was then considered transferred to Wĭs'kĭno. He brought Menominee men and women and seated them beside it, and his aid took the seat next to the entrance, where the Chippewa aid had been seated. All the gifts bestowed by the Chippewa were divided among the Menominee, Wĭs'kĭno himself superintending the distribution. While this was being done the Menominee erected the supports of the drum and put it in position; then they sang, drumming lightly on the edge of the drum.

After this song Wĭs'kĭno stood beside the drum, holding in his hand the long drumstick with the loon neck at the end (see p. 146). With this he pretended to strike the drum three times and as many times drew back. The fourth time he touched the drum lightly, and at the same time each of the four leading drummers struck it a sharp blow with his decorated drumstick. The Song of the Owner of the Drum (No. 57) burst forth, signifying that the drum belonged fully to the Menominee. The striking of the drum by Wĭs'kĭno was done with great dramatic effect; his feints at striking held the people in suspense, and the final tap was welcomed as a relief from the tension. The Menominee drummers took up their task with right good will, singing a number of Menominee songs.

It was then the turn of the Menominee to present gifts to the Chippewa, though it was not expected that a full equivalent would be given at that time. A blanket was spread on the ground, and on it were laid articles similar to those which the Chippewa had given to the Menominee.

Wĭs'kĭno made a speech concerning the drum, saying that he would take good care of it and that the persons whom he had selected as his drum party could use it whenever they desired to do so. He presented Bi'jĭkĕns with three or four new blankets and added several crisp bank notes which he took from his wallet. The two then shook hands and sat down side by side.

The day was wearing to a close. Rising in their places, the pipe bearers again presented their pipes to the circle of the sky, lighted them, and passed them from one to another in the assembly, each person puffing the pipe.

In a short time the leading singer started the Song of Departure, a signal that the day's ceremony was at an end. The Chippewa returned to their camp without the chief drum. This was placed with all the accustomed respect in the house of the Menominee chief and beside it as of old was the pipe, filled and ready for use.

On the following day took place the presentation of the warrior drum. This was given by a Chippewa to a member of the Menominee tribe from another part of the Menominee Reservation. The ceremony, which was not so impressive as that for the chief drum, lasted about the same time. The differences between the ceremonies were but slight. For instance, the drum was lifted from the ground and placed on the pile of gifts, all being presented together; and when the new possessor of the drum was about to strike it with the long drumstick, two of the leading drummers stood up, holding the drum.

The fourth day of the ceremony was occupied entirely with dancing, during which the Chippewa presented to the Menominee all their adornments, consisting of beaded belts and bags, gay headdresses, and other articles. On this day the Song of the Closed Door was sung, after which no one was allowed to leave the inclosure without paying a fee to the aid, who was seated at the entrance.

No. 71. Song of the Closed Door   (Catalogue No. S. 12)

Sung by Mec'kawiga'bau

Voice ♩ = 92
Drum ♩ = 92
(Drum-rhythm similar to No. 2)

Analysis.—This song begins on the seventh and the opening measures do not suggest the chord of F, which characterizes the close of the song. It is interesting to note, therefore, that the several renditions were begun on the same tone, the transition from the close of the song to the beginning being made with no break in the time and no apparent difficulty. The last tone in the first and fourth measures was slightly prolonged, while other tones also were prolonged but for periods too small to be indicated. All these variations from exact time were uniform in the several renditions. The song is major in tonality, melodic in structure, and contains all the tones of the octave.

Dog Feast

A Dog Feast is sometimes held on the fourth day of a drum-presentation. Such a feast was not held on the Menominee Reservation, but the writer witnessed one on the Leech Lake Reservation, Minnesota, during the celebration of the Fourth of July, 1910. Only Chippewa took part in this ceremony, two of them enacting the part of Sioux who were said to be "teaching them the ceremony." It was stated that the ceremony had been received from the Sioux and that the feather garments worn by the four leaders were given to the Chippewa by the Sioux about fifty years ago. The songs of the Dog Feast (sung by Mec'kawiga'bau) were recorded at Lac du Flambeau in October, 1910. His description of the ceremony as given on that reservation corresponded with the ceremony witnessed in Minnesota, and it may be assumed that the songs he furnished are the proper ones.

The four chief actors in the ceremony were two Chippewa representing respectively the oc'kabe'wĭs (aid or messenger) of the entire Drum-presentation Ceremony and the oc'kabe'wĭs of the Dog Feast, and two Chippewa representing the Sioux. These men wore elaborate native costumes, and feather garments of the kind described on page 168. The ceremony was held late in the afternoon. A large number of Chippewa were seated around the dancing circle, many having come from other reservations to attend the ceremony.

The first song was sung as the messenger of the Dog Feast brought in the kettle containing the cooked dog. He placed this kettle near the entrance of the circle and danced during the song; when the song was finished he removed the kettle to the western side of the inclosure.

(Catalogue No. S. 13)

No. 72. First Song of the Dog Feast

Sung by Mec'kawiga'bau

Voice ♩ 80
Drum ♩ = 88
(Drum-rhythm similar to No. 19)

Analysis.—This song was sung with great vibrato. The rhythm, which was clearly given, was uniform in all the renditions, but the time was not maintained with absolute regularity.

The following two songs were sung with no pause between them. During the first song the four men knelt on the ground, the two oc'kabe'wĭs on one side, and the two men representing the Sioux on the other side, of the kettle, at a distance of about 6 feet. As the song was sung they raised their arms high above their upturned faces, then lowered them until the palms of their hands almost touched the ground. This was repeated five or six times, the sweeping downward motion of the arms being simultaneous. Then the second of the group of songs was sung, the men rising and dancing around the drum, led by the oc'kabe'wĭs of the drum, with their hands extended in turn toward the north, east, south, and west.

(Catalogue No. S. 14)

No. 73. Second Song of the Dog Feast

Sung by MEC'KAWIGA'BAU

VOICE ♩ = 88

DRUM ♩ = 88

(Drum-rhythm similar to No. 19)

Analysis.—This song contains two rhythmic units, the first occurring four times, the second three times. A pleasing effect is produced by the succession of these units in the middle and latter part of the song. The rhythmic unit of No. 77 (S. 18) is similar to the second unit of this song and with one exception forms the only instance of duplication in either the present volume or Bulletin 45. The tempo of this song is slow; the song begins on the twelfth, ends on the tonic, and is melodic in structure.

(Catalogue No. S. 15)

No. 74. Third Song of the Dog Feast

Sung by Mec′kawiga′bau

Analysis.—This song, like the preceding, contains two rhythmic units; the last measure of these is the same while the first measure is in double time in the first unit and in triple time in the second. In the latter part of the song the division of the closing measure of the second unit is slightly changed, and the sixteenth note followed by a dotted eighth is transferred to the measures intervening between the units. The two renditions of the song are exactly uniform, a fact which shows that the rhythmic structure of the song was clear in the mind of the singer. The song is minor in tonality and contains the tones of the second five-toned scale. The tempo of both voice and drum is more rapid than in the next preceding song.

After dancing around the drum the four men side by side, with arms uplifted, advanced toward the kettle containing the dog. As they approached the kettle they lowered their hands, extending them over it. This was done several times, the men forcibly ejaculating *ho ho ho ho*, as described in connection with the Mīde′ ceremony.[1] The last time they lowered their hands rapidly, as though about to strike the kettle. This motion was the signal for the drumming and singing to cease. The following song was sung during this part of the ceremony.

---

[1] See Bulletin 45, p. 44.

(Catalogue No. S. 16)

No. 75. Fourth Song of the Dog Feast

Sung by Mec′kawiga′bau

Voice ♩ = 88
Drum ♩ = 88
(Drum-rhythm similar to No. 19)

Analysis.—The three recorded renditions of this song are uniform in every respect, the repetitions beginning with correct intonation and without break in the time. The opening measures in 5–4 time contain no secondary accent and are readily distinguishable from the triple measure followed by a double measure, which occurs later in the song. Attention is especially directed to the progressions in the fifth measure; these intervals were correctly sung, the accidental being given firmly and accurately. The song is transcribed in the key of C minor, but the fifth of that key does not occur in it.

This song was followed by a dancing song, the oc′kabe′wĭs signaling all to rise and dance.

(Catalogue No. S. 17)

No. 76. Fifth Song of the Dog Feast

Sung by Mec′kawiga′bau

Voice ♩ = 88
Drum ♩ = 96
(Drum-rhythm similar to No. 2)

Analysis.—A 5–4 measure characterizes this song, the only change of time being at the close, where three measures in double time occur. (Compare No. 78.) The tempo was strictly maintained in these double measures and the repetitions of the song began without a break in the time. It should be noted that the phrase which occurs on the fourth and fifth counts of the third measure is used on the third and fourth counts of the following measure. Three renditions of the song were recorded, which are uniform in every respect. The song is based on the fourth five-toned scale and is melodic in structure.

After the song was ended the oc′kabe′wĭs of the Dog Feast took a small piece of meat from the kettle. It was said that he selected the piece nearest the head of the dog and that he took it on a small spoon fastened at the end of a long stick. After dancing around the drum he presented the piece of meat to the owner of the drum, who accepted and ate it. The following song was sung as the oc′kabe′wĭs danced alone around the drum.

(Catalogue No. S. 18)

No. 77. Sixth Song of the Dog Feast

Sung by MEC′KAWIGA′BAU

VOICE ♩= 104
DRUM ♩= 104
(Drum-rhythm similar to No. 2)

Analysis.—The rhythmic unit of this song is the same as that of No. 73. The four renditions of the song recorded show no variation. All the tones of the octave except the seventh are found in the song, which is major in tonality and melodic in structure.

At the conclusion of the song the head of the dog was taken from the kettle and placed in a pan at the eastern side of the dancing circle. The oc′kabe′wĭs of the entire Drum-presentation Ceremony then danced several times around the drum, after which he selected four men from the assembly, leading them forward one at a time and seating them beside the pan. These were warriors of the tribe who had distinguished themselves by deeds of valor. They ate the meat from the dog's head as the following song was sung at the drum.

(Catalogue No. S. 19)

No. 78. Seventh Song of the Dog Feast

Sung by MEC'KAWIGA'BAU

VOICE ♩ = 88
DRUM ♩ = 96
(Drum-rhythm similar to No. 19)

Analysis.—This song begins in 5–4 time and ends in double time. (Compare No. 76.) Four renditions were recorded. There was no break in the time throughout the entire performance. The song is based on the fourth five-toned scale and is melodic in structure.

When the four warriors had finished eating, they returned to their places, and the following song was sung.

No. 79. Warriors' Song   (Catalogue No. S. 20)

Sung by MEC'KAWIGA'BAU

VOICE ♩ = 88
DRUM ♩ = 96
(Drum-rhythm similar to No. 19)

Analysis.—The rhythmic unit of this song occurs four times in a double, and once in a triple, measure. Four renditions were recorded.

The repetitions were exact, but the time was not maintained with absolute regularity. The song begins on the sixth above the tonic and ends on the fifth in the lower octave; thus about half the melody is above the tonic and half below it. The song is melodic in structure and contains the tones of the fourth five-toned scale.

After this song the warrior who was first selected danced around the dog's skull, which had been taken from the pan and laid on the ground. After dancing he made a speech regarding one of his most distinguished victories and sang a song commemorating the event. A similar course was followed by each of the three other warriors who had eaten of the dog's head.

The following song is typical of this class of war songs. It was recorded by Mec′kawiga′bau, who learned it from the composer, a prominent warrior among the Lac du Flambeau Chippewa, Memen′-gwa (Butterfly) by name.

No. 80. The Song of Butterfly   (Catalogue No. 437)

Sung by MEC′KAWIGA′BAU

VOICE ♩ = 84
DRUM ♩ = 84

(Drum-rhythm similar to No. 2)

Bi- gi - ja - te   gi - jĭg   *e*   tci- bi -na - ni - ba - wi - yan

WORDS

bi′gijate′..................... in the coming heat
gi′jĭg.......................... of the day
tcibinani′bawiyan′........... I stood there

Analysis.—In this melody it is interesting to note the influence of the rhythmic unit on parts of the song in which it is not repeated. Thus the sixth measure from the close of the song resembles the first measure of the rhythmic unit, the fifth and third measures from the close are similar to the last measure of the unit, and the measure next to the last is similar to the second measure of the unit. Obser-vation of many of these songs will detect separation of the rhythmic unit into phrases, one or two of which are combined with other measures to form the rhythm of the song as a whole. This song is classified as melodic with harmonic framework. The metric unit is unusually slow. Four renditions of the song were recorded; these show no important variation.

At the conclusion of this song the kettle containing the remainder of the dog was passed to the women of the company, some of whom ate small pieces. The kettle was then passed to the men and in a short time the feast was concluded.

———————

Returning to the narrative of the Drum-presentation Ceremony, as witnessed on the Menominee Reservation—the day after the drum-presentation was completed the writer went again to the place where the Indians were assembled. The Menominee had proved most gracious hosts, and the Chippewa had decided to remain four days longer. Custom required that each tribe dance four more days, and it was decided that they should dance together. It was a hospitable suggestion on the part of the Menominee, which promised much pleasure, but a gray cloud lay close to the horizon, and in a day or two the snow came, falling steadily in large, soft flakes. Several inches of snow covered the ground, but still they danced, as custom required that the dancing, once begun, be finished.

More difficult than the dancing was the weary tramp of 20 miles which the Chippewa must take in order to reach the railroad. Their packs were lighter than when they came, for the gifts they then carried had been given away and the Menominee had not yet returned the full equivalent, and, further, quantities of provisions had disappeared. The shawls which seemed a burden when the sun shone so warm were but a scanty protection from the keen north wind.

It was a rather forlorn company that returned to Lac du Flambeau; yet it was something to have been for a little while on the heights and to have given two drums to the Menominee.

Sioux Songs of Drum-presentation Ceremony

MELODIC ANALYSIS

TONALITY

	Numbers	Per cent.	Serial Nos. of songs
Major	11	*55*	56, 57, 58, 59, 70, 71, 72, 76, 77, 78, 79
Minor	9	*45*	54, 55, 60, 61, 62, 69, 73, 74, 75
Total.................................	20		

BEGINNINGS OF SONGS

	Numbers	Per cent.	Serial Nos. of songs
On the twelfth.............................	2	*10*	62, 73
On the fifth................................	3	*15*	57, 69, 76
On the eleventh............................	1	*5*	55
On the tenth...............................	2	*10*	74, 75
On the ninth...............................	2	*10*	72, 78
On the octave..............................	6	*30*	54, 56, 60, 61, 70, 77
On the seventh.............................	1	*5*	71
On the sixth...............................	3	*15*	58, 59, 79
Total.................................	20		

NOTE.—The Chippewa war songs occurring in the Drum-presentation Ceremony (Nos. 63, 64, 65, 66, 80) are included in the tabulated analysis of war songs on p. 195, and the divorce songs (67, 68) are included in the songs analyzed on p. 242.

ENDINGS OF SONGS

	Numbers	Per cent.	Serial Nos. of songs
On the tonic	13	*65*	55, 56, 60, 61, 62, 69, 70, 71, 72, 73, 74, 75, 77
On the fifth	6	*30*	54, 57, 58, 76, 78, 79
On the third	1	*5*	59
Total.................................	20		

TONE MATERIAL

	Numbers	Per cent.	Serial Nos. of songs
Second five-toned scale.....................	3	*15*	69, 73, 74
Fourth five-toned scale.....................	6	*30*	58, 59, 70, 76, 77, 79
Octave complete............................	2	*10*	54, 71
Octave complete except seventh............	2	*10*	72, 78
Octave complete except seventh and second.	1	*5*	62
Octave complete except sixth..............	2	*10*	56, 61
Octave complete except sixth and fifth.....	1	*5*	75
Octave complete except fifth and second....	1	*5*	75
Minor triad and fourth.....................	1	*5*	55
Other combinations of tone.................	1	*5*	60
Total.................................	20		

MELODIC ANALYSIS—continued
ACCIDENTALS

	Numbers	Per cent.	Serial Nos. of songs
Songs containing no accidentals............	18	90	54, 55, 56, 57, 58, 59, 60, 61, 62, 70, 71, 72, 73, 74, 76, 77, 78, 79
Songs containing seventh raised a semitone..	1	5	75
Songs containing sixth raised a semitone....	1	5	69
Total................................	20		

STRUCTURE

	Numbers	Per cent.	Serial Nos. of songs
Harmonic..............................	None	....	
Purely melodic..........................	17	85	54, 56, 57, 58, 59, 60, 61, 62, 69, 70, 71, 72, 73, 74, 75, 78, 79
Melodic with harmonic framework..........	3	15	55, 76, 77
Total................................	20		

FIRST PROGRESSION

	Numbers	Per cent.	Serial Nos. of songs
Downward..............................	12	60	54, 55, 58, 60, 62, 69, 71, 73, 76, 77, 78, 79
Upward................................	8	40	56, 57, 59, 61, 70, 72, 74, 75
Total................................	20		

RHYTHMIC ANALYSIS
PART OF MEASURE ON WHICH SONG BEGINS

	Numbers	Per cent.	Serial Nos. of songs
On accented part	8	40	54, 56, 59, 61, 62, 70, 72, 79
On unaccented part.......................	12	60	55, 57, 58, 60, 69, 71, 73, 74, 75, 76, 77, 78
Total................................	20		

RHYTHM OF FIRST MEASURE

	Numbers	Per cent.	Serial Nos. of songs
Songs beginning in 2–4 time...............	9	45	58, 59, 61, 62, 72, 73, 74, 78, 79
Songs beginning in 3–4 time...............	6	30	54, 56, 57, 62, 70, 71
Songs beginning in 5–4 time...............	4	20	55, 75, 76, 77
Songs beginning in 5–8 time...............	1	5	60
Total................................	20		

Rhythmic Analysis—continued

CHANGE OF TIME

	Numbers	Per cent.	Serial Nos. of songs
Songs containing a change of time..........	19	95	54, 56, 57, 58, 59, 60, 61, 62, 69, 70, 71, 72, 73, 74, 75, 76, 77, 78, 79
Songs containing no change of time.........	1	5	55
Total................................	20		

RHYTHMIC UNIT

	Numbers	Per cent.	Serial Nos. of songs
Songs containing a rhythmic unit..........	10	50	54, 58, 60, 62, 70, 72, 75, 76, 78, 79
Songs containing two rhythmic units.......	3	15	69, 73, 74
Songs containing no rhythmic unit.........	7	35	55, 56, 57, 59, 61, 71, 77
Total................................	20		

COMPARISON OF METRIC UNIT OF VOICE AND DRUM

	Numbers	Per cent.	Serial Nos. of songs
Metric unit of voice and drum the same.....	7	35	54, 59, 62, 71, 73, 75, 77
Metric unit of voice and drum different.....	13	65	55, 56, 57, 58, 59, 60, 69, 70, 72, 74, 76, 78, 79
Total................................	20		

SONGS OF THE LAC DU FLAMBEAU RESERVATION

In the north-central part of Wisconsin, about 80 miles southeast of Ashland, is the Lac du Flambeau Chippewa Reservation, formerly under the La Pointe Agency, but now in charge of the school superintendent. It is a beautiful region of pine forests and quiet lakes. A typical forest on the reservation is shown in plate 24. The principal Chippewa village (pl. 25) is several miles from the agency. The ceremonies of the Mĭde′wĭwĭn are held regularly and many other native customs are perpetuated. The gathering of wild rice forms an absorbing interest in autumn, followed by hunting expeditions. Deer are plentiful on the reservation and bears are not infrequent trophies of the chase. With these native avocations is mingled much that has been taught by the Government, many of the Indians cultivating little farms and even shipping potatoes with due regard to their market value.

Ĕ′niwûb′e ("sits farther along"), plate 26, the singer of many songs in the present series, is the owner of two houses, one in the Indian village, and one on his farm where he spends the summer. This farm of 4 or 5 acres is cultivated to the best of his ability. His house in the Indian village is ready for occupancy at any time, but he spends the long cold winter at his son's home near the agency. His own team of horses furnishes conveyance for himself and family when there is a gathering of Indians on a distant part of the reservation. He has never complained of being cheated by the white man, for he has been able to take care of his own interests. In his contact with civilization he has conceded comparatively little and gained much, standing to-day as a type of native manhood respected by all who know him.

Mec′kawiga′bau ("stands firmly"), plate 20, another singer, has a house and a few acres of cultivated land near the Indian village. The phonograph was taken to his house for recording many of his songs, which include those of the Drum-presentation Ceremony. His wife, Dji′siä′sĭno′kwe ("deceiving woman"), also sang two love songs, naively insisting that her husband depart while she recorded them, to be recalled when they were played on the phonograph.

Seventy-five songs were recorded at Lac du Flambeau. The personality of the other singers is described in connection with the analyses of the songs.

184

PINE FOREST, LAC DU FLAMBEAU RESERVATION, WIS.

LAC DU FLAMBEAU AND CHIPPEWA VILLAGE

WAR SONGS

No. 81. A Song of Indecision   (Catalogue No. 393)

Sung by MĬDE′WIGI′JĬG

VOICE ♩ = 96
DRUM ♩ = 96

(Drum-rhythm similar to No. 2)

Wi - na - wa - nin - da - ci - mi-gog   wi - na - wa - nin - da - ci - mi-gog

wi - na - wa - nin - da - ci - mi-gog   wi - na - wa - nin - da - ci - mi-gog

bĕ - sĭ- na - sĭ - wĭ-djĭg *e*   wi -na-wa-nin - da - ci- mi-gog   wi -na-wa - nin-

da- ci - mi-gog   wi-na -wa - nin- da - ci -mi-gog   wi- na-wa-nin - da- ci- mi-gog

WORDS

Part 1

[Free translation]

winawa′ninda′cimigog′...... they are talking about me
bĕsĭna′sĭwĭdjĭg′ .... saying "come with us"

This song was sung by the father of Ĕ′niwûb′e, a man said to be 90 years of age, whose name is Mĭde′wigi′jĭg ("Grand Medicine sky"). He is almost blind but remarkably active, feeling his way about the reservation with a stout cane. His voice was strong and he showed no hesitation in singing the song, saying that he remembered when the war parties went out to fight the Sioux and had heard the song at the preliminary dances. The words concern a man who is urged by friends to join the warriors but is not fully decided to go (see song No. 14). After singing the song twice with the first set of words the singer repeated it with the second set.

Part 2

owĭnĕn′dacnĭn′............ is there anyone who
ge′mawimĭd′............... would weep for me?
nindĭkwĕm′............... my wife
ge′mawimĭd′............... would weep for me

Analysis.—This melody is particularly simple in construction. The rhythmic unit comprises two measures and is repeated with only one interruption—the triple measure containing the change of words. (See Nos. 1, 8, 12, 13, 30, 39, 40, 105.)   A generally descending progression carries the melody along the fourth five-toned scale, beginning on the ninth and ending on the tonic.

No. 82. Song of the Sentry   (Catalogue No. 409)

Sung by Ĕ′NIWÛB′E

VOICE ♩ = 80
DRUM ♩ = 88
(Drum-rhythm similar to No. 19)

Ga-ye - nin

mĭ-stû-dĭ-moñg ba-ba mo - mi - go-yan - *e*

WORDS

gaye′nĭn..................... I also
mĭstû′dĭmoñg [1]............. on my horse
baba′momigoyan′........... carried around

Around the camp of the warriors nightly rode the sentry, singing this song. It·was said that the pony seemed to know the song and galloped in time to the music. The song indicates that the Wisconsin Chippewa had horses when they were at war with the Sioux. Odjĭb′we stated (see p. 61) that when he first led war parties against the Sioux in Minnesota the Chippewa had no horses and that very few were used by the Sioux.

Analysis.—This melody is broadly outlined by .two descending intervals of a fourth, C sharp–G sharp, and F sharp–C sharp. A similar prominence of the interval of a fourth has been noted in other songs which contain the idea of motion, either of.animals or of persons (see analysis of No. 22). No rhythmic unit occurs in the song, but a sixteenth note followed by a dotted eighth occurs frequently

---

[1] *Mĭstû′dĭm* (cf. *mistatim,* in Lacombe, *Dictionnaire de la Langue des Cris,* Montreal, 1874,) is a Cree word meaning "horse"; *oñg* is a Chippewa ending meaning, *inter alia,* "upon." See also pp. 72, 76, 108, 190, 230.

on the first count of the measure. The slow tempo suggests the leisurely gallop of the sentry's horse. There is no excitement in the idea of the song and none in the music. The phrase contained in the sixth and seventh measures is found also in the fourteenth, fifteenth, and sixteenth measures, one count being added, thus making the first part of the phrase in double instead of in triple time. Three renditions were recorded, with one repetition of the latter half of the song. The first count of each measure was emphasized, but the time was not maintained with absolute regularity.

No. 83. Song concerning Gwi′wizäns   (Catalogue No. 406)

Sung by Ĕ′niwûb′e

VOICE ♩= 92
DRUM ♩= 92

(Drum-rhythm similar to No. 19)

Gwi - wi-

zäns   gi - to - ta - ma - go - nañ   i - nĭ - nĭ - wûg

WORDS

Gwi′wizäns.................. Gwi′wizäns (man's name meaning "boy")
gigo′tama′gonañ′............ by his presence made them afraid
inĭ′nĭwûg.................. those men

This song was composed concerning a great warrior named Gwi′wizäns (Boy). It is said that when he led his men on the warpath he took his arrows, but did not fight; he stood still, watching his warriors. His will was so strong that he could make them win a fight without taking any part in it himself. His warriors were very proud of their leader. On the way home from a successful expedition they composed this song about him and sang it in the victory dance. The Chippewa words contain a play on the name of the leader. The word *inĭ′nĭwûg*, "men," is frequently used to designate warriors (see p. 69).

Analysis.—This song is minor in tonality and contains the first, second, third, fifth, and sixth tones of the diatonic minor scale, tone material occurring in only three other songs of the series of 340 (see Nos. 178 and 184 in Bulletin 45, and No. 125 of the present series). This is of special interest, as the omitted tones are the same intervals as in the fourth five-toned scale, which is major in tonality. The major third is a prominent progression in the opening phrases of this song (see Nos. 1, 9, 34, 94, 120), constituting 52 per cent of the entire number of progressions (31). (See also Nos. 29, 99.) The tempo was steadily maintained and the music admirably expresses the idea of the song.

No. 84. "The Sioux Follow Me"   (Catalogue No. 407)

Sung by Ĕ′NIWÛB′E

VOICE ♩ = 96
DRUM ♩ = 96
(Drum-rhythm similar to No. 19)

Ma - gi - ja - go ĭc - kwe - yañ   Si - si - ta - wañ bi - ä -

pi - si - ka - dog ĭc - kwe - yañ

WORDS

ma′gija′go	I think
ĭckwe′yañ	behind me
Sisi′tawañ (see p. 70)	the Sisseton Sioux
biäpi′sika′dog [1]	is no doubt following

Analysis.—This song is based on the chord of D major and would be classified as harmonic except for the presence of E flat as an accented tone. The phrases are of irregular length and the song contains no rhythmic unit, yet, as a whole, it has a certain rhythmic unity and completeness. The only tones used are those of the major triad and second.

The words of this and of the following song suggest that the songs were composed during dreams.

[1] The syllable *dog* affixed to a verb indicates lack of absolute knowledge, but confidence that the statement is correct.

No. 85. "Around the Sky"   (Catalogue No. 415)

Sung by Ĕ′NIWÛB′E

VOICE ♩ = 116
DRUM ♩ = 120
(Drum-rhythm similar to No. 19)

Gĭ - jĭ-guñg bi -

mĭ-se-yan   bĭ - nĕ - sĭ   nĭ - wi - dji- wa

WORDS

gi′jĭguñg′.................... in the sky
bimu′seyan′................. I am walking
bĭnĕ′sĭ........................ a bird
nĭwi′djiwa′................. I accompany

Analysis.—The rhythmic unit of this song occurs five times in the opening measures and is followed by a six-measure phrase, which is repeated at the close of the song. In this phrase we find part of the unit with a change of accent, the dotted eighth note falling on an unaccented instead of on an accented count. The melody is broadly outlined by two intervals of a fourth, B flat–E flat, and E flat–A flat. (See analysis of No. 22.) The song is minor in tonality and contains the progression 8–7–8; this is particularly effective, showing the interval of a whole tone, which is found between seven and eight in the second five-toned scale (see Nos. 9, 50, 100, 119, 124). The drum is slightly faster than the voice and seems constantly hurrying it forward.

No. 86. "If He is a Warrior" (Catalogue No. 419)

Sung by Ĕ′NIWÛB′E

VOICE ♩ = 126
DRUM ♩ = 126
(Drum-rhythm similar to No. 15)

O - gĭ - tcĭ-da-gwĕn na - *wa′* - wi-na-kwe - dag

WORDS

ogĭ′tcĭda′gwĕn [1] . . . . if he is a warrior
nawi′nakwedag′ . . . . he will answer me

Analysis.—This melody comprises the tones of the fourth five-toned scale. It will be readily seen that the progressions of the first six measures are outlined by the descending interval A–E, the principal tones being those of the triad, with the second as a passing tone. The next twelve measures are outlined by the descending interval E–B, which suggests in musical terminology the dominant chord in the key of A. We note, however, that G sharp, the third of that chord, does not appear and that F sharp is used as a passing tone, similar to B in the opening measures. Thus the framework of the melody consists of two descending intervals of the fifth—E–A and B–E, in both of which the second is used as a passing tone, the third occurring only in the opening section. (Compare Nos. 23 and 28, based on the interval of a fourth.) The rhythmic unit occurs three times. A triple followed by a double measure is found seven times in the song but the two unite to form a rhythmic unit only in the instances indicated by the bracket.

[1] From Sioux *aki′čita*, "warrior," + Chippewa suffix *-gwĕn*, subjunctive mode (with *kishpin*, "if," understood). See pp. 72, 76, 108, 186, 230.

No. 87. "In the South"   (Catalogue No. 426)

Sung by Ĕ′NIWÛB′E

VOICE ♩ = 112
DRUM ♩ = 120
(Drum-rhythm similar to No. 19)

WORDS

ca′wûnoñg′.................. in the south
bĭnĕ′sĭwûg.................. the birds
ge′binonda′goziwa′....:..... are heard singing

Analysis.—A peculiarity of this song is indicated in the second measure, the singer striking a tone above the proper pitch and descending *glissando*, apparently as an embellishment of the melody. The transcription is from the first rendition, the others differing in some unimportant note-values but not in the rhythm or in the embellishments. The song would be classified as harmonic in structure except for the accented E in next to the last measure. It is based on the fourth five-toned scale and contains no rhythmic unit.

No. 88. War Song   (Catalogue No. 411)

Sung by Ĕ′NIWÛB′E

VOICE ♩ = 120
DRUM ♩ = 132
(Drum-rhythm similar to No. 19)

Analysis.—This song is particularly definite in tonality and forceful in rhythm, seeming to retain some of the spirit of the warriors who sang it long ago. The song is characterized by syncopations, which are found but rarely in the songs under analysis (see No. 47 of the present book, and Nos. 123, 147, 152 in Bulletin 45). Attention is directed to the progressions above and below the tonic at the close of the song.

No. 89. War Song   (Catalogue No. 412)

Sung by Ĕ′NIWÛB′E

VOICE ♩ = 112
DRUM ♩ = 112
(Drum-rhythm similar to No. 19)

Analysis.—This song consists of eight three-measure phrases, the rhythmic unit being accurately repeated except in the third and the last phrase. So slight a change as the use of two eighth notes instead of one quarter note (ninth measure) swings the rhythm of the entire song clear of monotony and gives it character. Voice and drum have the same metric unit but the drum precedes the voice by

a perceptible interval of time.   The tonic chord is the evident framework of the melody.   From two of the four renditions the last six
measures are omitted.

No. 90. War Song   (Catalogue No. 416)

Sung by Ĕ′niwûb′e

VOICE ♩= 116
DRUM ♩= 132
(Drum-rhythm similar to No. 19)

Analysis.—The first measure of this song comprises a rhythmic
unit, which occurs only twice but forms the basis of the rhythm of
the entire song.   (See Nos. 94, 96, 103, 108, 109, 115, 123.)   The
second measure contains the same division of the counts but is a
double instead of a triple measure and the rhythmic unit is unfinished.   The fourth and opening of the fifth measure contain the same
division of the counts but with a change of accent.   Five complete
renditions were recorded with seven repetitions of the latter half of
the song, the singer seeming to have no preference whether he began
at the first or at the middle phrase in giving the repetitions.   This
peculiarity is occasionally noted in the performances of Chippewa
singers.

No. 91. War Song   (Catalogue No. 417)

Sung by Ĕ′niwûb′e

VOICE ♩= 126
DRUM ♩= 126
(Drum-rhythm similar to No. 19)

Analysis.—A strongly descending progression and a vigorous rhythmic unit characterize this song. A similarity between this and the next succeeding song (No. 92) suggests that they may have been composed by the same man, this being first in order of composition. It is a stirring melody, but lacks the smoothness and grace of No. 92. The rhythmic unit of the latter contains two measures instead of one, the division of the first measure being the same as that of the rhythmic unit of this song.

No. 92. War Song   (Catalogue No. 418)

Sung by Ĕ′NIWÛB′E

Voice ♩ = 126
Drum ♩ = 126
(Drum-rhythm similar to No. 19)

Analysis.—This is a particularly inspiring melody. The rhythmic unit comprises two measures and occurs five times with two quarter notes in the second measure. A rhythm similar to that of the first measure occurs three times, but is followed by a measure containing time-values differing from those in the rhythmic unit. The melody tones are those of the second five-toned scale. This scale is usually associated with a plaintive melody, but the present example shows it to be adapted as well to a stirring war cry. The similarity between this and No. 91 has been noted in the analysis of the preceding song.

No. 93. War Song   (Catalogue No. 420)

Sung by Ĕ′NIWÛB′E

VOICE ♩ = 108
DRUM ♩ = 112
(Drum-rhythm similar to No. 19)

Analysis.—The effect of this song is rhythmic, yet we find no phrase repeated accurately enough to constitute it a unit of rhythm. The opening measure of the repeated part contains a succession of note-values in triple time, which is twice repeated in double time, and which forms an interesting example of freedom in rhythmic treatment. The song contains one accidental, which was sung distinctly in all the renditions.

War Songs—Lac du Flambeau Reservation

MELODIC ANALYSIS

TONALITY

	Number of songs	Serial Nos. of songs
Major	10	63, 66, 80, 81, 84, 86, 87, 88, 91, 93
Minor	8	64, 65, 82, 83, 85, 89, 90, 92
Total	18	

NOTE.—The following songs, included in this table, are found in the account of the Drum-presentation Ceremony (pp. 158–161, 179): Nos. 63, 64, 65, 66, 80.

MELODIC ANALYSIS—continued

BEGINNINGS OF SONGS

	Number of songs	Serial Nos. of songs
On the twelfth	8	64, 65, 66, 80, 86, 87, 89, 93
On the fifth	2	88, 90
On the tenth	2	83, 92
On the ninth	1	81
On the octave	4	63, 82, 84, 85
On the sixth	1	91
Total	18	

ENDINGS OF SONGS

	Number of songs	Serial Nos. of songs
On the tonic	14	64, 65, 66, 80, 81, 82, 83, 85, 86, 87, 89, 90, 92, 93
On the fifth	3	63, 84, 88
On the third	1	91
Total	18	

TONE MATERIAL

	Number of songs	Serial Nos. of songs
Second five-toned scale	3	82, 89, 92
Fourth five-toned scale	6	63, 66, 80, 81, 86, 87
Major triad and second	1	84
Minor triad and fourth	1	90
Octave complete	1	93
Octave complete except seventh	4	64, 65, 88, 91
Octave complete except seventh and fourth	1	83
Octave complete except seventh and second	1	85
Total	18	

ACCIDENTALS·

	Number of songs	Serial Nos. of songs
Songs containing no accidentals	17	63, 64, 65, 66, 80, 81, 82, 83, 84, 85, 86, 87, 88, 89, 90, 91, 92
Songs containing the seventh lowered a semitone	1	93
Total	18	

MELODIC ANALYSIS—continued

STRUCTURE

	Number of songs	Serial Nos. of songs
Harmonic	1	83
Purely melodic	9	63, 81, 82, 84, 85, 88, 90, 91, 92
Melodic with harmonic framework	8	64, 65, 66, 80, 86, 87, 89, 93
Total	18	

FIRST PROGRESSION

	Number of songs	Serial Nos. of songs
Downward	15	63, 64, 65, 66, 80, 81, 82, 84, 85, 86, 87, 88, 89 91, 93
Upward	3	83, 90, 92
Total	18	

RHYTHMIC ANALYSIS

PART OF MEASURE ON WHICH SONG BEGINS

	Number of songs	Serial Nos. of songs
On accented part	12	63, 64, 80, 81, 82, 84, 87, 88, 89, 90, 92, 93
On unaccented part	6	65, 66, 83, 85, 86, 91
Total	18	

RHYTHM OF FIRST MEASURE

	Number of songs	Serial Nos. of songs
Songs beginning in 2–4 time	12	63, 64, 65, 66, 80, 81, 85, 87, 88, 89, 91, 92
Songs beginning in 3–4 time	6	82, 83, 84, 86, 90, 93
Total	18	

CHANGE OF TIME

	Number of songs	Serial Nos. of songs
Songs containing a change of time	16	63, 64, 65, 66, 81, 82, 83, 84, 85, 86, 87, 88, 90, 91, 92, 93
Songs containing no change of time	2	80, 89
Total	18	

RHYTHMIC ANALYSIS—continued

RHYTHMIC UNIT

	Number of songs	Serial Nos. of songs
Songs containing a rhythmic unit.....................	14	63, 64, 65, 66, 80, 81, 83, 85, 86, 88, 89, 90, 91, 92
Songs containing no rhythmic unit....................	4	82, 84, 87, 93
Total..	'8	

COMPARISON OF METRIC UNIT OF VOICE AND DRUM

	Number of songs	Serial Nos. of songs
Metric unit of voice and drum the same..............	9	64, 80, 81, 83, 84, 86, 89, 91, 92
Metric unit of voice and drum different..............	9	63, 65, 66, 82, 85, 87, 88, 90, 93
Total..	18	

DREAM SONGS

The following is the dream song of a man who painted his face with charcoal and endured a fast of ten days. At the end of that time he dreamed that he saw clouds rising in the south. There were manido' in the clouds who spoke to him, saying, "Brother, come here with us." So the man went up into the clouds. There he saw the thunderbirds, who taught him this song which they were singing.

No. 94. Song of the Thunderbirds   (Catalogue No. 394)

Sung by Ĕ′NIWÛB′E

VOICE ♩ = 116

DRUM ♩ = 116

(Drum-rhythm similar to No. 19)

Analysis.—This song is vigorous and clear in rhythm and tonality. The first 12 measures are based on the triad G–B flat–D, these tones occurring in descending progression in the third and eighth measures. The last five measures of the song are based on the descending chord G–D–B flat–G. The song is minor in tonality, yet the major third is the opening interval. (See Nos. 1, 9, 34, 83, 120.) The entire song is thus shown to be harmonic in framework. The song contains four phrases of five measures each. The first phrase comprises a rhythmic unit, which is repeated practically without change in the second phrase. The third phrase (measure 3) shows a reversal of the couplet and triplet division which occurs in the corresponding measure of the rhythmic unit, the two following measures being practically the same as in the unit. The variations in the final phrase are readily discerned. The variation of a rhythmic phrase is a feature of special importance in the study of primitive musical development. (See Nos. 90, 96, 103, 108, 109, 115, 123.)

Other songs supposed to be the musical expression of animals are Nos. 34, 41, 58, 68, 88, 119, and 197, in Bulletin 45, and Nos. 95, 96, 97, 98, 99, 114, and 115 of the present work.

The following song was heard by a man when he was fasting and seeking a dream. As he was walking around he heard voices which seemed to come from beyond a hill. Stealthily climbing this hill, he saw a herd of deer standing in a circle. One said, "Now we will dance. We always have a dance at this season, when the leaves have fallen from the trees." All the deer pointed to a little buck whose pointed horns rose somewhat higher than his ears, saying he should be the one to sing; thereupon he sang this song. Thus the man learned it and afterward it became his dream song. He sang it when he hunted the deer. There were two parts to the song: First, the little deer sang about himself and then about the other deer. Only the first part is transcribed, as the second was not an interesting melody. Before singing this and the two next succeeding songs the singer "imitated the noise made by the deer." (See pp. 101, 203.)

No. 95. Song of the Deer (a)   (Catalogue No. 398)

Sung by Ĕ′niwûb′e

VOICE ♩ = 104
DRUM ♩ = 104
(Drum-rhythm similar to No. 2)

Ki-we-wi-na - ko-wi - nĕ   be - jĭg ai-ya - bĕ   ki-we - wi-na -

ko-wi - nĕ   be - jĭg ai-ya - bĕ   ki-we - wi-na - ko - wi - nĕ

be-jĭg ai-ya-bĕ

WORDS

kiwe′wina′kowinĕ′........... straight-horned
be′jĭg .... one
aiya′bĕ..................... buck

Analysis.—Although minor in tonality this song is bright and full of action. The descending interval of the fourth, which occurs frequently, has been noted in other songs concerning animals (see No. 22). The rhythmic unit, which is clear and vigorous, is found three times in this song.

No. 96. Song of the Deer (b)   (Catalogue No. 402)

Sung by Ĕ′niwûb′e

VOICE ♩ = 100
DRUM ♩ = 108
(Drum-rhythm similar to No. 2)

Ki -

we-wi-na-ko-wi-nĕ   be - jĭg ai-ya-bĕ

Analysis.—This song, like the preceding, was heard by the man in his dream of the deer. The words are the same as in the preceding song. The first two measures contain four descending tones similar to the successive tones of the scale, a progression rarely found in the songs under analysis.   The interval of the fourth is prominent in the framework of this melody (see No. 22), the descending intervals D flat–A flat, A flat–E flat being similar to the intervals C sharp–G sharp, G sharp–D sharp in the preceding melody, yet this song is in the key of A flat and the preceding song is in the key of B, and the characteristics of the two melodies are entirely different.   (See Nos. 105, 106.)   This song contains no rhythmic unit, but the treatment of its opening phrase is worthy of observation.   It will be noted that the phrase contained in the first and second measures is repeated in the fifth measure and in the first part of the sixth measure, with a change of accent.   (See Nos. 90, 94, 103, 108, 109.)   The same phrase occurs with other changes in the third and fourth measures.

Similar to the preceding are two songs by another singer.   The narrative concerning the first song is as follows:

Long ago an old man made a feast and invited all the men and women.   He did not tell them why they were asked; he only said there would be a dance.   When they were all assembled the old man who had asked them sang this song, which had come to him in a dream, and another old man led the dance, acting like a deer.   The men followed him, acting like the buck deer and the women acted like the doe.   In old times the hunters had a dance like this in the evening and went out to hunt the deer the next morning.[1]

No. 97. Song of the Deer Dancing   (Catalogue No. 433)

Sung by MEC′KAWIGA′BAU

VOICE ♩ = 104
DRUM ♩ = 112
(Drum-rhythm similar to No. 19)

Ti - bi-wĕn-da - ba - no-gwĕn ai - ya - bĕ   ti - bi - wĕn-da -

ba-no-gwĕn ai-ya - bĕ   ai-ya - bĕ   ai-ya - bĕ

WORDS

ti′biwĕnda′banogwĕn′.............. whence does he dawn? [2]

aiya′bĕ............................ the buck?

Analysis.—The rhythm of this song is somewhat expressive of the dance and its pantomime.   The interval of the fourth is prominent, as in many songs concerning animals.   (See No. 22.)

---

[1] Compare the dance of the warriors before a fight, imitating the action of the buffalo (p. 101); also the imitation of the plover, in the pipe dance (p. 295).

[2] This is an idiomatic phrase in common use among the Chippewa.   It is not unlike the expression, "Where did he spring from?"

No. 98. "My Shining Horns"   (Catalogue No. 434)

Sung by MEC'KAWIGA'BAU

VOICE ♩ = 108
DRUM ♩ = 108
(Drum-rhythm similar to No. 19)

Wĕn-dji-we - ä - sa-ko-nes-we-yan

WORDS

wĕn'djiweä'sako'nesweyan'............. my shining horns

Analysis.—This song was said to represent the deer "walking alone, singing to himself, and proud of his shining horns." The melody is harmonic in structure and contains a short rhythmic unit. In general outline it presents a descending progression along the intervals of the tonic chord. It is minor in tonality and is based on the second five-toned scale. The six renditions recorded show no important variation.

Like the two songs next preceding, this song had its origin in a dream. A man who was fasting is said to have heard the buffalo sing and to have learned their song. As he was wandering about he heard sounds which seemed to come from some gathering of Indians. On going to the place he saw a herd of buffalo walking in a circle, knee-deep in mud, with swaying heads and lashing tails; all were singing as they walked around. The Indian joined the herd and thereupon became a buffalo. For this reason they gave him the song which they were singing.

No. 99. Song of the Buffalo   (Catalogue No. 399)

Sung by Ĕ′NIWÛB′E

VOICE ♩ = 96
DRUM ♩ = 100
(Drum-rhythm similar to No. 2)

Bi - jĭ - ḳi - wûg

we - ya - ka - ga - bû - wi - wa - djĭn

wa - do - ka - wa-gwa-nĭn -

e   he   wa   ni   e   wa   ni   e   wa - do - ka - wa - gwa-nĭn - e

ä   hwi   ä   wi   hi   ä   hwi   ä

WORDS

bi′jĭki′wûg′ .... the buffalo
we′yaka′gabûwiwa′djĭn .... as they stand in a circle
wa′doka′wagwa′nĭne................ I join with them

Analysis.—Except in the last nine measures, the principal tones of this melody are those of the triad of F sharp minor; the song is therefore transcribed in that key, although the second and seventh of the key do not occur. This is an instance in which "key" can scarcely be said to exist, and the signature should be understood as indicating merely the pitch of certain tones. The formation of the melody is essentially that of successive intervals, in a descending progression: First, C sharp–A, second A–F sharp, and lastly F sharp–D. As an example of interval formation this offers an interesting contrast to songs based on the interval of the fourth (see No. 22). Although the song is minor in tonality, it is found that 50 per cent of the intervals are major thirds, the song containing 18 intervals and 9 minor thirds (see Nos. 29, 83). Before the recording of this song, and also before the final word, the singer "imitated the noise made by the buffalo." Several renditions were recorded, interspersed with these peculiar "noises."

SONGS CONCERNING A BOY'S FAST

This and the song next following are associated with the old Indian custom requiring youths to hold fasting vigils in the wilderness. These are songs which Ĕ′niwûb′e's grandfather sang to him when he was a boy and were secured only after the latter's confidence in the writer was fully established. The first song was sung when the boy had blackened his face and was ready to go forth alone from the camp. Ĕ′niwûb′e said that he danced, and his grandfather sang the song. The meaning of the words is obscure. We can not understand what boyhood vision rose in the mind of the aged man as he asked a boon for the child whose vision was yet to come.

No. 100. Song Before a Boy Goes Out to Fast

(Catalogue No. 421)

Sung by Ĕ′NIWÛB′E

VOICE ♩ = 84
DRUM ♩ = 88
(Drum-rhythm similar to No. 2)

A - ni - nĕn-we-we   a - ni - nĕn-we - we   wa - zi-swûn nim-bi - zĭn-

da - go - ne

WORDS

a′ninŏn′wewe′.............. the receding sound
wa′ziswûn′................ of the nest [1]
nim′bizĭnda′gone′.......... I listen to it

Analysis.—The compass of this song is only four tones, comprising the first, second, third, and seventh of the minor scale; it begins on the third, descends to the second, and ends on the tonic. Eight renditions of the song were recorded; these are uniform in rhythm but uncertain in the intonation of the opening measures, the singer seeming to have difficulty in giving intervals so small, with distinctness. (See Nos. 54, 55, 61, 64.) In contrast to this uncertainty as to semitones and whole tones, we find the accidental in the third measure and A flat near the close of the song given firmly and unmistakably. The whole tone between 7 and 8 is prominent in this song. (See Nos. 9, 50, 85, 119, 124.) The melody forms a good example

---

[1] This may refer to the "nest" which a man built in a tree, in which he waited, fasting, for a vision (see p. 84), though the use of the word "sound" in this connection is obscure.

of the entire song as a rhythmic unit, complete and homogeneous. The metric unit of both voice and drum is slow and the general effect of the song is different from that of the majority of songs under analysis.

When the boy Ĕ′niwûb′e returned from his fasting vigil his grandfather insisted that he dance before tasting food; he also talked with him, asking long life for him and saying that he needed water to drink. Other boys returned at the same time from their fasts and Ĕ′niwûb′e's grandfather talked to them all. Near his door there was a medicine pole (similar to those described on p. 248), around which the boys danced while Ĕ′niwûb′e's grandfather sang the following song. There was a hole through the medicine pole just below the banner of deerskin. At the foot of the pole the old man placed a birchbark dish. As the boys danced and the old man sang a strange thing happened—water flowed from the hole in the pole and fell into the dish.[1] When it was full Ĕ′niwûb′e's grandfather stopped the dancers and gave them this water to drink. In this manner their fast was broken. Both these fasting songs by Ĕ′niwûb′e's grandfather were "composed in his dreams," and the medicine pole was made to correspond to that which he saw in one of his visions. (Compare Me′dweya′sûñ's medicine pole, p. 249.)

No. 101. Song After a Boy Returns from Fasting

(Catalogue No. 422)

Sung by Ĕ′NIWÛB′E

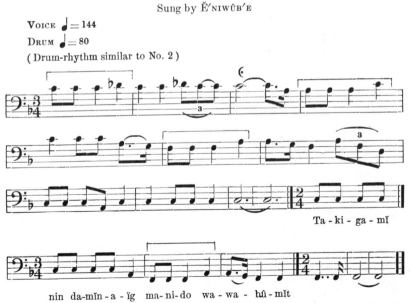

Voice ♩ = 144
Drum ♩ = 80
(Drum-rhythm similar to No. 2)

Ta - ki - ga - mĭ

nin da-mĭn - a - ĭg ma - ni - do wa - wa - bû - mĭt

---

[1] A similar practice is said to exist among the Assiniboin of Montana, a medicine-man tracing a zigzag line on the Sun-dance pole, drawing his feather fan down this line, and causing water to flow from the pole for the refreshment of those taking part in the Sun dance.

taki′gamĭ′.................. cool water

nin....................... }he will give me to drink
da′mĭna′ĭg..................

manido′..................... manido′

wawa′bûmĭt................ where he sees me

Analysis.—The voice tempo is much more rapid in this than in the preceding song, while the tempo of the drum remains about the same.[1] (Compare Nos. 103, 104; 121, 122; also No. 168.) The first measure forms a rhythmic unit which occurs four times and clearly influences the rhythm of the entire song. The flatted sixth is found twice and was given in all of the six renditions of the song; it is not correct in intonation, being somewhat less than a semitone above C. The song is harmonic in structure and contains the tones of the fourth five-toned scale. Attention is directed to the very low note at the close of the song; this was sung softly but was clear and approximated accuracy of intonation.

GAME SONGS

It is the belief of the Chippewa that gambling was taught the Indians by a manido′ in order to relieve their distress from hunger and ill fortune. Three games were taught them for this purpose—the hand game (*onĭn′jiwatage′wĭn*), the moccasin game (*makĭzĭn′ata′-diwĭn′*), and the plate game (*bûgese′wĭn*). Songs were sung during the first two games, but there was no music with the plate game, as the play was very brief and the computing of the score required considerable time. All these games are played by the Chippewa of the present day and are commonly regarded as mere pastimes, but it is said that "the older Indians who understand the origin of the games and songs still hold them in reverence as a gift from the Manido′."

The following narrative concerning the origin of gambling was given by Ē′niwûb′e (pl. 26):

Long ago there was a Chippewa who had two wives, each of whom had two children. The man was a great hunter and could kill any animal that he desired. He once took his family and went on a hunting expedition. They went far away from all other Indians. Suddenly one of his children died and the next day another died. He and his wives buried them. The third day another child died and on the following day the last of his children died. The fourth day one of his wives died and on the following day his other wife died. He buried them both. Then he wondered what would become of him. Should he kill himself with his knife or with his arrow? He decided not to do so. A death as certain awaited him if he wandered about the country until worn out with exhaustion, and he decided on this course. Day after day he walked continuously. If he saw water he did not drink, for he was determined to die. He staggered on his way until at last he fell and could not rise. His clothing of skins had

---

[1] In his description of Iroquois Music (in *Archæological Report of Ontario* 1898, p. 145) Mr. A. T. Cringan states: "The rate of movement in the melody may be accelerated or retarded but that of the accompaniment remains constant throughout."

Ĕ′NIWŬB′E

be̱ n̊ e̥ tirely torn from him. He had lost everything—his family, his strength, his tattered raiment; at length life itself departed.

As he lay dead he heard some one coming toward him, stamping heavily on the earth. With returning consciousness he saw a man standing before him. The stranger was dressed all in black, even to his mittens. The stranger (who was a manido') spoke, saying, "Brother, why do you lie here?" He who had been dead then rose to a sitting posture. The stranger said, "Brother, let us gamble." The man answered, "Very well," though he did not know what game was to be played. The stranger, seating himself opposite the man, took a skunk-skin bag from his hip pocket. In this were a piece of flint and a small screw-shaped piece of metal used in removing the wad from a gun.[1] The stranger tossed the flint to the man, saying, "You may use this;" he himself used the piece of metal.

The stranger showed the man how to play the hand game. Laying his coat across his knees, he concealed his hands beneath it; in one hand was the metal object. He then passed his closed hands rapidly before his opponent. Skill in the game consisted in transferring this from one hand to the other while both were closely watched by the opponent, who attempted to guess in which hand the object was concealed. The man who had been dead won the game from the stranger, although it had just been taught him.[2]

The stranger, though defeated by the man who had been dead, asked him to try another kind of game. The stranger then took off his moccasins, and, laying them on the ground, taught the man to play the moccasin game exactly as it is played by the Chippewa at the present time.[3] At this, as well as at the first game, the man who had been dead was victorious.

Then the stranger took from his belt a small shallow wooden plate, which hung there by a cord, and from his tobacco bag some tiny figures made of bone. Placing these figures in the plate, he showed the man how to toss them in the air and note their positions as they fell. The former dead man was winner in this game also.[4]

After being defeated at the plate game the mysterious stranger rose and said to his opponent: "Brother, we will part now. Look, yonder is an Indian village. Go there and gamble as I have taught you. I will now tell you who I am. Watch me as I depart."

The man looked up and saw a large black bear walking away from him. The bear turned and said, "Brother, do you know me?" and the man answered, "Yes, I know now who you are."

The man then went to the Indian village and began to gamble. According to Ĕ′niwûb′e "the man won back his dead—that is, two women and four children were staked on the game, and he won; so he felt as though he had the same ones back again."

---

[1] These spiral pieces of metal, ending in a sharp point, called "gun worms," were secured from traders at an early day.

[2] The hand game is probably the oldest and most widely distributed of Indian games. Culin states (in *Twenty-fourth Ann. Rep. Bur. Amer. Ethn.*, p. 267) that the game has been found among 81 tribes, belonging to 28 linguistic stocks, adding: "This extensive distribution may be partially accounted for by the fact that, as it was played entirely by gesture, the game could be carried on between individuals who had only the sign language in common."

According to Ĕ′niwûb′e, the hand game, taught by the manido', soon came into general use among the Chippewa. The numerous players were seated in two long rows facing each other, while the pile of wagered articles, placed between them, was often so high that the opposing players could scarcely look over it. The spectators danced around the players, singing the hand game songs.

[3] Ibid., pp. 340–342.

[4] According to Culin, a game or games of this type exist "among 130 tribes, belonging to 30 linguistic stocks, and from no one tribe does it appear to have been absent." (Ibid., p. 45.) The plate game among the Chippewa received attention from Schoolcraft (see Oneo′ta, or Characteristics of the Red Race of America, New York, 1845, p. 85), whose description of the game and its implements corresponds with observations made by the writer on the Leech Lake Reservation, in Minnesota, in 1910.

No. 102. Song of the Hand Game   (Catalogue No. 395)

Sung by Ĕ′NIWÛB′E

VOICE ♩ = 120
DRUM ♩ = 120
(Drum-rhythm similar to No. 19)

Analysis.—This is said to be the identical song which was taught by the mánido′ to the man who had been dead. No words were recorded. Drum and voice have the same metric unit but the drum is constantly in advance of the voice, seeming to urge it forward. The rhythmic unit in the first phrase of the song is once repeated accurately, varied somewhat in the third phrase, and disappears entirely in the final phrase of the song. Only one tone other than those of the tonic triad occurs in the melody. The singer stated that when the players "make a guess" in the game it is customary for the song to stop at once and for the drum to beat rapidly while the score is counted. In illustration of this he interrupted the singing of the song with an exclamation and beat the drum very rapidly for several seconds; he then resumed the song, beginning at the first measure instead of at the measure where he made the pause. This appears in the phonographic record of the song.

No. 103. Moccasin Game Song (a)   (Catalogue No. 396)

Sung by Ĕ′NIWÛB′E

VOICE ♩ = 88
DRUM ♩ = 104
(Drum-rhythm similar to No. 19)

Analysis.—This and the following moccasin game song were said to have been taught by the stranger (or manido′) to the man who had been dead. The stranger taught him to sing these songs in order that he might play the game successfully. This song is in 5–4 time. The first measure constitutes a rhythmic unit, which is twice repeated accurately. The other measures show divisions which closely resemble those of the unit but are not complete repetitions. (See Nos. 90, 94, 96, 108, 109, 115, 123.) It is interesting to note these variations and also to observe the rhythmic effect of the song as a whole. The interval of the fourth is prominent in the formation of the melody. This is found in many songs concerning animals and it will be remembered that the manido′ appeared to this man in the form of a bear. (See No. 22.) A slow tempo in songs of controlled excitement is noted also in Nos. 30, 51, 52, 161.

No. 104. Moccasin Game Song (b)   (Catalogue No. 397)

Sung by Ĕ′NIWÛB′E

VOICE ♩ = 100
DRUM ♩ = 104
(Drum-rhythm similar to No. 19)

Analysis.—This song was said to be sung alternately with the one next preceding and was so recorded on the phonograph cylinder. The rhythm of the two songs forms a sequence, the first being agitated and irregular and the second confident and emphatic but closing with a rhythm resembling that of the first. This ending gives unity to the group. The drum has the same metric unit in the two songs, but the voice is faster in the second song. (See Nos. 100, 101; 121, 122; also No. 168.) The structure of both songs is characterized by the compass of an octave and the interval of the fourth. (See No. 22.)

The Moccasin Game

This game is frequently played by the Chippewa at the present time, but has ceased to be a serious occupation and has become a mere diversion. The days are past when men sought success in dreams and lost or won fortunes in a day. Yet many of the characteristics of the game remain unchanged. In July, 1910, the writer saw a party of Chippewa from Bear Island playing the moccasin game with a party from the Leech Lake Agency. One side had won 11 games and the other had not won a single game, yet from the faces of the players it was impossible to tell who had won and who had lost. Additional games were scored without change of countenance by the winners, while the losers met continued defeat with equal stoicism.

The following incident indicates the manner in which the game was formerly regarded:

It is said that one of the most successful players of the game at Leech Lake in the early days obtained the secret of his success from his wife, who returned to him in a dream after death. He had been a gambler for many years before her death and had been fairly successful, but after she died he met with nothing but failure until finally he lost everything. ' In despair he went into the woods to fast and "dream." After a

HIDING THE BULLETS

GUESSING THE LOCATION OF THE MARKED BULLET

MOCCASIN GAME AT WHITE EARTH, MINN.

HIDING THE BULLETS

AFTER THE BULLETS ARE HIDDEN

MOCCASIN GAME AT WHITE EARTH, MINN.

time his wife appeared to him and told him that somewhere in the woods were hidden four bullets, which would bring him success in the moccasin game, and that he must let them lie in the water before using them. Then the man began his search for the bullets. He had no further clew to their whereabouts, but he searched constantly, wandering in the woods day after day. At last he found four bullets and, as he had been directed, placed them in the water at the edge of the lake. He then announced that in a certain number of days he would have a moccasin game. By using the bullets which had been in the water he won everything and thereafter was always successful.

With this incident began the custom of soaking the bullets. Many players do so now, believing this procedure will bring them success in the game.

It was stated that another successful player had a dream in which he saw a row of moccasins and that as he took them up, one after another, he found a piece of money under each. This dream gave him confidence in his playing of the game.

Two men may play the game, but the contestants are usually four men, two playing as partners against the others. Each side in turn hides four bullets under as many moccasins laid in a row on a blanket (pls. 27, 28); one of the bullets is marked. Skill in the game consists in placing the marked bullet in such a manner that it can not be readily located by the opposing players.

Other implements of the game are 20 counting-sticks, each about 9 inches long, and one slender striking-stick, about 36 inches long. The writer has seen a set of moccasin game bullets made of solid steel, which were very heavy. Such a set is valued at one blanket. In addition to the bullets which are hidden, it is customary for the guessing side to use four bullets in indicating its guess, as explained below. The qualities required in playing the game are self-control and keenness of observation; the prize is given to him who conceals, not to him who discovers. The side which hides the bullets is the side which scores.

There are many involuntary signs which may indicate the placing of the marked bullet, and the mannerisms of various players are closely studied. Some affect many gesticulations and hide the bullets with great rapidity; with others a slight motion of the head, a change of facial expression, a slower or a more rapid motion of the right hand may accompany the hiding of the marked bullet. It is said that some players allow it to slip between the fingers when placing it beneath the moccasin. Ki'ose'wini'ni ("good hunter"), a successful player of the game, said that he always "watched the *chest* of the man who hid the bullets," as a player who could control every other muscle would often hold his breath for an instant when he placed the marked bullet. He said further that some players looked at the moccasin under which they had hidden the bullet, and that others as systematically looked at some other moccasin. Still others always hold the marked bullet in a certain part of the hand,

and a close observer learns to look there for a betraying muscular movement.

In preparation for a moccasin game a blanket is spread on the ground, beside which are placed the articles staked on the result of the game. A rifle is usually wagered on the result of six consecutive games, a blanket on three games, and a shirt on one game, while a beaded bag is staked on two or three games, according to its value.

Before beginning the game a knife is tossed to decide which side shall be first to hide the bullets. On the side which is to hide the bullets one player holds a drum; the other lays four moccasins in a row on the blanket and takes in his hand the four bullets which he is to hide. On the side which is to guess, one player holds the striking-stick with which to toss aside the moccasins, and the other, seated at his left, holds in his left hand the four bullets with which he will indicate his guess. Beside these players are laid the 20 sticks with which the score is kept.

When all is ready the drummer sings a moccasin game song and beats the drum while his partner lifts the toe of each moccasin with his left hand and slips a bullet under it with his right hand, his opponents watching closely to detect some change of manner or facial expression when the marked bullet is placed in position. (Pls. 27, 28.)

If the guessing player who holds the striking-stick is sure that he knows under which moccasin the marked bullet is hidden and is willing to risk the score on his own judgment, he extends his right hand with two fingers spread. In this case his partner does not indicate his guess, and if the leading player's guess is correct the score is the same as for a "double crack." This course is seldom followed, however, usually each of the guessing players deciding where he thinks the marked bullet is hidden.

The guesser holding the bullets slips the marked one into a position corresponding to the moccasin under which he thinks the other marked bullet is concealed. For instance, if the guesser thinks his opponent has hidden the marked bullet under the moccasin next to the right end of the row, he places the marked bullet in his own hand between the first and second fingers, the position corresponding to that moccasin when his open hand is extended toward his opponents. The man holding the bullets is allowed only one guess. The man with the striking-stick is allowed three guesses; if he tosses aside two moccasins without disclosing the marked bullet, he may turn another, on which the score is made. His partner then indicates his own guess; if correct, he opens his hand and shows the marked bullet in the right position; if incorrect, he extends his hand with the thumb down, meaning "I have guessed wrong" (pl. 29).

A correct guess by both players is called a "double crack," which entitles them to an additional turn at hiding the bullets, provided

SIGNAL "I GUESSED WRONG"

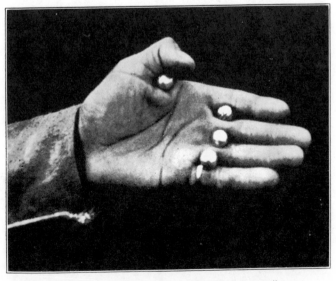

ARRANGEMENT OF BULLETS INDICATING A "GUESS"

MOCCASIN GAME AT WHITE EARTH, MINN.

their opponents do not make a "double crack" in the meantime to counterbalance the first. The "double crack" is mentioned in the words of song No. 175, Bulletin 45. One side continues to hide the bullets until the guessing side guesses correctly, after which the score is counted. The guesser who holds the striking-stick in his right hand holds in his left hand the counting-sticks, at first 20 in number. From these sticks each side receives the number to which it is entitled by the score. When the counting-sticks which remain are three or fewer in number the man holding the bullets does not guess, the game depending on the player who holds the striking-stick. If the marked bullet is under either moccasin at the end of the row and he guesses right, the game is his; if it is under either of the middle moccasins and he fails to locate it, the game is won by his opponents.

The score is complicated, depending on the position of the moccasin under which the marked bullet was hidden—whether at the end or in the middle of the row, also on the number of guesses required by the man with the striking-stick in locating the marked bullet and on the agreement or disagreement of himself and his partner in their choice. For instance, if the bullet is under one of the middle moccasins and both guessers fail to locate it, the side which hid the bullet adds eight counting-sticks to its score. If the bullet is in the same location and only one guesser fails to locate it, the score is six.

At the conclusion of each game a stick about 10 inches long is stuck into the ground at the edge of the blanket. The stakes are settled after the playing of a number of consecutive games agreed on in the beginning.

Dream Songs—Lac du Flambeau Reservation

MELODIC ANALYSIS

TONALITY

	Number of songs	Serial Nos. of songs
Major	2	96, 101
Minor	9	94, 95, 97, 98, 99, 100, 102, 103, 104
Total	11	

BEGINNINGS OF SONGS

	Number of songs	Serial Nos. of songs
On the twelfth	2	94, 101
On the fifth	3	95, 99, 102
On the octave	4	97, 98, 103, 104
On the fourth	1	96
On the third	1	100
Total	11	

MELODIC ANALYSIS—continued

ENDINGS OF SONGS

	Number of songs	Serial Nos. of songs
On the tonic	8	94, 97, 98, 99, 100, 101, 103, 104
On the fifth	3	95, 96, 102
Total	11	

TONE MATERIAL

	Number of songs	Serial Nos. of songs
Second five-toned scale	1	97
Fourth five-toned scale	2	98, 101
Minor triad and sixth	1	94
Minor triad and fourth	3	95, 102, 104
Octave complete except seventh	1	96
Octave complete except seventh and second	1	99
Octave complete except sixth	1	103
Octave complete except sixth and fourth	1	100
Total	11	

ACCIDENTALS

	Number of songs	Serial Nos. of songs
Songs containing no accidentals	9	94, 95, 96, 97, 98, 99, 102, 103, 104
Songs containing the seventh raised a semitone	1	100
Songs containing the sixth lowered a semitone	1	101
Total	11	

STRUCTURE

	Number of songs	Serial Nos. of songs
Harmonic	3	97, 98, 101
Purely melodic	8	94, 95, 96, 99, 100, 102, 103, 104
Total	11	

FIRST PROGRESSIONS

	Number of songs	Serial Nos. of songs
Downward	8	94, 95, 96, 99, 100, 102, 103, 104
Upward	3	97, 98, 101
Total	11	

Rhythmic Analysis

PART OF MEASURE ON WHICH SONG BEGINS

	Number of songs	Serial Nos. of songs
On accented part	11	94, 95, 96, 97, 98, 99, 100, 101, 102, 103, 104
On unaccented part	None	
Total..	11	

RHYTHM OF FIRST MEASURE

	Number of songs	Serial Nos. of songs
Songs beginning in 2–4 time...........................	7	95, 96, 97, 98, 99, 102, 104
Songs beginning in 3–4 time...........................	3	94, 100, 101
Songs beginning in 5–4 time...........................	1	103
Total..	11	

CHANGE OF TIME

	Number of songs	Serial Nos. of songs
Songs containing a change of time.....................	11	94, 95, 96, 97, 98, 99, 100, 101, 102, 103, 104
Songs containing no change of time...................	None	
Total..	11	

RHYTHMIC UNIT

	Number of songs	Serial Nos. of songs
Songs containing a rhythmic unit.....................	9	94, 95, 97, 98, 99, 101, 102, 103, 104
Songs containing no rhythmic unit...................	2	96, 100
Total..	11	

COMPARISON OF METRIC UNIT OF VOICE AND DRUM

	Number of songs	Serial Nos. of songs
Metric unit of voice and drum the same...............	4	94, 95, 98, 102
Metric unit of voice and drum different...............	7	96, 97, 99, 100, 101, 103, 104
Total..	11	

LOVE SONGS[1]

No. 105. "Go with Me"   (Catalogue No. 400)

Sung by Ĕ′NIWÛB′E

VOICE ♩ = 72

Recorded without drum

Ma - dja - ya - ni - ne   ma - - dja - ya - ni - ne   ma -

dja - ya - ni - ne   ma - - dja - ya - ni - ne   ma -

dja - ya - ni - ne   ma - - dja - ya - ni - ne   ki - ga - mi-nĭn go-cû

ga - bi - zi - ka - mûn ma- dja - ya - ni - ne   ma - - dja - ya - ni - ne

WORDS

madja′yanine′....................... when I go
ki′gami′nĭn......................... I will givė you
gocû′............................... surely
gabi′zika′mûn...................... what you will wear
wi′djiwiyûn′....................... if you go with me

Analysis.—This is the only love song in the present series that can be called a "courting song," unless the "Song of an ambitious mother" (No. 112) be included under this head. The last word was not sung, but was given by the singer as one of the words of the song. The progressions are characterized by the interval of the fourth, which has been noted in other songs concerning motion (see No. 22). In several instances the intervals were sung *glissando*, a feature which can be indicated only imperfectly in musical notation. The metric unit is slow and not rigidly maintained by the singer, all the Chippewa love songs being sung somewhat *rubato*. The rhythmic unit, which is clear, occurs three times; it comprises the entire song except the third section, in which a change of words is found. (See Nos. 1, 8, 12, 13, 30, 39, 40, 81.) The melody is distinctly major in tonality and contains an indefinable element of pleading. After singing the song as transcribed the singer repeated the various phrases and sections in an irregular order, seeming to sing them as suggested by his fancy.

No. 106. "Do not Weep"   (Catalogue No. 401)

Sung by Ĕ′NIWÛB′E

VOICE ♩ = 72
Recorded without drum

WORDS

caïgwû′............................ now
nimadja′........................... I go
ke′gosû′............................ do not
ma′wikĕn′.......................... weep

Analysis.—This melody is transcribed in the key of C minor, although the third of that key occurs only next to the last note of the song. The descending fourths C–G, F–C mark the broad outlines of the melody, which has a compass of an octave. It will be noted that the same octave represents the compass of the preceding song, but the two melodies are in different keys. (See Nos. 95, 96.) As in the preceding song, the interval of the fourth is of frequent occurrence. (See No. 22.) The rhythmic unit, which occurs five times, is accurately repeated. The prominence of the subdominant is noted in this and in other songs of sadness. (See Nos. 109, 110, 170.)

No. 107. "You Desire Vainly"   (Catalogue No. 430)

Sung by MEC′KAWIGA′BAU

VOICE ♩= 92

Recorded without drum

Gi - da - ga - wa - dañ   djĭ - mĭ - sû - wĭ - no -

nan   gi-da-ga- wa - dañ   djĭ-mĭ - sû -wĭ-no - nan

a - nĭ - ca   gi - ci - mĕ   ba- ön- djĭ - ĭ - ka - yan

WORDS

gi′daga′wadañ′....................	you desire vainly
djĭ′mĭsûwĭ′nonan′................	that I seek you
a′nĭca′............................	the reason is
gici′mĕ...........................	I come
baön′djikayan′....................	to see your younger sister

Analysis.—The three recorded renditions of this song differ only in the length of the prolonged tone in the fifth and sixth measures, one rendition giving this tone the value of four instead of five quarter notes. The rhythm of the song is smooth and flowing, the irregular divisions blending in an effective whole. The song is distinctly minor in tonality and freely melodic in structure.

No. 108. "He is Gone"   (Catalogue No. 431)

Sung by MEC′KAWIGA′BAU

VOICE ♩ = 92

Recorded without drum

Na - nin -a - nĕn-da-wen-dûm   na - nin-a - nĕn - da-wen-

dûm nin - da   ya   nin - ga-cken-dûm   gi - ma-djad nin -

i - mu - ce

WORDS

nanin′anĕn′dawen′dûm.............⎫
ninda′.................................⎬ I might grieve
ninga′cken′dûm.................... I am sad
gi′madjad′.......................... that he is gone
nin′imu′ce .... my lover

It was said that this song was sung by either a man or a woman whose lover was dead.

Analysis.—This song contains 29 measures and comprises five periods of irregular lengths. The rhythmic unit occurs only three times, but it is interesting to observe that the rhythm of the intervening parts of the song resembles the rhythm of this unit. For instance, in the phrase which includes measures 6 to 13 we note that the opening and the close of the phrase correspond to the beginning and the end of the unit, respectively, but the phrase contains eight measures while the unit contains only five. (See Nos. 90, 94, 96, 103, 109, 115, 123.) Two consecutive syllables of the third word are equally accented.

No. 109. "I am Thinking of Her"   (Catalogue No. 442)

Sung by Mec'kwawiga'bau

VOICE ♩ = 92

Recorded without drum

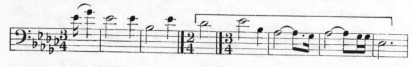

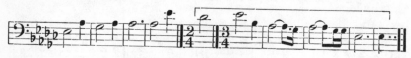

WORDS (FREE TRANSLATION)

I sit here thinking of her
I am sad as I think of her

Analysis.—This was said to be a particularly old song. It contains an unusual number of intervals of a whole tone—14 (58 per cent) of the 24 intervals in the song. Reference to Tables Nos. 11 and 12 will show that only 42 per cent of the ascending, and 35 per cent of the descending, intervals in the 340 songs under analysis are intervals of a second, either a whole tone or a semitone. The prominence of the subdominant is noted in this, as in other songs of sadness. (See Nos. 106, 110, 170). The melody tones are those of the second five-toned scale. The rhythmic unit, although repeated only once, clearly influences the rhythm of the entire song. (See Nos. 90, 94, 96, 103, 108, 115, 123.) The interval of the fourth in the formation of a melody is considered in the analysis of No. 22.

No. 110. "Weeping for My Love"   (Catalogue No. 443)

Sung by Dji'siä'sino'kwe ("DECEIVING WOMAN")

VOICE ♩ = 92

Recorded without drum

I go around weeping for my love

Analysis.—The three recorded renditions of this song vary slightly in the length of the sustained tones. The transcription is from the second rendition. The rhythmic unit, which is long, occurs four times. The middle part of the song contains progressions similar to those of the unit, but having a different rhythm. All the tones of the octave are contained in the song, which is melodic in structure. The subdominant is given special prominence. (Compare Nos. 106, 109, 170.) The interval of the fourth appears in the formation of the melody (see No. 22).

No. 111. "Come, Let Us Sing"   (Catalogue No. 444)

Sung by DJI'SIÄ'SĬNO'ḲWE

VOICE ♩ = 96

Recorded without drum

WORDS

umbe'bĭna	come, I beseech you
nagûmo'da	let us sing
wegonĕn'wĕndjĭ'da	why are you offended?

Analysis.—This song consists of three parts, the first two chiefly in double, and the last in triple, time. There is no rhythmic unit, and the rhythm of the song as a whole is smooth and graceful. The wide intervals suggest to the eye a certain awkwardness not present, however, in the rendition by the Indian singer, who sang the melody with sweetness and good intonation. The words, which were sung indistinctly, are not transcribed. The interval of the fourth occurs frequently in the middle part of the song (see No. 22).

No. 112. Song of an Ambitious Mother

(Catalogue No. 445)

Sung by Mrs. GAUTHIER [1]

Voice ♩ = 176

Recorded without drum

Nin nun - do - da - ma - ge - nŭn nin nun - do - da - ma -

ge - nŭn Bu - gac o - da - nŭn nin - gĭ - tcĭ i - nin - a - kik

nin - gĭ - tcĭ nin - a - kik o - gĭ - mĭ - gi - we - nŭn

WORDS

nin..........................	I am asking for
nundo′damage′nûn..........	
Bugac′..........................	Bugac′'s
oda′nûn..........................	daughter
ningĭtcĭ′..........................	my big
inin′akik [2]....................	brass kettle
ogĭmĭ′giwe′nûn..............	he is giving

The singer stated that this song was a memory of her earliest childhood, when she heard her mother sing it. A brass kettle is said to have been one of the first manufactured articles secured by the Chippewa and was a highly valued possession. The words of the song suggest that the woman singer is bestowing her own property, yet the last line indicates that in doing so she is representing her son.

Analysis.—This song begins and ends on the same tone, a peculiarity found in only 11 songs of the series of 340, namely, Nos. 132, 142, 149, 150, 170, 174, 197 in Bulletin 45 and Nos. 53, 112, 125, 127 of the present work, No. 127 being a duplicate of No. 149 in Bulletin 45. All these songs begin and end on the tonic. This is one of the comparatively few songs composed by women (see Nos. 31, 39, 40, 127, 151, 177, 178). The last measure of the rhythmic unit varies slightly in its repetitions, a measure being added in the second occurrence of the unit. A peculiarity of this song is that it contains only

---

[1] Mrs. Benjamin Gauthier (see pl. 30), who sang this song, is known also by her Chippewa name Bĭ′tawagi′jĭgo′kwe ("double sky woman"). She is a granddaughter of Ginĭc′tano ("wind-bound"), who was chief of the Mă′nĭtowĭc′ and Bimidjĭg′amag bands of Wisconsin Chippewa, and who several times visited Washington with tribal delegations. Mrs. Gauthier is a progressive member of the Lac du Flambeau village, but retains her interest in tribal traditions and customs.

[2] Said to be a compound of the words inĭ′nĭ ("man") and wa′bĭk ("metal"), the large brass kettles obtained from the traders in the early days being called "man-kettles."

MRS. BENJAMIN GAUTHIER

CHIPPEWA DRESS

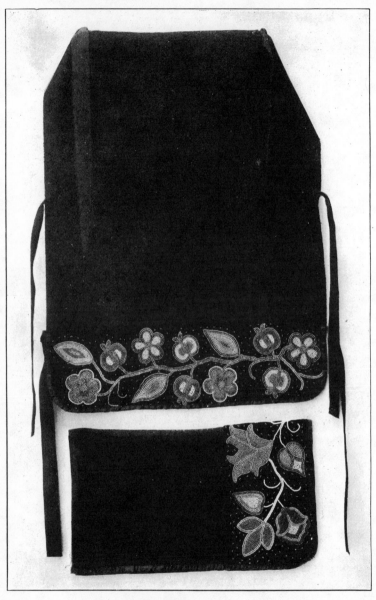

SLEEVE (ABOVE) AND LEGGING—CHIPPEWA

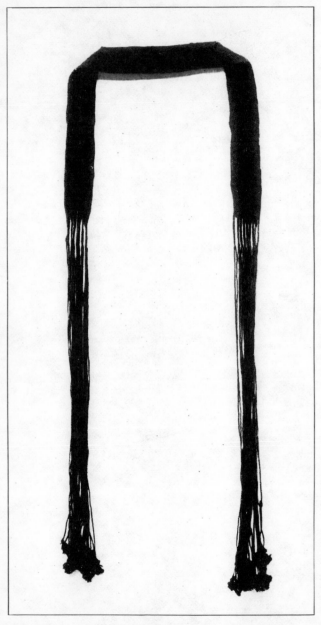

CHIPPEWA SASH

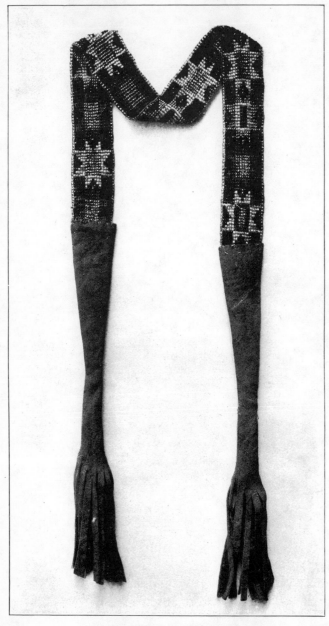

CHIPPEWA HEADBAND

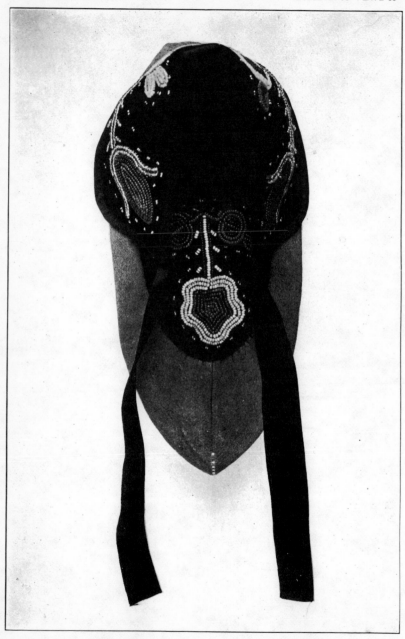

CHIPPEWA MOCCASIN (PRESENT STYLE)

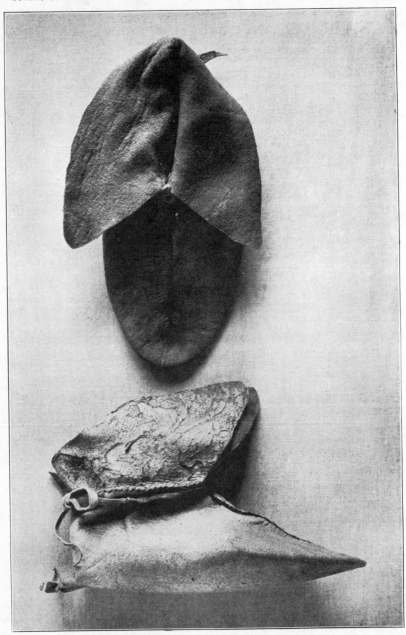

CHIPPEWA MOCCASIN (OLD PATTERN)

the first, second, fifth, and sixth tones of the diatonic scale, the third
being omitted. This is fully considered in the analysis of No. 53.
The interval of the fourth is prominent and has been noted in other
songs concerning motion (see No. 22). Thus we find in the analysis
of this melody a peculiarity noted in other songs composed by women
and in other songs concerning motion.

At the time this song was used the Chippewa women were wearing
the old, tribal style of dress. Mrs. Gauthier recalled her mother's
description of this dress, and the costume she wears (pl. 30) was made
under her own direction, no fewer than seven Chippewa women con-
tributing their skill. The several parts of the costume (dress, sleeves,
leggings, sash, headband, and moccasins) are shown in plates 31–35.
Before securing broadcloth the Chippewa made a garment of similar
design from a blanket. Ĕ′niwûb′e offered to explain this to the
writer and requested his wife to stand while he put a blanket
around her, fastening it at the waist with a scarf and arranging long
folds under each arm to dispose of the fullness. His wife merrily
agreed that he remembered the dress she wore when they both were
young. The surplus length of the blanket was folded over and allowed
to hang loosely on the chest, the garment being held in place by
shoulder bands. In the old days the only ornamentation was on this
piece which hung over the chest, the depth of which depended on the
height of the person. Later, when broadcloth was used for the garment, this was replaced by a strip of that material, beaded, and still
later by beaded velvet. The sash worn by Mrs. Gauthier is of yarn,
woven in an ancient manner by the wife of Ĕ′niwûb′e, the singer.

A somewhat later type of Chippewa woman's dress is shown in plate
16. This costume is decorated at the hem of the skirt, a style said to
be comparatively recent, and the sleeves, instead of being separate,
are joined together in the back to form a short jacket. The floral
designs which form the decoration of Mrs. Gauthier's costume (pls.
30, 32, 35) are typical of the designs in use among the Chippewa at
the present time, which are frequently copied from natural leaves
and flowers. Similar designs appear in plates 11, 20, and 39. A
floral design said to be older than these may be seen on the sleeve
pieces of the woman's costume in plate 16; these pieces were brought
from Mille Lac many years ago. It is said that geometric designs
preceded floral patterns among the Chippewa. Perhaps the simplest
of the former was the "zigzag pattern," which is shown on the piece
across the chest, in the woman's costume in plate 16 and also on the
ma′kûk (pl. 37). The "star pattern" is said to have been originally
a dream symbol (pl. 33). The decoration on Odjĭb′we's war drum
also was the outcome of a dream (see p. 62).

Plate 35 shows the type of moccasin now in use among the Chippewa, and plate 36 the type from which some writers have believed

that the tribe derived its name, many Indians holding the same opinion (see footnote [1], p. 59). In figure 4 is shown a pattern, cut by the aged woman at Lac du Flambeau who made the moccasins. Speaking through an interpreter, she said that in the old days they had no shears and cut the deerskin with a knife. No pattern was used, as they "just made a covering for the feet and gathered it up." She said that she sewed the moccasin up the instep and "piped it to hold it firm," the shortest of the three strips being used for that purpose. She then moistened the moccasin on the inside and molded the outline with the back of a knife placed inside the moccasin. The gathered front also was moistened with tepid water and flattened by pressing it on her knee. The seam up the back was curved below the heel, leaving the small triangle of deerskin. She cut patterns for two strips to be used in fastening the moccasin, but one long strip was used in the pair illustrated, being passed through two little slits at the front of the instep and tied, leaving the long ends to be passed

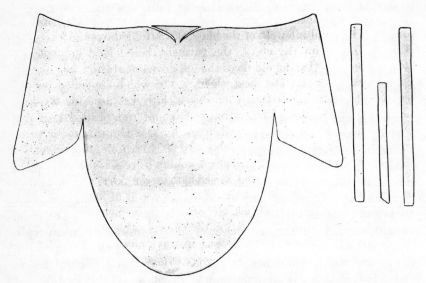

FIG. 4. Pattern of moccasins.

around the ankle and tied at the back when the moccasin was worn. In the old days, when deerskin was plentiful, the moccasins were cut in one piece; it is said that one deerskin would make only two pairs of moccasins. In the pair illustrated the flaps are separate from the feet. The sewing was done with sinew, according to the old custom.

After much discussion and with no little hesitation on her part, a blind woman sang the following song, which was recorded by the phonograph.

No. 113.   Love Song   (Catalogue No. 446)

Sung by O′GABEÄ′SĬNO′KWE ("WOMAN OF THE BREEZE THAT BLOWS TO THE END")

VOICE ♩ = 160

Recorded without drum

Nin-ga-da-wĭ-ga-ga-no-na   nin-i-mu-ce

nin-ga-da-wĭ-ga-ga-no-na   bi-jĭ-go-kwe

nin-ga-da-wĭ-ga-ga-no-na   bi-jĭ-go-kwe

sa-gi-ä   nin-i-mu-ce   ning-ga-wĭ-ga-ga-no-na

bi-jĭ-go-kwe   sa-gi-ä   nin-i-mu-cc

WORDS

ningadawĭ′gagano′na................ I will go and talk with
nin′imu′ce......................... my sweetheart
bi′jĭgo′kwe........................ the widow
sagiä′............................. I love
nin′imu′ce......................... my sweetheart
bi′jĭgo′kwe........................ the widow

Analysis.—The metric unit is more rapid in this than in most of the love songs, but this is compensated for by the frequent occurrence of prolonged tones.   All the tones of the octave except the third occur in the song, which is freely melodic in structure.   (See No. 53.)

67996°—Bull. 53—13——15

Love Songs—Lac du Flambeau Reservation

MELODIC ANALYSIS

TONALITY

	Number of songs	Serial Nos. of songs
Major	3	105, 112, 113
Minor	6	106, 107, 108, 109, 110, 111
Total...	9	

BEGINNINGS OF SONGS

	Number of songs	Serial Nos. of songs
On the octave...	4	106, 107, 109, 111
On the seventh...	1	113
On the fifth..	4	105, 108, 110, 112
Total...	9	

ENDINGS OF SONGS

	Number of songs	Serial Nos. of songs
On the tonic	5	106, 107, 109, 110, 111
On the fifth	4	105, 108, 112, 113
Total...	9	

TONE MATERIAL

	Number of songs	Serial Nos. of songs
Second five-toned scale................................	2	108, 109
Octave complete..	1	105
Octave complete except seventh and sixth............	2	106, 111
Octave complete except fourth........................	1	110
Octave complete except third.........................	1	113
Octave complete except second.......................	1	107
First, second, fifth, and sixth tones..................	1	112
Total...	9	

ACCIDENTALS

	Number of songs	Serial Nos. of songs
Songs containing no accidentals.......................	9	105, 106, 107, 108, 109, 110, 111, 112, 113

MELODIC ANALYSIS—continued

STRUCTURE

	Number of songs	Serial Nos. of songs
Harmonic	None	
Purely melodic	9	105, 106, 107, 108, 109, 110, 111, 112, 113
Total	9	

FIRST PROGRESSION

	Number of songs	Serial Nos. of songs
Downward	4	106, 107, 108, 111
Upward	5	105, 109, 110, 112, 113
Total	9	

RHYTHMIC ANALYSIS

PART OF MEASURE ON WHICH SONG BEGINS

	Number of songs	Serial Nos. of songs
On accented part	4	106, 108, 112, 113
On unaccented part	5	105, 107, 109, 110, 111
Total	9	

RHYTHM OF FIRST MEASURE

	Number of songs	Serial Nos. of songs
Songs beginning in 2–4 time	4	107, 108, 110, 111
Songs beginning in 3–4 time	5	105, 106, 109, 112, 113
Total	9	

CHANGE OF TIME

	Number of songs	Serial Nos. of songs
Songs containing a change of time	9	105, 106, 107, 108, 109, 110, 111, 112, 113
Songs containing no change of time	None	
Total	9	

RHYTHMIC ANALYSIS—continued

RHYTHMIC UNIT

	Number of songs	Serial Nos. of songs
Songs containing a rhythmic unit......................	6	105, 106, 108, 109, 110, 112
Songs containing no rhythmic unit....................	3	107, 111, 113
Total...	9	

NOTE.—No drum was used in connection with love songs.

BEGGING DANCE SONGS [1]

The first of the following group of songs used in the begging dance is said to have come from the Assinniboin, or Rock Sioux, many years ago. The dance also was derived from the same tribe but has been practised among the Chippewa for so many generations that it may be regarded as one of their tribal dances. This song was said to be connected with the origin of the dance.

Ě'niwûb'e stated that it was the custom among the Sioux to lay a new-born baby boy on the ground about as far from the wigwam door as the dogs usually lie. A place was made comfortable for the child, who did not enter the wigwam until he could creep, when it was said that he "entered the wigwam as the dogs enter." While the child lay on the ground outside the door the dogs formed a circle around him with their heads toward him, and their breath helped to keep him warm. It was said that the dogs gave this song to a boy during the time that he spent among them. Ě'niwûb'e said that the dogs did not *sing* the song but *willed* the boy to know it and he did. When the latter reached manhood he went from camp to camp singing this song, followed by the dogs. In his hand he carried a rattle of deer hoofs which he shook as he sang. When he finished the song he was given food and his dogs also were fed. This was the origin of the begging dance. In its later use it was considered a legitimate way for the needy members of the tribe to secure food and was also practised for pleasure. A begging dance could be started at any time, a leader and a small company going from one wigwam to another, dancing and singing. If the occupants of the wigwam were asleep the dancers entered and danced around their fire. The people then arose and gave them food, for those who danced the begging

[1] See p. 171, Bulletin 45, and p. 47 of the present work.

dance were never refused. If the people had no cooked food, the visitors took such provisions as they had, placing them in a birch-bark bag which an old woman carried for the purpose.

No. 114. Song of the Dogs   (Catalogue No. 403)

Sung by Ĕ′niwûb′e

WORDS

a′nimokan′ûg................ the dogs
ningawi′djiwigog′............. will go with me

Analysis.—In structure this song is classified as melodic with harmonic framework. It contains no rhythmic unit and the time was not steadily maintained. It is interesting to note that a variation in time occurs on corresponding measures in the four renditions of the song.

No. 115. "Here I Come Again"   (Catalogue No. 438)

Sung by MEC'KAWIGA'BAU

VOICE ♩ = 84
DRUM ♩ = 84
(Drum-rhythm similar to No. 19)

Ca - ĭ - gwû mĭ - na - wa   ni - ga - bi - dwe - we - dûm   o - gĭ - tcĭ - da - dog

e   a he   ca - ĭ - gwû mĭ - na - wa   ni - ga - bi - dwe - we -

dûm   o - gĭ - tcĭ - da - dog   e   ca - ĭ - gwû mĭ - na -

wa   a he

WORDS

caïgwû'......................'.... here
mĭnawa'........................ I come again
ni'gabidwe'wedûm........... howling as I come
ogĭ'tcĭda'dog [1].............. O you warriors

Analysis.—Those who take part in the begging dance represent themselves as dogs, using the term (*ogĭ'tcĭda'dog*) which dogs are supposed to use toward their masters.

The first two measures of this song comprise the rhythmic unit. These are followed by a triple measure containing the note-values of the rhythmic unit but showing a change of accent. (Compare Nos. 90, 94, 96, 103, 108, 109, 123.) The ninth measure contains a peculiar rhythm which does not vary in the six renditions of the song; the first tone of the triplet is accented, and the note-values are steadily maintained. The song contains all the tones of the octave and is purely melodic in structure.

---

[1] *Ogĭ'tcĭda* (from Sioux *aki'ćita*, warrior) is a word which has come into common use among the Chippewa. The ending *dog* in the case of a noun is a vocative, having a different significance than when used with a verb (see No. 84). For other instances of words from Indian languages incorporated, with some modification, into Chippewa, see pp. 76, 186, 190.

MA'KÛK FOR MAPLE SUGAR

No. 116. "Maple Sugar"   (Catalogue No. 439)

Sung by Mec′kawiga′bau

VOICE ♩ = 88
DRUM ♩ = 88
(Drum-rhythm similar to No. 19)

Sĭn - zi-ba-kwat e - ta me-no - ka - go-yan

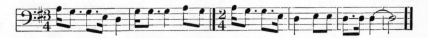

WORDS

sĭn′ziba′kwat................ maple sugar
e′ta........................ is the only thing
me′noka′goyan′.............. that satisfies me [1]

Analysis.—This song contains the tones G, A, C, D, E. Although the song begins and ends on D, the tone acceptable to the ear as a keynote is G. The tone material thus comprises the tones of a major scale lacking the third and seventh, a sequence of tones designated by Helmholtz [2] as the first five-toned scale. Other songs lacking the third are considered in the analysis of No. 53. The influence of the rhythmic unit is evident throughout the song, though the variation of the phrases is less interesting than in the group of songs mentioned in connection with No. 90.

The maple sap (*sinziba′kwadwabo′*) is boiled into sirup (*jiwagûm′-izigûn*) and then prepared in three forms, the most common being the grained sugar (*nasa′igûn*), which is stored in *ma′kûks* (pl. 37), varying in size from very small ones to large ones holding 20 pounds or more. With the covers sewed down the *ma′kûks* afford a convenient method of storing the sugar. In the old days they were

---

[1] A pail or *ma′kûk* of maple sugar was a gift highly valued by those who joined in the begging dance.
[2] In *Sensations of Tone*, p. 260.

sewed with spruce roots.   The "molded sugar" (*zi'gaïgûn*) was packed in cones of birch bark (fig. 5) fastened with tiny wooden pegs and

hung by narrow strips of bark; several of these cones were sometimes hung together. A duck's bill was frequently used to hold the "molded sugar." A third method of preparing the sugar was in the form of a sticky gum or "taffy" (*bĭgĭ-yuwĭ'zigûn*), which was placed in small folded packets of birch bark and tied with strips of the bark. At the close of the sugar-making the Chippewa went to their summer camps

FIG. 5.   Birch-bark cone filled with maple sugar.

(pl. 38), which were usually situated on the shores of lakes. In the illustration a man is shown mending his canoe by holding a charred stick near the pitch which covers the seams; the heat softens the pitch so that it can be rubbed into the seams with the fingers, making them watertight.

No. 117. "My Travels"   (Catalogue No. 440)

Sung by MEC′KAWIGA′BAU

VOICE ♩ = 88
DRUM ♩ = 88
(Drum-rhythm similar to No. 19)

A - ga-wa-ni - gi-ken-dan   be - ba - ma - di - zi-yan *e   a   he*

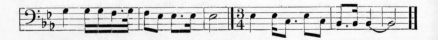

CHIPPEWA SUMMER CAMP, LEECH LAKE, MINNESOTA

aga′wanigikendan′.................. I can scarcely remember
bebama′diziyan′................... my travels

Analysis.—The words of this song suggest that the singer is emphasizing his need of food by referring to the length of his journey. This song contains no rhythmic unit but is characterized by a sixteenth note at the beginning of the measure, followed by a dotted eighth. Double and triple measures alternate throughout the song. This succession of measure-lengths is uniform in the several renditions on the phonograph cylinder. The song is purely melodic in structure and contains the tones of the fourth five-toned scale.

No. 118. Song of Thanks for Food   (Catalogue No. 441)

Sung by MEC′KAWIGA′BAU

VOICE ♩ = 120
DRUM ♩ = 138
(Drum-rhythm similar to No. 19)

Analysis.—This song marks the close of the begging dance at a house and is sung only once. The people have eaten the food given them and sing this before proceeding on their way.

The rhythmic unit occurs in the opening measures and also at the close of the song. The fourth and fifth measures bear resemblance to the rhythmic unit, but show a change of time from double to triple. The song contains only the tones of the major triad and sixth, and would be classified as harmonic in structure except for the accented F in the fourth measure from the close. Eleven renditions of the song were recorded, which are identical in every respect.

SOUTHERN DANCE SONGS[1]

No. 119   (Catalogue No. 404)

Sung by Ĕ′NIWÔB′E

VOICE ♩ = 144
DRUM ♩ = 120
(Drum-rhythm similar to No. 19)

Analysis.—In this song the metric unit of the drum is slower than that of the voice. The melody contains all the tones of the octave, an unusual feature in songs of minor tonality. In one measure we find C sharp, which characterizes the key of D minor in musical usage. The other measures contain C natural, giving a whole tone between 7 and 8 (see Nos. 9, 50, 85, 100, 124). The rhythmic unit consists of two parts, the first of which contains four measures and is based on the descending fifth D–G, while the second part contains a short answering phrase on D in the lower octave. The melody is unusually pleasing and effective.

[1] See pp. 45, 129.

No. 120. "Invite Our Sweetheart" (Catalogue No. 405)

Sung by Ĕ′NIWÛB′E

VOICE ♩ = 184
DRUM ♩ = 116

(Drum-rhythm similar to No. 19)

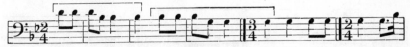

A-wi-nûn-do-ma-keg a-wi-nûn-do-ma - keg ki ni-mu - ce-nan o-

gĭ - tci-mĭn-wen - da go - cû o ca-wûn-o - ka - zi - wĭn o-

gĭ - tci-mĭn-wen - da go - cû o ca-wûn-o - ka - zi - wĭn

WORDS

a′winûn′doma′keg	go and invite
ki	our
nin′imuce′nan	sweetheart
ogĭ′tcimĭnwen′da	she enjoys
gocû′	truly
ca′wûnoka′ziwĭn	the dance called ca′wûno′ga

Analysis.—In this, as in the preceding song, the metric unit of the drum is slower than that of the voice. Five renditions of the song were recorded, the peculiar rhythm being steadily maintained. The song is harmonic in structure, the melody moving along the intervals of the chord of G minor. The first progression is a major third (see Nos. 1, 9, 34, 83, 94). There is no rhythmic unit after the fourth measure, yet the song as a whole has a rhythmic swing.

No. 121. Southern Dance Song   (Catalogue No. 413)

Sung by Ĕ′ɴɪᴡÛʙ′ᴇ

Analysis.—The singer stated that this and the following song were always sung together and at his request they were recorded consecutively on the phonograph cylinder. Throughout this song a double measure follows a triple measure, the accent being so clearly defined that the two can not be combined in a 5–4 measure. Two rhythmic units are contained in the song, the division of the last measure being somewhat similar in the two but each having a character of its own. It is said that "the Indians were so carried away with the ca′wûno′ga that frequently they danced all night." The songs of this dance contain a rhythm which would tend to produce this result. Each song was sung an indefinite number of times, with no interruption of the time.

No. 122. Southern Dance Song   (Catalogue No. 414)

Sung by Ĕ′ɴɪᴡÛʙ′ᴇ

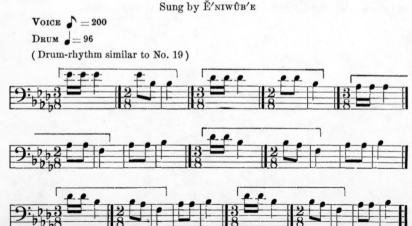

Analysis.—Between the recording of this and the preceding song the pause was sufficient only for the prolonged call with which an Indian frequently closes a song. It is impossible to transcribe this call, or ejaculation, which begins on a high tone and descends *glissando*, the syllables being *yu-u-u, wa!* Sometimes such a close is given with the syllables *wa-a-a, hi!* accompanied by a rapid beating of the drum.

This song contains the same drumbeat as the preceding; the voice-rhythm is more rapid than in the preceding song, and can be measured only by an eighth note as the metric unit. (See Nos. 100, 101; 103, 104; also No. 168.) Five renditions of the song were recorded and the metric unit was steadily maintained, the only difference in the renditions being that the last phrase was omitted from the first three. Comparison with the preceding song will show the rhythmic unit of each to consist of triple followed by double time, but in the first song there is one, and in the second there are two, double measures. The dance seems to gather speed until it ends in a veritable whirlwind, but through it all the stolid drum retains its even, moderate beat.

Songs Concerning the Gift of a Pony

When the people at a dance hear the following song they know that a pony is to be given away. A man dances around the drum with a little stick in his hand with which he whips an imaginary pony; then he presents this stick to a friend, the actual transfer of the pony taking place later.

It sometimes happens that the people are slow in volunteering to part with their ponies. In that event the head drummer may start this song and one of the assembly may present a beaded suit to a man who owns a particularly desirable pony. The proper return for this gift is a pony and in this manner the presentation of one may be forced. All who have given away ponies join in the dance and if others dance at this time they are required to part with their ponies.

No. 123. Song Accompanying the Gift of a Pony

(Catalogue No. 435)

Sung by MEC′KAWIGA′BAU

VOICE ♩ = 96
DRUM ♩ = 100

(Drum-rhythm similar to No. 19)

Analysis.—This song opens with a two-measure phrase, which is repeated. This is followed by a phrase of two measures, which reappears near the close of the song. The first phrase is not regarded as a rhythmic unit, as it is found only at the opening and does not influence the rhythm of the remainder of the song. The second phrase has an evident relation to the rhythm of the entire song, measures 7 and 11 containing a division of the count similar to that in the first part of the unit, and the third measure from the close containing the sixteenth followed by a dotted eighth note, which characterizes the latter part of the unit. (See Nos. 90, 94, 96, 103, 108, 109, 115.) The song is minor in tonality and contains only the tones of the minor triad and fourth.

The man who has received the pony-stick leads the dance as the following song is sung, carrying the stick in his hand. All who have ever given away ponies dance with him, many holding up fingers to indicate the total number of ponies thus presented at various dances.

No. 124. Song of Thanks for the Gift of a Pony

(Catalogue No. 436)

Sung by Mec′kawiga′bau

VOICE ♩ = 96
DRUM ♩ = 100
(Drum-rhythm similar to No. 2)

Analysis.—This song is particularly rhythmic. The unit of rhythm is in double time and is repeated once, followed by a section in triple time in which is noted the triplet in the first count of the measure which characterized the rhythmic unit. The song is minor in tonality and contains a whole tone between 7 and 8 (see Nos. 9, 50, 85, 100, 119).

Moccasin Game Songs

This and the following song are ordinary songs of the game, and no dream origin is attributed to them (compare Nos. 103, 104).

No. 125. Moccasin Game Song   (Catalogue No. 410)

Sung by Ĕ′NIWÛB′E

VOICE ♩ = 84
DRUM ♩ = 92
(See drum-rhythm below)

Drum-rhythm

 etc.

Analysis.—This song is minor in tonality and contains the first, second, third, fifth, and sixth tones of the diatonic minor scale, a tone material occurring in only three other songs of the series of 340 (see Nos. 178 and 184 of Bulletin 45, and No. 83 of the present work). This is of special interest, as the omitted tones are the same intervals as in the fourth five-toned scale, which is major in tonality. The melody begins with an upward progression of an octave (see Nos. 170 and 174 of Bulletin 45, and Nos. 9, 31, 53 of the present book); it also begins and ends on the same tone (see No. 53). The rhythmic unit is steadily repeated except in two measures in which the division of the last count is changed, this slight change giving character to a melody which otherwise would be monotonous. The entire song is in triple time. Four renditions were recorded, the repetitions usually succeeding each other without a long closing tone. Such a tone is indicated in the transcription, but appears only once on the phonograph cylinder.

CHIPPEWA CRADLE-BOARDS

No. 126. Moccasin Game Song   (Catalogue No. 427)

Sung by MEC'KAWIGA'BAU

VOICE ♩ = 96
DRUM ♩ = 104
(Drum-rhythm similar to No. 125)

Analysis.—This song is based on the tones of the minor triad. The rhythmic unit occurs seven times, with a slight variation in the division of the first count.   The speed of the phonograph was greatly reduced in order to test this variation, which was found to be clearly and uniformly given throughout the several renditions.   The intonation on the sixteenth notes occurring at the close of the measures was uncertain, these being given with a "toss of the voice."

SONG FOR THE ENTERTAINMENT OF CHILDREN [1]

No. 127. Lullaby   (Catalogue No. 447)

Sung by O'GABEÄ'SĬNO'KWE

VOICE ♩ = 96
Recorded without drum

we we we we we   we we we we we   we we we we

Analysis.—The only two songs which the Lac du Flambeau Chippewa were found to have in common with the White Earth Chippewa are the lullaby and the song accompanying the folk tale of We'nabo'jo and the ducks (Bulletin 45, No. 197).   This lullaby was first recorded at White Earth, Minnesota (see ibid., p. 193).   On comparing the two transcriptions it will be seen that the first four measures are identical and that the latter parts differ, though both renditions end on the same tone.   This is one of the few songs composed by women (see Nos. 31, 39, 40, 112, 151, 177, 178).   No words are used in this song, *wewe* [2] being continuously repeated.

---

[1] See also songs Nos. 51, 52, 53, 179, 180.

[2] *Wewe* is a root, the meaning of which implies a swinging motion; thus, *wewe'bizun* signifies a child's swing or hammock.   The writer has frequently seen a Chippewa mother put her baby, still fastened in its cradle-board (*aťĭk'ana'gŭn*), plate 39, into a hammock crudely made of a blanket stretched open with a stick, which she swung back and forth until the baby fell asleep.   Still more primitive is the method also shown in the same plate; here the woman is seated on the ground with feet extended in front and the cradle-board resting against them, enabling her to move the cradle-board slightly back and forth by a motion of the feet.

Unclassified Songs—Lac du Flambeau Reservation [1]

MELODIC ANALYSIS

TONALITY

	Number of songs	Serial Nos. of songs
Major	8	68, 115, 116, 117, 118, 121, 122, 127
Minor	8	114, 119, 120, 123, 124, 125, 126, 171
Beginning major, ending minor (same keynote).......	1	67
Total.............................	17	

BEGINNINGS OF SONGS

	Number of songs	Serial Nos. of songs
On twelfth..............................	2	68, 115
On fifth...............................	4	116, 118, 120, 125
On ninth..............................	2	67, 117
On octave.............................	5	114, 119, 123, 124, 126
On fourth.............................	2	121, 122
On third..............................	1	171
On tonic..............................	1	127
Total.............................	17	

ENDINGS OF SONGS

	Number of songs	Serial Nos. of songs
On tonic	12	67, 68, 114, 115, 119, 121, 122, 123, 124, 126, 127, 171
On fifth	4	116, 117, 120, 125
On third	1	118
Total.............................	17	

TONE MATERIAL

	Number of songs	Serial Nos. of songs
First five-toned scale............................	1	116
Second five-toned scale............................	1	122
Fourth five-toned scale............................	3	68, 117, 127
Major triad and sixth............................	1	118
Minor triad and fourth............................	2	120, 123
Octave complete............................	1	119
Octave complete except seventh............................	1	115
Octave complete except seventh and second............	1	126
Octave complete except sixth............................	2	114, 124
Minor third and fourth............................	1	171
First, second, and fifth tones............................	1	121
Other combinations of tones............................	2	67, 125
Total.............................	17	

[1] The following songs included in this table are described in other chapters: Nos. 67 and 68 are divorce songs, found in the Drum-presentation Ceremony, while No. 171 is a song of the pipe dance.

MELODIC ANALYSIS—continued
ACCIDENTALS

	Number of songs	Serial Nos. of songs
Songs containing no accidentals....................	16	67, 68, 114, 115, 116, 117, 118, 120, 121, 122, 123, 124, 125, 126, 127, 171
Songs containing seventh raised a semitone...........	1	119
Total........................	17	

STRUCTURE

	Number of songs	Serial Nos. of songs
Harmonic...............................	3	120, 123, 124
Purely melodic...........................	11	67, 68, 115, 116, 117, 119, 121, 122, 125, 127, 171
Melodic with harmonic framework....................	3	114, 118, 126
Total...........................	17	

FIRST PROGRESSION

	Number of songs	Serial Nos. of songs
Downward	10	68, 114, 117, 118, 119, 120, 121, 122, 123, 126
Upward	7	67, 115, 116, 124, 125, 127, 171
Total...........................	17	

RHYTHMIC ANALYSIS
PART OF MEASURE ON WHICH SONG BEGINS

	Number of songs	Serial Nos. of songs
On accented part	12	68, 115, 116, 117, 118, 121, 122, 123, 124, 125, 126, 171
On unaccented part	5	67, 114, 119, 120, 127
Total...........................	17	

RHYTHM OF FIRST MEASURE

	Number of songs	Serial Nos. of songs
Songs beginning in 2–4 time............................	12	67, 114, 115, 116, 117, 118, 119, 120, 123, 124, 127, 171
Songs beginning in 3–4 time....................	4	68, 121, 125, 126
Songs beginning in 3–8 time....................	1	122
Total...........................	17	

CHANGE OF TIME

	Number of songs	Serial Nos. of songs
Songs containing change of time......................	14	67, 68, 114, 115, 116, 117, 118, 119, 120, 121, 122, 123, 124, 171
Songs containing no change of time...................	3	125, 126, 127
Total..	17	

RHYTHMIC UNIT

	Number of songs	Serial Nos. of songs
Songs containing rhythmic unit.......................	14	67, 68, 115, 116, 118, 119, 120, 122, 123, 124, 125, 126, 127, 171
Songs containing two rhythmic units.................	1	121
Songs containing no rhythmic units...................	2	114, 117
Total..	17	

COMPARISON OF METRIC UNIT OF VOICE AND DRUM

	Number of songs	Serial Nos. of songs
Metric unit of voice and drum the same...............	5	115, 116, 117, 121, 122
Metric unit of voice and drum different...............	11	67, 68, 114, 118, 119, 120, 123, 124, 125, 126, 171
Recorded without drum.............................	1	127
Total..	17	

COMBINED ANALYSES OF WAR, DREAM, LOVE, AND UNCLASSIFIED SONGS [1]—LAC DU FLAMBEAU RESERVATION

MELODIC ANALYSIS

TONALITY

	War songs	Dream songs	Love songs	Unclassi- fied songs	Total	Per cent.
Major......................................	10	2	3	8	23	42
Minor......................................	8	9	6	8	31	56
Beginning major, ending minor (same key- note)......................................	....	....	....	1	1	2
Total..................................	18	11	9	17	55	....

[1] Given separately on pages 195, 213, 226, 242.

MELODIC ANALYSIS—continued

BEGINNINGS OF SONGS

	War songs	Dream songs	Love songs	Unclassified songs	Total	Per cent.
On the twelfth	8	2		2	12	*22*
On the fifth	2	3	4	4	13	*24*
On the tenth	2				2	*4*
On the third		1		1	2	*4*
On the ninth	1			2	3	*5*
On the octave	4	4	4	5	17	*30*
On the seventh			1		1	*2*
On the sixth	1				1	*2*
On the fourth		1		2	3	*5*
On the tonic				1	1	*2*
Total	18	11	9	17	55	

ENDINGS OF SONGS

	War songs	Dream songs	Love songs	Unclassified songs	Total	Per cent.
On the tonic	14	8	5	12	40	*72*
On the fifth	3	3	4	4	13	*24*
On the third	1			1	2	*4*
Total	18	11	9	17	55	

TONE MATERIAL

	War songs	Dream songs	Love songs	Unclassified songs	Total	Per cent.
First five-toned scale				1	1	*2*
Second five-toned scale	3	1	2	1	7	*13*
Fourth five-toned scale	6	2		3	11	*20*
Major triad and sixth				1	1	*2*
Major triad and second	1				1	*2*
Minor triad and sixth		1			1	*2*
Minor triad and fourth	1	3		2	6	*10*
Octave complete	1		1	1	3	*5*
Octave complete except seventh	4	1		1	6	*10*
Octave complete except seventh and sixth			2		2	*4*
Octave complete except seventh and fourth	1				1	*2*
Octave complete except seventh and second	1	1		1	3	*5*
Octave complete except sixth		1		2	3	*5*
Octave complete except sixth and fourth		1			1	*2*
Octave complete except fourth			1		1	*2*
Octave complete except third			1		1	*2*
Octave complete except second			1		1	*2*
Minor third and fourth				1	1	*2*
First, second, and fifth tones				1	1	*2*
First, second, fifth, and sixth tones			1		1	*2*
Other combinations of tones				2	2	*4*
Total	18	11	9	17	55	

MELODIC ANALYSIS—continued

ACCIDENTALS

	War songs	Dream songs	Love songs	Unclassified songs	Total	Per cent.
Songs containing no accidentals............	17	9	9	16	51	*92*
Songs containing seventh raised a semitone.	....	1	....	....	1	*2*
Songs containing seventh lowered a semitone...................................	1	....	....	1	2	*4*
Songs containing sixth lowered a semitone.	....	1	....	....	1	*2*
Total.................................	18	11	9	17	55	....

STRUCTURE

	War songs	Dream songs	Love songs	Unclassified songs	Total	Per cent.
Harmonic..................................	1	3	....	3	7	*13*
Purely melodic............................	9	8	9	11	37	*67*
Melodic with harmonic framework........	8	....	....	3	11	*20*
Total.................................	18	11	9	17	55	....

FIRST PROGRESSION

	War songs	Dream songs	Love songs	Unclassified songs	Total	Per cent.
Downward	15	8	4	10	37	*67*
Upward....................................	3	3	5	7	18	*33*
Total.................................	18	11	9	17	55	....

RHYTHMIC ANALYSIS

PART OF MEASURE ON WHICH SONG BEGINS

	War songs	Dream songs	Love songs	Unclassified songs	Total	Per cent.
On accented part..........................	12	11	4	12	39	*71*
On unaccented part.......................	6	....	5	5	16	*29*
Total.................................	18	11	9	17	55	....

RHYTHM OF FIRST MEASURE

	War songs	Dream songs	Love songs	Unclassified songs	Total	Per cent.
Songs beginning in 2–4 time...............	12	7	4	12	35	*63*
Songs beginning in 3–4 time...............	6	3	5	4	18	*33*
Songs beginning in 5–4 time...............	....	1	....	....	1	*2*
Songs beginning in 3–8 time...............	....	....	....	1	1	*2*
Total...........................	18	11	9	17	55	....

CHANGE OF TIME

	War songs	Dream songs	Love songs	Unclassified songs	Total	Per cent.
Songs containing change of time...........	16	11	9	14	50	*91*
Songs containing no change of time.......	2	....	....	3	5	*9*
Total...........................	18	11	9	17	55	....

RHYTHMIC UNIT

	War songs	Dream songs	Love songs	Unclassified songs	Total	Per cent.
Songs containing rhythmic unit...........	14	9	6	14	43	*78*
Songs containing two rhythmic units......	....	....	....	1	1	*2*
Songs containing no rhythmic unit........	4	2	3	2	11	*20*
Total...........................	18	11	9	17	55	....

COMPARISON OF METRIC UNIT OF VOICE AND DRUM

	War songs	Dream songs	Love songs	Unclassified songs	Total	Per cent.
Metric unit of voice and drum the same....	9	4	....	5	18	*33*
Metric unit of voice and drum different....	9	7	....	11	27	*49*
Recorded without drum....................	....	....	9	1	10	*18*
Total...........................	18	11	9	17	55	....

The Symbols of Songs Which Never Were Sung

In passing through the Chippewa village at Lac du Flambeau tall poles may be seen standing beside many of the houses. Surmounting each pole is a cloth-covered frame which resembles a small flag and is so fastened as to permit it to swing with the wind. On gray weather-beaten poles only part of the frame and a few tatters of cloth remain (pl. 40), but from the newer ones fly banners bearing strange figures outlined in red and blue.   Symbols of the sun, moon, and stars are easily recognized and there are also crude drawings of birds.   High up on many of the poles are tied bundles of faded rags that flutter in the breeze and suggest mystery.

Inquiry as to the significance of the poles will probably be met with evasive answers.   The writer heard a white person ask an Indian whether the fluttering rags were "supposed to frighten away evil spirits."   One who had lived in the vicinity many years said, "The Indians put up a new pole when anyone dies; there is always a new pole after a death at the village."   Such is the superficial impression regarding the medicine poles, showing how well the Indian has guarded the things which concern his deeper nature.

If the entire story of one of these medicine poles could be written, it would be the history of a man's life—his boyhood dream, his failure to fulfill that dream, and his struggle against sickness and death.

It is said that the custom of erecting a medicine pole beside a house had its origin many generations ago, and was as follows: A young man blackened his face and went away to fast, according to the custom of the tribe (see pp. 83, 204).   He dreamed a dream, in which he saw the thunderbirds and the tall tree on which they lived.   Returning to his home, he cut down a tall straight tree and trimmed off the branches, making a pole, which he placed in the ground at his door. He pictured on a deerskin the birds he had seen in his dream.   This he stretched on a frame and fastened at the top of the pole, completing the representation of his dream.   The later custom differed, in that the young man did not erect the medicine pole as soon as he returned from his fasting vigil, but waited to see whether his dream would come true.   The dream usually concerned war and promised success on the warpath.   If he went to war and "fulfilled his dream," he did not erect a pole, but while on the warpath he sang for the first time the song which came to him in his dream (see p. 71).   The words had reference to the birds, the sun, or the stars which he saw in his dream.   If he lacked the opportunity to go to war, he pictured these objects on a deerskin or a cloth, but the song was never sung. Such a man was supposed to have special power to cure the sick. To one who understands its symbolism the pole beside a house says: "Here lives a man who dreamed a dream and the mysterious strength of his vision is in him.   He never used it against human foe, but more than other men he has power against that greater enemy—death."

In the springtime the owner of a pole frequently takes it down, lays it on the ground, and makes a feast.   He asks his friends to come and "preaches about the pole."   If some one "wishes to secure

CHIPPEWA MEDICINE POLES

In the picture on the right a Chippewa cemetery is shown in the background.

CHIPPEWA MEDICINE POLES

long life," he brings one of his garments with tobacco folded in it and ties the garment around the pole. In the autumn a similar feast is often held, but the frozen state of the ground makes it impossible to take down the pole.

When the friends of a sick person are anxious about his condition, they put tobacco in one of his garments, which they fasten high on one of these poles. Sometimes they scrape a weatherworn pole so that it is white and smooth, or even replace it with a new pole, on which they tie a garment belonging to the sick person.

The writer saw a pole which appeared to have been recently erected; it was painted with bands of red and blue and the figures on the banner were clearly outlined in blue. (Pl. 41.) On inquiry the information was given that it was not a new pole but one which had been scraped a few months previously, when Me′dweya′sûñ ("the sound of the wind"), the chief or "speaker" of the village, was very ill. The pole belonged to one of his relatives. It had been freshened and redecorated, the cloth of the banner renewed, and an offering fastened on the pole. But Me′dweya′sûñ did not recover; he had lived the full measure of allotted years and died of old age.

At another house the writer saw the peculiar medicine pole which Me′dweya′sûñ himself erected; on this too were fluttering strips of cloth, portions of garments he had worn, placed there by his friends in the effort to prolong his life. This medicine pole consisted of an uprooted tree placed horizontally between two forked poles as braces at a height of about 5½ feet from the ground. (Pl. 41.) In his youth Me′dweya′sûñ dreamed of war; he dreamed that he was leader of a war party, that he conquered the enemy, and in pursuing them leaped over a fallen tree. Years passed. The call to battle did not come, the tribes were at peace, and there were no war parties for him to lead. At length he put up this tree as his medicine pole, placing it at the same height as the fallen tree over which he leaped in his dream.[1] He felt obliged to do this because he "had not fulfilled his dream," but the song which should have inspired his warriors was buried in his heart.

Kĭ′tciödja′nimwewegi′jĭg ("sky in terrible commotion") told the writer that when he was a boy he fasted and dreamed of a bird. As he never went to war, he later erected a medicine pole beside

---

[1] See description preceding No. 101.

his dwelling, drawing on the cloth banner a picture of the bird he saw in his dream. Although the cloth was torn and the drawing almost effaced by sun and storm, he drew again the outline of the bird (fig. 6), that the story of his dream and his medicine pole

FIG. 6.   Design on cloth attached to medicine pole (native drawing).

might be known to his white brethren far away.   His is the monotonous life of a reservation Indian who can not fully adapt himself to the white man's way, yet beneath it is the memory of a dream and above it is the symbol of the song that never was sung.

RED LAKE, AT WABA'CIÑG, MINN.

CHIPPEWA CAMP AT WABA'CIÑG, MINN.

SONGS OF THE CHIPPEWA AT WABA'CĬÑG VILLAGE, RED LAKE RESERVATION

The songs comprised in this group were recorded at the Chippewa village on Red Lake, in northern Minnesota, called by the Indians Waba'cĭñg ("where the wind blows from both sides"), and known among the white people as "Cross Lake Settlement," a convenient designation, as the village lies across the lake from the Agency. The Indian title is derived from the location of the village on a point of land which divides the upper and lower sections of Red Lake. (Pl. 42.) This point is narrow and several miles in length, so the village is fully exposed to the winds. Twelve miles of open water separate it from Red Lake Agency in summer and the means of transportation are limited. In winter the village is somewhat more accessible, as the ice forms a highway.

These songs were recorded during a gathering of Indians for the celebration of the Fourth of July, 1910. (Pl. 43.) All the singers live near the village of Waba'cĭñg, except one, a Canadian Chippewa from the Rainy River country, who was camping on the upper lake and came to attend the celebration. These Indians seldom hear the music of the white race and may be considered comparatively free from its influence, a feature which adds interest to the analysis of the songs.

The Indians at Waba'cĭñg are estimated at about 350 in number. They are acknowledged to be above the average in character and intelligence. Most of them are full-blood Chippewa. The first encroachment of civilization occurred in 1901 when the Government established a day school at the settlement. The Indians opposed this to the full extent of their power. To-day they are tractable and contented and are interested in keeping their children at school. Some of the younger men work in the logging camps during the winter.

Most of the Indians at Waba'cĭñg are members of the Mĭde'wĭwĭn, and its rites are closely observed. The writer saw two women tending a fire at the head of a newly made grave. According to the teaching of the Mĭde', this fire must be kept burning four nights. Near this was the grave of a little child, with only the embers of the fire remaining. On the grave was a crude rattle which the little one had loved, and beside it was a paper bag containing food.

The dancing of the Waba'cĭñg Chippewa was characterized by freedom and individuality, the best dancers using the muscles of the entire body.   With some the motion seemed to begin in the shoulders and progress with sinuous grace to the feet, while in others shrugging and twisting of the shoulders were seen.   (Pls. 44, 45.)

The drum used, which was of native manufacture, was about 24 inches in diameter and 12 inches in height; it was covered with untanned hide.   The drum was suspended between four crotched sticks driven firmly into the ground (see p. 147).   The singers at the drum usually numbered six or eight.   In beginning the leaders sang a few bars alone, after which the others took up the song.

During the dancing food consisting of slices of beef boiled without salt, triangular pieces of bread cooked in skillets beside the campfire, and bits of bread dough fried in hot fat, considered a special delicacy, was distributed.   The older Waba′cĭñg Indians have not yet acquired a liking for salt, which was unknown to them until a few years ago (see No. 168).

According to the Canadian Indian Awûn′akûm′ĭgĭckûñ′ ("fog covering the earth"), his people have rarely heard a piano, organ, or any other tuned instrument.   He has always lived with the same group of Chippewa, drifting with them from one camp to another. He was a man about 30 years old, who appeared to be a full-blood Chippewa.   He spoke no English.   He said that when he was a little boy he "sat with the old men," listening to their singing and learning their songs, but that now he sang the songs which the men of his village "made up in their dreams."   He sang in falsetto voice with a peculiar throaty *vibrato*.   He said that he discovered his ability to do this when he was a boy and had cultivated it ever since.

The other singers were A′jide′gijĭg ("crossing sky"), an old man who seldom leaves Waba′cĭñg and who wears his hair in long braids; Ki′miwûn ("rainy"), a man of middle age who is prominent in the tribal councils; Ki′miwûna′nakwad ("rain cloud"), who had a particularly good voice, and Gegwe′djibi′tûñ ("sitting near it"), who sang only one song.

Reproduction of these songs by the phonograph afforded the Indians much pleasure.   The phonograph was placed in the door of the little carpenter shop in which the songs had been recorded.   The Indians were grouped outside and the sunset light rested on their eager, intent faces.   Beyond were the wigwams and the shining lake. It was a picture long to be remembered.

DREAM SONGS [1]

Forty songs were recorded at Waba′cĭñg, 26 of which were said to have been composed in dreams.   It is probable that most of the Chippewa dream songs were used in war.   This is not difficult to understand.   The young man who had a dream in his fasting vigil

---

[1] See p. 37.

WAR DANCE OF WABA'CIŊG CHIPPEWA

WAR DANCE

WOMAN'S DANCE

DANCES OF WABA'CĬÑG CHIPPEWA

was usually an individual of character and strength of purpose. War was the principal career which offered itself in the old days and the man of the dream had the qualifications which made for success. After he had sung his dream song on the warpath he sang it at the dances preparatory to war, and in time it became the common property of the tribe.

The dream songs recorded at Waba′cĭñg are arranged according to the uses indicated by the singers. The first four were said to have been used in war dances; these are followed by five songs used in the woman's dance; by six songs used by the Chippewa doctor, whose songs were always received in dreams, and one song of the moccasin game, by which some successful player secured his advantage in the old days. The uses of the remaining songs were not designated but many such are undoubtedly the dream songs of forgotten warriors.

No. 128. A Song of Spring   (Catalogue No. 289)

Sung by A′JIDE′GIJĬG ("CROSSING SKY")

VOICE ♩ = 108
DRUM ♩ = 108
(Drum-rhythm similar to No. 2)

Wa-pa-ba i-na-bi - yan mûc-ko-de

noñ-go-mi-go-dji-ni - bĭn

WORDS

wa'paba'...................... as my eyes
ina'biyan'..................... search
mûc'kode'................... the prairie
noñgo'migodjini'bĭn......... I feel the summer in the spring

Analysis.—This song consists of nine phrases, seven of which contain three measures each. From the beginning of the song to the close of the eighth measure the melody contains only the tones of the minor triad F sharp A–C sharp. In the ninth measure F descends to E, introducing the chord of A major, which forms the basis of the next two phrases. The second section of the song opens with the minor triad, changing after two phrases to the major triad, with which the song closes. (Compare No. 33.) The song contains two rhythmic units, one being used in the minor measures and (with a slight change) in what might be termed the transitional measures, and the other in the measures which contain only the tones of the major triad. Upward progressions are more strongly marked in the second unit than in the first, whose general progression is downward. It is interesting to note the two eighth notes in the last measure of the rhythmic unit, second section, which take the place of the unequal division of the corresponding count in the first section, the song seeming to grow more steady as it draws to a close. In the ca'wûno'ga songs Nos. 121 and 122 it was noted that the songs gained in excitement as they proceeded. The melody is marked by simplicity and well reflects the mood of one who discerns the first signs of spring on the familiar prairie.

No. 129. Dream Song
(Catalogue No. 315)

Sung by Kɪ′mɪwûna′nakwad ("RAIN CLOUD")

VOICE ♩ = 116
DRUM ♩ = 116

(Drum-rhythm similar to No. 19)

Analysis.—The tones comprised in this song are those of the fourth five-toned scale, the melody being based on the tonic triad and the other tones being used as passing tones. The rhythm of the entire song constitutes a unit. On its first occurrence the lower tone of the minor third was slightly flatted but during the remainder of the song was given with correct intonation. (See analyses of Nos. 54, 133, 146, 164.)

No. 130. Dream Song   (Catalogue No. 321)

Sung by Awûn′akûm′ĭgĭckûñ′ ("FOG COVERING THE EARTH")

VOICE ♪ = 184
DRUM ♪ = 152
(Drum-rhythm similar to No. 2)

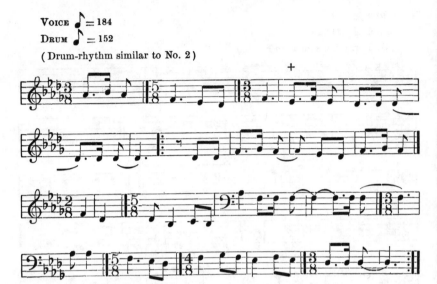

Analysis.—The metric unit of this song was difficult to recognize in the tempo at which the song was sung. By greatly reducing the speed of the phonograph it was possible to detect this unit, and the relative note-values were thus transcribed. The metric unit is ♪=184, which is unusually rapid. The tempo of the original rendition was determined in the usual manner, that is, by adjusting the speed of the phonograph at 160 revolutions per minute, so that the tone C′ as registered on the cylinder corresponded to the same tone as given by the pitch pipe. The metric unit was steadily maintained throughout the two renditions of the song, which were identical in every respect. The song is melodic in structure and has a compass of twelve tones, beginning on the twelfth and ending on the tonic.

No. 131. Dream Song   (Catalogue No. 324)

Sung by AwÛn′akÛm′ĭgĭckÛñ′

VOICE ♩= 69
DRUM ♩= 80
(Drum-rhythm similar to No. 2)

Analysis.—This song was said to have been used in the victory dances which followed a successful war expedition, but never in the dances preparatory to war. The rhythm of the song is forceful and triumphant. Four renditions were recorded. The melody tones are those of the fourth five-toned scale, the melody being based on the tonic triad, and the second and sixth used as passing tones.

No. 132. Dream Song   (Catalogue No. 327)

Sung by AwÛn′akÛm′ĭgĭckÛñ′

VOICE ♩= 108
DRUM ♩= 88
(Drum-rhythm similar to No. 2)

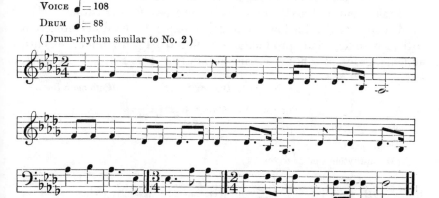

Analysis.—This melody contains the tones of the fourth five-toned scale, beginning on the twelfth and ending on the tonic, the tones being grouped around the intervals of the tonic triad. The opening measures were not included in the repetitions of the song.

This and the following four dream songs are said to have been used in the woman's dance.

No. 133. Dream Song   (Catalogue No. 317)

Sung by AwÛn′akÛm′ĭgĭckÛñ′

VOICE ♩ = 104
DRUM ♩ = 108
(Drum-rhythm similar to No. 19)

Analysis.—The first two renditions of this song were faulty in intonation, being sung a tone lower than the transcription; after a pause the singer gave the song as transcribed, with more correct intonation. (See Nos. 54, 129, 146, 164.) This is interesting, as the singer stated that he was not accustomed to hearing tuned instruments. The song is harmonic in structure, contains only the tones of the tonic triad and sixth, and has a compass of eleven tones. The submediant, or third below the tonic, is frequently used in connection with the tonic triad, producing a minor triad with minor seventh added, a group of tones occurring also in Nos. 147, 151, 152, 153, 154, 163.

No. 134. Dream Song   (Catalogue No. 320)

Sung by AwÛn′akÛm′ĭgĭckÛñ′

VOICE ♩ = 120
DRUM ♩ = 120
(Drum-rhythm similar to No. 19)

Analysis.—Three renditions of this song were recorded, the first three and a half measures being omitted in the repetitions. The range of the song is unusually high and the first two tones were slightly flatted. The short repeated tones were individualized by a muscular action of the throat. The melody is strongly harmonic in character, but the presence of accented E and A cause it to be classified as melodic with harmonic framework. The rhythmic unit is short and the rhythm of the song as a whole is distinctive and clearly marked.

No. 135. Dream Song   (Catalogue No. 323)

Sung by Awûn′akûm′ĭgĭckûñ′

VOICE ♩ = 100
DRUM ♩ = 100
(Drum-rhythm similar to No. 19)

Analysis.—This song is a particularly good example of a melody based on the second five-toned scale. The first measure contains the rhythmic unit of the song, which occurs five times. The first part of the melody is based on the chord of C minor and the latter part suggests the chord of E flat, though the tone E flat does not appear. In the absence of this tone, which would be the tonic of the major chord, the song is considered to be minor in tonality; this is, however, an instance in which what we term "key" can not be said to be established. The relation of the tones is an interval-relation rather than a key-relation (see pp. 7, 8).

No. 136. Dream Song   (Catalogue No. 325)
Sung by Awûn′akûm′igĭckûñ′

VOICE ♩ = 112

DRUM ♩ = 112

(Drum-rhythm similar to No. 19)

Analysis.—The intervals of progression in this melody are unusually large and would present some difficulties to a singer of the white
race. It is, however, a bright and attractive melody, lively in
tempo, and strongly rhythmic in character. The tones are those of
the tonic triad and sixth. The first measures were not included in
the repetitions of the song.

No. 137. Dream Song   (Catalogue No. 326)
Sung by Awûn′akûm′igĭckûñ′

VOICE ♩ = 112

DRUM ♩ = 112

(Drum-rhythm similar to No. 19)

Analysis.—In this song the signature of the transcription should be regarded as indicating the pitch of certain tones and not as implying an established key. The transcription merely represents the tones sung by the Indian singer.

The framework of this melody is characterized by the interval of the third. The first seven measures are based on the descending third F sharp–D sharp, with G sharp as a tone of approach (see analysis of No. 53). This is followed by the descending thirds B–G sharp; D sharp–B; B–G sharp, with a return to the third F sharp–D sharp, with G sharp as a tone of approach. The second section of the song has essentially the same framework.

This song and the following five dream songs are said to have been used by a Chippewa doctor during his treatment of the sick. (See Bulletin 45, pp. 119, 120.)

No. 138. "My Body Lies in the East"   (Catalogue No. 308)

Sung by KI′MIWÛN ("RAINY")

Wa-bûn-oñg a - te   ni-au *e*

WORDS

wabûnoñg′.................... in the east
ate′.......................... lies
ni-au′ .... my body

Analysis.—The two renditions of this strange melody secured are identical. The song is based on the minor triad, the fourth and sixth being used as passing tones. The tempo is slow, with long swinging cadence. The rhythm is characterized by the triplet, which occurs frequently on the last count of the measure. The song contains no rhythmic unit, but the rhythm of the entire song constitutes a homogeneous whole. In this group of six "doctor's songs" it is noted that vowel syllables distinctly enunciated are used on the tones not supplied with words, resembling the Mïde' songs, and differing from the majority of Chippewa songs, in which the separation of tones is produced by muscular action of the throat (see No. 134).

No. 139. "Sitting with the Turtle"   (Catalogue No. 309)

Sung by KI'MIWÛN

WORDS

mĭkĭnak'...................... turtle
niwi'tabimû'.................. I am sitting with him

Analysis.—Five renditions of this song were recorded. In the first and fourth renditions no words were used; in the second and fifth the words occurred as transcribed, and in the third the words were used in the seventh and eighth measures instead of at the opening of the song. The first rendition begins on D flat instead of E flat, a fact which suggests that D flat is felt to be the principal tone, E flat being used as an approach to that tone. (See analysis of No 53.)

No. 140. "Carried Around the Sky" (Catalogue No. 310)

Sung by KI′MIWÛN

VOICE ♩ = 116
DRUM ♩ = 116
(Drum-rhythm similar to No. 19)

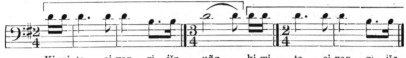

Ki-wi- ta - ci-yan gi - jĭg - uñg   ki-wi - ta - ci-yan gĭ - jĭg -

uñg   ki-wi - ta - ci-yan gi - jĭg - uñg   ki-wi - ta - ci -

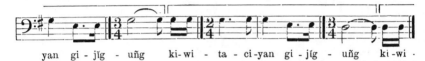

yan gi - jĭg - uñg   ki- wi - ta - ci -yan gi - jĭg - uñg   kĭ -wi -

ta - ci - yan gĭ - jĭg - uñg   ki-wi - ta - ci-yan gĭ - jĭg- uñg

WORDS

kiwita′yaciyan′ [1]............ as the wind is carrying me
gi′jĭguñg′.................. around the sky

Analysis.—This is an example of a song showing an interval formation and containing what would be called in musical terms "the
tonic of the key" only in the middle part of the song. Chippewa
songs with this characteristic have been noted only among those collected at Waba′cĭñg; these are Nos. 135, 137, 139, 141, 142, 165. If
we depend on the musical ear in determining the key of a song, we
place this song in the key of G major, yet 85 per cent of the intervals
are minor. The song contains 13 intervals, of which 9 (70 per cent)
are minor thirds and 2 (15 per cent) are minor seconds, the other
intervals being a major third and a major second. (See Nos. 141,
151, 161, 163.) The rhythmic unit contains three measures and
occurs seven times, being accurately and continuously repeated. The
accidental tone (A sharp) was given with correct intonation. No
differences appear in the four renditions of the song.

This and the two following songs are said to be sung after the
"doctor" has "swallowed" the bones and during the treatment of

[1] One syllable of this word was omitted by the singer.

the sick person. After the second rendition of the song there is recorded on the phonograph cylinder a sharp hissing sound which the doctor makes as he breathes, or "blows," on the person receiving treatment; after the third rendition there is recorded a shrill whistle, which he is said to make as the bones issue from his mouth. It is said that in the old days the "doctor" did not take the bones in his hand before swallowing them, but drew them directly into his mouth from a shallow dish of water. The writer has been informed by more than one eyewitness that when the medicine-men were in possession of their former powers the bones, many of which were much larger than those used in recent years, were actually swallowed by them.

No. 141. "The Approach of the Thunderbirds"

(Catalogue No. 311)

Sung by KI'MIWÛN

VOICE ♩ = 88
DRUM ♩ = 138
(Drum-rhythm similar to No. 2)

Ka - bĭ - de - bwe - we - da - mo - wad bĭ - nĕ - sĭ - wûg

WORDS

kabĭde′bwewe′damowad′......the sound approaches
bĭnĕ′sĭwûg..................the (thunder) birds draw near

Analysis.—This song contains a short rhythmic unit, which occurs only twice. The song is major in tonality, but is characterized by the frequent occurrence of the interval of the minor third, 67 per cent of the intervals being minor thirds. (See Nos. 140, 151, 161, 163.) Harmonic in structure, the melody contains only the tones of the tonic triad and sixth. Attention is directed to the rapid drumbeat in this and the following two songs. The approach to the harmonic tone by the tone above is discussed in the analysis of No. 53.

No. 142. "White-haired Raven"   (Catalogue No. 312)

Sung by Kī′mīwûn

Voice ♩ = 160
Drum ♩ = 120
(Drum-rhythm similar to No. 2)

Kwe wa - bi-kwe - ka - ga - gi kwe ba - ba- mac nin - de - go   kwe

wa - bi - kwe - ka - ga - gi kwe ba - ba- mac nin - de - go   kwe

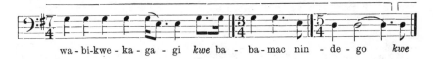

wa - bi-kwe - ka - ga - gi kwe ba - ba- mac nin - de - go   kwe

wa - bi - kwe - ka - ga - gi kwe ba - ba- mac nin - de - go

WORDS

wa′bikwe′kaga′gi..............."white-haired raven
babamac′.....................flying around the sky"
nin′dego′.....................I am called

Analysis.—The four recorded renditions of this song are identical in all respects except that in one instance D instead of B was sung on the last count of the first measure. This is unimportant except that it is the only variation. At the close of the second rendition is recorded the peculiar whistle described in connection with the preceding song. There is no perceptible secondary accent in the measures marked, respectively, 7–4 and 5–4. The rhythmic unit comprises three measures and occurs four times. The measures in 3–4 time were sung with a slightly slower metric unit than those in 7–4 time. The melody is particularly striking and forceful.

No. 143. Dream Song   (Catalogue No. 313)

Sung by Kɪ'ᴍɪᴡûɴ

VOICE ♩ = 144
DRUM ♩ = 120
(Drum-rhythm similar to No. 2)

Analysis.—Four renditions of this song were recorded; the second and third renditions were followed by the peculiar whistle and hiss already described. The song contains the tones of the tonic triad and sixth and is harmonic in structure. The rhythmic unit contains four measures, its repetitions comprising the entire song.

The following is a song of the moccasin game. It is unusual to find a moccasin game song which is said to have had its origin in a dream. Long ago the players sought skill by means of fasts and dreams, but at present the game is regarded less seriously. This song was recorded by a member of a Canadian band of Chippewa, among whom the moccasin game may have retained its original status (see p. 206).

No. 144. Dream Song   (Catalogue No. 319)

Sung by Aᴡûɴ'ᴀᴋûᴍ'ɪɢïᴄᴋûɴ'

VOICE ♩ = 72
DRUM ♩ = 104
(Drum-rhythm similar to No. 19)

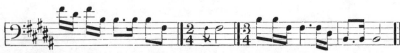

Analysis.—The entire trend of the melody is downward, along the intervals of the tonic triad. The metric unit of the voice is slow and that of the drum is rapid, a peculiarity found in most of the moccasin game songs and suggesting the mingled control and excitement of the game. A song closely resembling this but in a different rhythm was recorded on the White Earth Reservation (compare No. 176).

The singers did not state on what occasions the remaining songs of this group were sung, but it is probable that they were used in the dances preparatory to war. The words are of interest, in many instances suggesting the confidence which makes for leadership in any undertaking and becomes the more inspiring when it is believed to be of supernatural origin.

No. 145. "Into the Several Heavens"   (Catalogue No. 288)

Sung by A′JIDE′GIJĬG

Voice ♩ = 104
Drum ♩ = 104
(Drum-rhythm similar to No. 19)

O - gi -ma   gi - jĭg - uñg   en - ga - ba - bi - ni -go

WORDS

o′gima........................the chief
gi′jĭguñg′.....................into the heavens
engaba′binigo′..............will take me

Analysis.—This song contains a peculiarity which occurs frequently in songs recorded at Waba′cĭñg, namely, the approach to a harmonic tone by means of the tone above it. For instance, this melody is based on the triad of E flat major, yet the first tone is an accented C. This is discussed in the analysis of No. 53 and is found also in Nos. 29, 45, 51, 53, 65, 137, 139. The sixth was sung slightly sharp when reached by an ascending progression, this feature being uniform throughout the two renditions of the song. Faulty intonation on the interval of a second is noted in Nos. 54, 55, 61, 64, 100, 145, 166. The closing tone was sung with good intonation, representing an unusually low range of voice.

(Catalogue No. 290)

No. 146. "Two Foxes Face Each Other"

Sung by A'JIDE'GIJÏG

VOICE ♩ = 112
DRUM ♩ = 112

(Drum-rhythm similar to No. 2)

Wĕ -on-da-sû-ma-bi - wad   wa-guc-ûg   mi - ma-dji-ä - bi - yan

WORDS

wĕonda'sûma'biwad'.............. they face each other
wagucûg'......................... two foxes
mima'djiä'biyan'................. I will sit between them

Analysis.—This song contains no rhythmic unit, though a dotted eighth followed by a sixteenth note occurs with frequency. It should be noted that the lower tone of the minor third was slightly flatted on its first occurrence in each octave, though sung afterward with correct intonation. (See Nos. 54, 129, 133, 164.) The tonic chord forms the framework of the melody, with the second and sixth as unaccented passing tones.

No. 147. "One Bird"   (Catalogue No. 291)

Sung by A'JIDE'GIJĬG

VOICE ♩= 108

DRUM ♩= 108

(Drum-rhythm similar to No. 2)

Be - jĭg bĭ-nĕ - si   ni-wi-djĭ - wa

WORDS

be'jĭg............................ one
bĭnĕ'si............................ bird
niwi'djĭwa'........................ I am going with him

Analysis.—The rhythmic unit of this song contains six measures and occurs five times; its repetitions constitute the entire song. The first section of the song is outlined by the interval of the fourth, representing the descent from the tonic to the dominant; the second section is based on the descending interval of the fifth and contains the tones of the tonic triad; and the third contains the descent in the lower octave from the tonic to the dominant. The outline of the second and third sections is repeated, and the dominant is the closing tone of the song. Thus the melody, in its broad outline, is seen to have a definite relation to the tonic chord, yet within this outline we find another characteristic. The tone D flat appears with prominence, and in its connection with the tonic triad forms a group of the minor triad and minor seventh, which has been noted in songs of the Chippewa and also in the music of other primitive people. (See footnote, p. 130, Bulletin 45.) This group is noted also in Nos. 133, 151, 152, 153, 154, and 163 of the present work.

No. 148. "The Sky Will Resound"   (Catalogue No. 296)

Sung by KĬ′MIWÛN

VOICE ♩ = 100
DRUM ♩ = 100
(Drum-rhythm similar to No. 19)

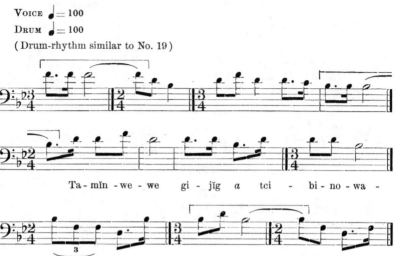

Ta - mĭn - we - we   gi - jĭg   a   tci - bi - no - wa -

da - go - si - nan

WORDS

ta′mĭnwe′we...................... it will resound finely
gi′jĭg............................ the sky
tci′binonda′gosinan′.............. when I come making a noise

Analysis.—This song is harmonic in structure and is based on the chord of B flat major. The rhythmic unit is not strongly marked, yet the song as a whole has a rhythmic effect which is particularly pleasing. The metric unit was maintained with absolute regularity by the singer.

No. 149. "One Wind"   (Catalogue No. 298)

Sung by Kɪ′ᴍɪᴡûɴ

VOICE ♩ = 100
DRUM ♩ = 104
(Drum-rhythm similar to No. 19)

Be - jĭg no-dĭn nin-ga - na -

wĕn - dan

WORDS

be′jĭg............................. one
no′dĭn............................. wind
ninga′nawĕndan′.................. I am master of it

Analysis.—Three renditions of this song were recorded. The time
was not steadily maintained, and it is noted that variations from
exact time occur in corresponding measures in the several renditions.
The song contains the tones of the fourth five-toned scale, is harmonic
in structure, and is based on the tonic triad, the second and sixth
appearing only as passing tones. No rhythmic unit occurs in the
song, although the rhythm of the song as a whole is strongly marked.

No. 150. "An Overhanging Cloud"   (Catalogue No. 299)

Sung by KI′MIWÛN

VOICE ♩ = 120
DRUM ♩ = 120
(Drum-rhythm similar to No. 19)

Ka - bi -ba -bam -a - go - deg   a - na -kwad tci -ba -ba - mi -no   -   ta -

gwûn

WORDS

ka′bibabam′agodeg′................ an overhanging
a′nakwad.......................... cloud
tcibaba′minota′gwûn.............. repeats my words with pleasing sound

Analysis.—This melody consists of two sections, the first comprising six measures and the second comprising eight measures. The melody-tones are those of the fourth five-toned scale, and the song is harmonic in structure. The rhythm is so decided that one looks for a rhythmic unit or some regularity in the succession of double and triple measures, but neither is present.

No. 151. "Heaps of Clouds"   (Catalogue No. 314)

Sung by KI′MIWÛNA′NAKWAD ("RAIN CLOUD")

VOICE ♩ = 112
DRUM ♩ = 112
(Drum-rhythm similar to No. 19)

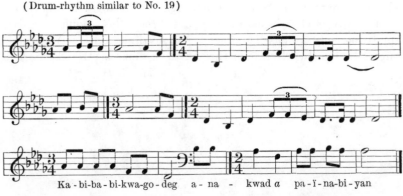

Ka - bi -ba - bi -kwa -go - deg   a - na -   kwad a   pa - ï -na -bi - yan

ka′bibabi′kwagodeg′......... great heaps
a′nakwad..................... of clouds
pa′ïna′biyan′................. in the direction I am looking

Analysis.—This song is said to have been composed by a woman.
(See Nos. 31, 39, 40, 112, 127, 177, 178.)   The melody contains only
three descending progressions larger than a minor third; these are
major thirds, occurring between the lower tone of one minor third
(F–A flat) and the upper tone of another minor third (B flat–D flat).
The song is major in tonality, yet 13 of the intervals (36 per cent)
are intervals of the minor third, 9 descending and 4 ascending.   (See
Nos. 140, 141, 161, 163.)   The last four measures of the song consist
of the tones of the major triad on D flat, yet observation of the first
part of the song shows the prominence of the outline A flat–F–D
flat–B flat, which forms a minor triad with minor seventh added.
This is a chord of strong barbaric color, which has been found in the
music of many primitive peoples; it is noted in Bulletin 45 (footnote,
p. 130), also in Nos. 133, 147, 152, 153, 154, 163 of the present series.
In the song under analysis this chord resolves into the tonic chord
by the progression of B flat to A flat in the seventh measure from the
close.   The song is harmonic in structure, the only tones accented
being the tones of the tonic triad.   The melody tones are those of
the fourth five-toned scale.   The intonation of the singer was most
nearly accurate on the tonic and fifth and most uncertain on the
third of the key.

No. 152. "Around the Sky"   (Catalogue No. 318)

Sung by AWÛN′AKÛM′ÏGÏCKÛÑ′

VOICE ♩ = 80
DRUM ♩ = 104
(Drum-rhythm similar to No. 19)

Ki-wi-ta- gi -jĭg *e*   ka-bi- de -

bwe-wi-da - mon

WORDS

ki'witagi'jĭg................. around the sky
ka'bidebwe'widamon'....... I come to you with my sound

Analysis.—This is a particularly graceful melody and was sung with regularity of rhythm and good intonation. The downward progressions E–C sharp–A–F sharp form the minor triad with minor seventh added, which resolves into the tonic chord by the tone E in the eighth and eighteenth measures (compare Nos. 133, 147, 151, 152, 154, 163). At the opening of the seventh measure occurs a peculiar division of the count, which is found also in Nos. 153, 157, 159, 161, 163.

No. 153. "The Thunderbirds"   (Catalogue No. 322)

Sung by Awûn'akûm'ĭgĭckûñ'

Voice ♩ = 72

Drum ♩ = 144

(Drum-rhythm similar to No. 2)

Bĭ - nĕ - sĭ - wûg ni - koc - ko -

ĭ - a - gog

WORDS

bĭnĕ'sĭwûg.................. the (thunder) birds
nikoc'koĭgog'................ startle me

Analysis.—The first three measures of this song contain the downward progression G–E–C–A, comprising the minor triad with minor seventh added (see Nos. 133, 147, 151, 152), the tonic chord of C major being established in the ninth measure. The remainder of the song is based on the tonic triad, the sixth occurring only as a passing tone. The rhythm is characterized by a peculiar division of the first count of the measure. This occurs in the opening of the rhythmic unit and has been noted also in Nos. 152, 157, 159, 161, 163.

Dream Songs—Waba'cĭñg Village, Red Lake Reservation

MELODIC ANALYSIS

TONALITY

	Number of songs	Serial Nos. of songs
Major	25	128, 129, 130, 131, 132, 133, 134, 136, 137, 138, 139, 140, 141, 142, 143, 144, 145, 146, 147, 148, 149, 150, 151, 152, 153
Minor	1	135
Total	26	

BEGINNINGS OF SONGS

	Number of songs	Serial Nos. of songs
On thirteenth	1	145
On sixth	5	137, 139, 141, 147, 152
On twelfth	11	129, 130, 132, 138, 143, 144, 146, 148, 150, 151, 153
On fifth	4	133, 140, 142, 149
On tenth	3	128, 134, 136
On third	2	131, 135
Total	26	

ENDINGS OF SONGS

	Number of songs	Serial Nos. of songs
On tonic	14	128, 129, 130, 132, 136, 138, 143, 144, 145, 146, 148, 150, 151, 153
On tonic fifth	2	131, 134
On tonic third	10	133, 135, 137, 139, 140, 141, 142, 147, 149, 152
Total	26	

MELODIC ANALYSIS—continued

TONE MATERIAL

	Number of songs	Serial Nos. of songs
Fourth five-toned scale	15	128, 129, 130, 131, 132, 135, 140, 142, 146, 147, 148, 149, 150, 151, 153
Major triad	1	144
Major triad and sixth	9	133, 134, 136, 137, 139, 141, 143, 145, 152
Minor triad, sixth and fourth	1	138
Total	26	

ACCIDENTALS

	Number of songs	Serial Nos. of songs
Songs containing no accidentals	24	128, 129, 130, 131, 132, 133, 134, 135, 136, 137, 138, 139, 141, 143, 144, 145, 146, 147, 148, 149, 150, 151, 152, 153
Songs containing second raised a semitone	2	140, 142
Total	26	

STRUCTURE

	Number of songs	Serial Nos. of songs
Harmonic	14	129, 133, 134, 138, 140, 141, 143, 144, 146, 148, 149, 150, 151, 152
Purely melodic	4	132, 142, 135, 137
Melodic with harmonic framework	8	128, 130, 131, 134, 135, 136, 137, 139
Total	26	

FIRST PROGRESSION

	Number of songs	Serial Nos. of songs
Downward	21	128, 129, 130, 132, 134, 135, 136, 137, 139, 140, 141, 142, 143, 144, 145, 146, 148, 149, 150, 152, 153
Upward	5	131, 133, 138, 147, 151
Total	26	

Rhythmic Analysis

PART OF MEASURE ON WHICH SONG BEGINS

	Number of songs	Serial Nos. of songs
On accented part	17	128, 129, 130, 133, 135, 136, 137, 139, 141, 144, 145, 146, 147, 148, 149, 150, 152
On unaccented part	9	131, 132, 134, 138, 140, 142, 143, 151, 153
Total..	26	

RHYTHM OF FIRST MEASURE

	Number of songs	Serial Nos. of songs
Songs beginning in 2–4 time	13	129, 131, 132, 134, 135, 137, 138, 139, 140, 141, 147, 150, 152
Songs beginning in 3–4 time..........................	10	128, 133, 136, 144, 145, 146, 148, 149, 151, 153
Songs beginning in 4–4 time..........................	1	143
Songs beginning in 7–4 time..........................	1	142
Songs beginning in 3–8 time..........................	1	130
Total..	26	

RHYTHMIC UNIT

	Number of songs	Serial Nos. of songs
Songs containing rhythmic unit.......................	9	131, 134, 135, 140, 141, 142, 143, 147, 153
Songs containing two rhythmic units..................	1	128
Songs containing no rhythmic unit....................	16	129, 130, 132, 133, 136, 137, 138, 139, 144, 145, 146, 148, 149, 150, 151, 152
Total..	26	

COMPARISON OF METRIC UNIT OF VOICE AND DRUM

	Number of songs	Serial Nos. of songs
Metric unit of voice and drum the same...............	13	128, 129, 134, 135, 136, 137, 140, 145, 146, 147, 148, 150, 151
Metric unit of voice and drum different...............	13	130, 131, 132, 133, 138, 139, 141, 142, 143, 144, 149, 152, 153
Total..	26	

RHYTHMIC ANALYSIS—continued

CHANGE OF TIME

	Number of songs	Serial Nos. of songs
Songs containing change of time......................	26	128, 129, 130, 131, 132, 133, 134, 135, 136, 137, 138, 139, 140, 141, 142, 143, 144, 145, 146, 147, 148, 149, 150, 151, 152, 153
Total..	26	

MĬDE′ SONGS

This and the following song were said to form part of a ceremony which is held soon after the death of a member of the Mĭde′wĭwĭn (Grand Medicine Society), and which has for one of its objects the direction of the spirit on its journey.   (See Bulletin 45, p. 54.)

No. 154. "The Noise of the Village"   (Catalogue No. 306)

Sung by KĬ′MIWÛN

VOICE ♩=56
DRUM ♩=112
(Drum-rhythm similar to No. 2)

WORDS

a′nina′nibawiyan′............ whenever I pause
de′bwewe′................... the noise
ode′na....................... of the village

Analysis.—The tempo of this song is very slow, the metric unit being a half note. The rhythmic unit occurs five times, as indicated. The melody comprises the tones of the fourth five-toned scale, yet the progressions are grouped about the minor triad with minor seventh added. (See Nos. 133, 147, 151, 152, 153.) The several renditions recorded show the rhythm unchanged but the intonation varying, a *glissando* being frequently introduced.

No. 155. Mĭde′ Song   (Catalogue No. 304)

Sung by Kɪ′ᴍɪᴡûɴ

Voice ♩ = 72
Drum ♩ = 112
(Drum-rhythm similar to No. 2)

Analysis.—Three renditions of this song were recorded at Waba′cĭñg. A few weeks later the phonograph record was played for a member of the Mĭde′wĭwĭn on the White Earth Reservation, who said that the melody was correct, but that the words were not. As he was a particularly good authority, the words are omitted in the transcription. The melody is simple, containing only the tonic triad and sixth and moving along harmonic lines. Attention is directed to the slow metric unit of the voice and the rapid unit of the drum. The rhythmic unit is unusually long and its repetitions embrace the entire song.

No. 156. "Be Kindly"   (Catalogue No. 307)

Sung by Ki 'MIWÛN

Outline of melody-progressions

WORDS

wewe′mi.................... be kindly
nimanido′.................... my manido′
nikân′....................... my Mïde′ brother

Analysis.—This song is transcribed in outline, quarter notes without stems being used to indicate the trend of the melody, but not the length of the tones. The first interval of the descending fourth is somewhat unusual. The flatted sixth, which was accurately sung, gives an effect of sadness to the close of the song. The words are broken by interpolated syllables and the rhythm contains little of interest.

LOVE SONGS

No. 157. "I Have Lost My Sweetheart"   (Catalogue No. 300)

Sung by KI′MIWÛN

VOICE ♩ = 66

Recorded without drum

Ke - ä - bi - go   ni - wa - ni - ä   nin - i - mu - ce

WORDS

keä′bigo′...................... and still
niwa′niä.................... I have lost
nin′imu′ce.................... my sweetheart

Analysis.—This song contains three rhythmic units, and its melodic formation shows the triads of B minor and G major. The first section comprises three phrases on the triad of B minor and one on the triad of G major, the first rhythmic unit being steadily maintained. In the second section we note two phrases in B minor and one in G major, the second rhythmic unit being used; this is followed by the third section, on the chord of B minor without the third, the song closing with two phrases in B minor, using the second and third rhythmic units. The second rhythmic unit opens with a division of the count, which occurs also in Nos. 151, 152, 159, 161, 163.

No. 158. "I Will Not Drink"   (Catalogue No. 301)

Sung by Kɪ′ᴍɪᴡûɴ

VOICE ♩ = 66
Recorded without drum

Ka - wĭn - ga - na-ge   nin - ga - mi - na-kwe - sĭ

WORDS

kawĭn′ganage′................ I will not
ninga′minakwe′sĭ............. drink at all′

Analysis.—This song was given with much freedom of tempo. It begins with an upward progression to an accidental, an opening which is unusual. The song is minor in tonality, melodic in structure, and contains all the tones of the octave except the second.

No. 159. Love Song   (Catalogue No. 302)

Sung by Kɪ′ᴍɪᴡûɴ

VOICE ♩ = 63
Recorded without drum

Analysis.—This song is unusually regular in form. It has 16 measures and 4 periods, the first, second, and last periods containing the rhythmic unit. In the third period the phrases of the rhythmic unit are found in a reversed order. The metric unit was not steadily maintained, but the rhythmic unit shows no variation in the five renditions of the song. The division of the last count of the third measure is noted also in Nos. 152, 153, 157, 161, 163.

No. 160. Love Song   (Catalogue No. 303)

Sung by Kı′ᴍɪᴡûɴ

Voice ♩ = 96

Recorded without drum

Analysis.—This song consists of five sections, each of which contains four measures. Each section is designated as a rhythmic unit although the measure-divisions differ somewhat in the latter part of the song. The accidentals were sung with correct intonation and the effect of the song is pleading and plaintive.

Moccasin Game Songs

No. 161   (Catalogue No. 292)

Sung by A′ᴊɪᴅᴇ′ɢɪᴊîɢ

Voice ♩ = 63

Drum ♩ = 112

(Drum-rhythm similar to No. 125)

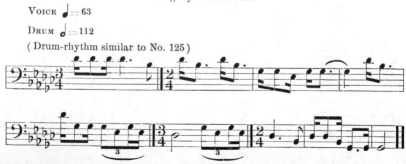

Analysis.—This song has the slow voice-rhythm which character-izes the moccasin game songs and which is noted also in Nos. 30, 51, 52, 103. The melody comprises the tones of the fourth five-toned scale and is harmonic in structure. Although the song is major in tonality a large majority of the intervals are minor thirds. The song contains 24 melodic progressions, 17 (71 per cent) of which are minor thirds, 7 being ascending and 10 descending intervals (see Nos. 140, 141, 151, 163). There is no rhythmic unit, but the division of the first count of the measure recurs with frequency (see Nos. 152, 153, 157, 159, 163).

No. 162. "The Sound of His Footsteps" (Catalogue No. 293)

Sung by A′JIDE′GIJĬG

VOICE ♪ = 192

DRUM ♩ = 112

(Drum-rhythm similar to No. 125)

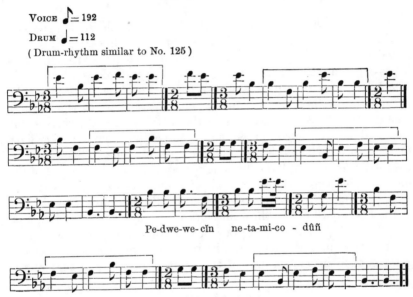

Pe-dwe-we-cĭn   ne-ta-mi-co - dûñ

WORDS

pe′dwewe′cĭn...................... the sound of his approaching footsteps
neta′micodûñ′...................... who always hits the mark

Analysis.—The tempo of this song is so rapid that it was necessary to reduce the speed of the phonograph in order to detect the metric unit and indicate the note-values. The rhythm was given uniformly in the two renditions of the song, showing that it was clear in the mind of the singer. The fourth is the principal interval of progression (see No. 22).

No. 163. Moccasin Game Song   (Catalogue No. 305)

Sung by KI′MIWÛN

VOICE ♩ = 96
DRUM ♩ = 108

(Drum-rhythm similar to No. 125)

Analysis.—This song contains only the tones of the tonic triad and sixth, the melody moving freely along harmonic lines. It has been noted that in some songs containing these tones the sixth is used as a passing tone, the melody being based on the tonic triad, while in other instances the sequence of the tones is such as to produce the minor triad with minor seventh as an integral part of the melodic framework. This song belongs to the latter group, the sixth being accented in the fourth measure and appearing again in the sixth measure, after which it is used only as a passing tone. (See Nos. 133, 147, 151, 152, 153, 154.) The song is major in tonality, yet 12 of the intervals (55 per cent) are intervals of a minor third. (See Nos. 140, 141, 151, 161.) The song contains no rhythmic unit. The division of the first count of the third measure is also noted in Nos. 152, 153, 157, 159, 161. Three renditions of the song were recorded, which are identical in every respect. In this, as in most of the moccasin game songs, the metric unit of the drum is faster than that of the voice.

DANCE SONGS

The woman's dance is a feature of every gathering of the Minnesota Chippewa, but has never been introduced on the Lac du Flambeau Reservation in Wisconsin. This dance is said to have been acquired from the Sioux (see pp. 45, 46; also Bulletin 45, p. 192). The dancers face the drum, moving clockwise, in a circle. In plate 45 are shown the Waba′cĭñg Chippewa in a woman's dance. A shade of branches has been erected over the drummers, but the women wear their plaid woolen shawls. In this instance the men and women are dancing by themselves. A more common arrangement, when gifts are being freely exchanged, is for a man and a woman to dance together, the men and women alternating around the circle.

No. 164. Woman's Dance Song   (Catalogue No. 295)

Sung by A'ʝɪᴅᴇ'ɢɪʝɪɢ

Voice ♩ = 108
Drum ♩ = 108

(Drum-rhythm similar to No. 19)

Analysis.—This song is strongly rhythmic in character but contains no rhythmic unit. It comprises the tones of the second five-toned scale and is definitely minor in tonality. The accented tones in the last seven measures correspond to the descending intervals of the tonic chord. The faulty intonation in the first measure was corrected in the second measure. (See Nos. 54, 129, 133, 146.)

No. 165. "He Killed a Man"   (Catalogue No. 294)

Sung by A'ʝɪᴅᴇ'ɢɪʝɪɢ

Voice ♩ = 168
Drum ♩ = 100

(Drum-rhythm similar to No. 2)

Ca - mau-ga-nĭc *a*   gi - nĭc - i - wed *i* -

na gi - nĭc - i - wed

WORDS

camau'ganĭc........................ a soldier
ginĭ'ciwed'........................ killed a man in war

Analysis.—This very old song was sung by the women who went to meet a war party on its return to the village (see p. 118). The same song was recorded at White Earth (see Bulletin 45, p. 143), the two records being identical except that the former record includes the shrill falsetto cry given by the women. The structure of the melody is interesting. In the first six measures the rhythmic unit is repeated with regularity and the first note of that unit (which is also the first note of the measure) follows the descending intervals of the fourth five-toned scale. The remainder of the song is harmonic in outline, comprising first the chord on the sixth and then the third D sharp–F sharp, suggesting the chord of B major. Attention is directed to the interesting rhythm of the part of the song containing the words.

No. 166. "I Carry It Away"   (Catalogue No. 316)

Sung by GEGWE′DJIBI′TÛÑ ("SITTING NEAR IT")

VOICE ♩ = 100
DRUM ♩ = 100
(Drum-rhythm similar to No. 2)

Nin-da-ma-dji-don

WORDS

nin′dama′djidon′................... I carry it away

Analysis.—This is a song of the ca′wûno′ga (southern dance) (see p. 129). The song was recorded on the White Earth Reservation also and the records were found to be identical. The rhythmic unit is not continuous but gives character to the song. The melody tones are those of the fourth five-toned scale and the effect of the song is that usually associated with this scale. Faulty intonation on the interval of the second is noted also in Nos. 54, 55, 61, 64. 100, 145, 166.

No. 167. "The Entire World"   (Catalogue No. 297)

Sung by KɪʹMIWÛN

VOICE ♩ = 100
DRUM ♩ = 100
(Drum-rhythm similar to No. 19)

Ĕ - nĕ - go-kwag   a - ki ni-ma-

wi - mi - gun

WORDS

ĕʹnĕgokwagʹ........................ the entire
akiʹ................................ world
nimaʹwimigunʹ..................... weeps for me

Analysis.—This was said to be the music of a dance much older than the caʹwûnoʹga. The three renditions of the song recorded are identical except that the tone before the words is prolonged in the first rendition. The song is characterized by a vigorous rhythm, with a distinct unit which occurs three times in entirety and parts of which are found throughout the song. The melody is minor in tonality and contains only the tones of the tonic triad and sixth.

COMBINED ANALYSES OF DREAM, MĬDE′, LOVE, MOCCASIN GAME, AND
DANCE SONGS—WABA′CĬÑG VILLAGE, RED LAKE RESERVATION

MELODIC ANALYSIS

TONALITY

	Dream songs	Mĭde′ songs	Love songs	Moccasin game songs	Dance songs	Total	Per cent.
Major	25	3	1	3	2	34	85
Minor	1		3		2	6	15
Total	26	3	4	3	4	40	

BEGINNINGS OF SONGS

	Dream songs	Mĭde′ songs	Love songs	Moccasin game songs	Dance songs	Total	Per cent.
On thirteenth	1					1	2.5
On sixth	5					5	12.5
On twelfth	11	1	4	2	2	20	50
On fifth	4	2				6	15
On tenth	3					3	7.5
On third	2				1	3	7.5
On tonic				1	1	2	5
Total	26	3	4	3	4	40	

ENDINGS OF SONGS

	Dream songs	Mĭde′ songs	Love songs	Moccasin game songs	Dance songs	Total	Per cent.
On tonic	14	2	4	2	2	24	60
On fifth	2	1		1		4	10
On third	10				2	12	30
Total	26	3	4	3	4	40	

TONE MATERIAL

	Dream songs	Mĭde′ songs	Love songs	Moccasin game songs	Dance songs	Total	Per cent.
Second five-toned scale					1	1	2.5
Fourth five-toned scale	15	2	1	2	2	22	55
Major triad	1					1	2.5
Major triad and sixth	9	1		1		11	27.5
Minor triad and sixth			1		1	2	5
Minor triad sixth and fourth	1					1	2.5
Minor triad and fourth			1			1	2.5
Octave complete except second			1			1	2.5
Total	26	3	4	3	4	40	

MELODIC ANALYSIS—continued

ACCIDENTALS

	Dream songs	Mĭde′ songs	Love songs	Moccasin game songs	Dance songs	Total	Per cent.
Songs containing no accidentals.	24	2	2	3	3	34	*85*
Songs containing sixth raised a semitone			1			1	*2.5*
Songs containing second raised a semitone	2				1	3	*7.5*
Songs containing second raised a semitone and sixth lowered a semitone			1			1	*2.5*
Songs containing sixth lowered a semitone		1				1	*2.5*
Total	26	3	4	3	4	40	

STRUCTURE

	Dream songs	Mĭde′ songs	Love songs	Moccasin game songs	Dance songs	Total	Per cent.
Harmonic	14	1	1	2	2	20	*50*
Purely melodic	4	2	3	1	2	12	*30*
Melodic with harmonic framework	8					8	*20*
Total	26	3	4	3	4	40	

FIRST PROGRESSION

	Dream songs	Mĭde′ songs	Love songs	Moccasin game songs	Dance songs	Total	Per cent.
Downward	21	3	3	3	2	32	*80*
Upward	5		1		2	8	*20*
Total	26	3	4	3	4	40	

RHYTHMIC ANALYSIS

PART OF MEASURE ON WHICH SONG BEGINS

	Dream songs	Mĭde′ songs	Love songs	Moccasin game songs	Dance songs	Total	Per cent.
Beginning on accented part of measure	17	1	3	3	3	27	*67*
Beginning on unaccented part of measure	9	2	1		1	13	*33*
Total	26	3	4	3	4	40	

Rhythmic Analysis—continued

RHYTHM OF FIRST MEASURE

	Dream songs	Mĭde′ songs	Love songs	Moccasin game songs	Dance songs	Total	Per cent.
Beginning in 2–4 time	15	2	2	1	1	21	52.5
Beginning in 3–4 time	9		1	2	2	14	35
Beginning in 4–4 time	1					1	2.5
Beginning in 5–4 time			1		1	2	5
Beginning in 7–4 time	1					1	2.5
Transcribed in outline		1				1	2.5
Total	26	3	4	3	4	40	

CHANGE OF TIME

	Dream songs	Mĭde′ songs	Love songs	Moccasin game songs	Dance songs	Total	Per cent.
Songs containing change of time.	26	1	3	3	4	37	92.5
Songs containing no change of time		1	1			2	5
Transcribed in outline		1				1	2.5
Total	26	3	4	3	4	40	

RHYTHMIC UNIT

	Dream songs	Mĭde′ songs	Love songs	Moccasin game songs	Dance songs	Total	Per cent.
Songs containing rhythmic unit.	9	2	2	1	2	16	40
Songs containing two rhythmic units	1					1	2
Songs containing three rhythmic units			1			1	2
Songs containing no rhythmic unit	16		1	2	2	21	53
Transcribed in outline		1				1	2
Total	26	3	4	3	4	40	

COMPARISON OF METRIC UNIT OF VOICE AND DRUM

	Dream songs	Mĭde′ songs	Love songs	Moccasin game songs	Dance songs	Total	Per cent.
Metric unit of voice and drum the same	13				3	16	40
Metric unit of voice and drum different	13	2		3	1	19	47.5
Transcribed in outline		1				1	2.5
Recorded without drum			4			4	10
Total	26	3	4	3	4	40	

SONGS OF WHITE EARTH RESERVATION

This group contains songs of several classes, comprising all the material in this work collected on White Earth Reservation, Minn., except songs connected with war (pp. 59–141).

No. 168. "We Have Salt" (Catalogue No. 268)

Sung by HENRY SELKIRK

VOICE ♩= 160
DRUM ♩= 104
(Drum-rhythm similar to No. 19)

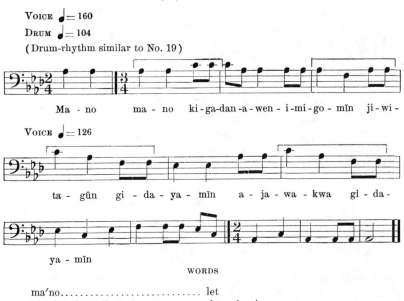

Ma - no   ma - no   ki - ga-dan -a - wen - i -mi - go - mĭn   ji - wi -

VOICE ♩= 126

ta - gûn   gi - da - ya - mĭn   a - ja - wa - kwa   gi - da -

ya - mĭn

WORDS

ma′no............................ let
kigadeän′awen′imĭgo′mĭn.......... them despise us
ji′wita′gûn......................... salt
gi′dayamĭn′........................ we have
a′jawa′kwa......................... here, beyond the belt of timber
gi′dayamĭn′ .... we live

In the early days the Minnesota Chippewa had no salt, and some of the older Indians have not yet acquired a taste for it.   In a treaty known as the "Salt Treaty," [1] concluded at Leech Lake, August 21, 1847, with the Pillager Band of Chippewa, there was a stipulation that the Indians should receive 5 barrels of salt annually for five years.

---

[1] *A compilation of all the treaties between the United States and the Indian tribes now in force as laws*, Washington, 1873, p. 212.

Analysis.—Four renditions of this song were recorded. In all these the drumbeat was steadily maintained but the voice tempo changed as indicated. (See the following groups, each comprising two songs: Nos. 100, 101; 103, 104; 121, 122.) The melody contains the tones of the major triad and sixth and would be classified as harmonic in structure except for the accented F in the fourth measure from the last. Meaningless syllables were used in the closing measures of the song.

No. 169. "If I Were a Son-in-law"

(Catalogue No. 269)

Sung by HENRY SELKIRK

VOICE ♩ = 184
DRUM ♩ = 108
(Drum-rhythm similar to No. 19)

WORDS

kozigwa′kominûg′.................. June berries
ninda′nawapo′kinûg[1].............. I would take to eat on my journey
naängûb′iyan′ [2].................... if I were a son-in-law

June berries, which are abundant in the Chippewa country, constitute the simplest possible form of refreshment. "Take some June berries with you," is a common saying among the Chippewa. These berries grow on tall bushes; they are small and red, have firm white meat and very little juice, and are sweetish in taste.

Analysis.—This song contains the major triad and fourth, tone material found in only one other song of the series of 340. It is rhythmic in character but contains no unit of rhythm. The voice tempo is rapid and the song has a marked individuality.

---

[1] One syllable of this word was omitted by the singer.

[2] Two consecutive syllables of this word are accented. The Chippewa word meaning "son-in-law" is *naäng'ic.* The word occurring in the song contains also the root *ûb,* meaning "to sit," and would be literally translated, "if I were sitting as a son-in-law." In the old days each member of a Chippewa family had his or her seat in the wigwam, and the son-in-law, coming into the home of his wife, had a seat assigned him, and was referred to as "sitting." This indicated that he had been received as a member of the family.

No. 170. "Work Steadily"   (Catalogue No. 270)

Sung by MAIÑ'GANS

VOICE ♩ = 60
Recorded without drum

A - yañ-gwa-mĭ-sĭn   tci - ä - no - ki - yûn   e   ge -

ga - ma - ka - mi - go   ni - au   e

WORDS

ayañgwa'mĭsĭn'....................	be very careful
tciäno'kiyûn'......................	to work steadily
gegama'kamigo'....................	⎱ I am afraid they will take you away from
niau...............................	⎰ me

Many of the Chippewa love songs can be sung by either a man or a woman, but this is a woman's song.

Analysis.—This song is slow in tempo and mournful in character. The tonality is minor, and the melody contains all the tones of the octave except the second. The subdominant is especially prominent and the song has a pleading quality. This peculiarity is noted in other love songs also (see Nos. 106, 109, 110). The time was not rigidly maintained on the eighth notes, which occur on the unaccented parts of the measure.

PIPE DANCE SONGS

The pipe dance was said to be the principal "good time dance" of the early Chippewa. It is very old and, like all other dances, is believed to have come from the manido'. In this dance a man carried a pipestem and his body was supposed to represent a pipe. The dancer never rose erect, but took a crouching or squatting posture, trying to assume the form of a pipe as nearly as possible. Many contortions of the body were used, and the antics of the dancers were considered very amusing. Only one man danced at a time. When he had finished dancing he presented the pipestem to another, who was obliged to accept it and dance; he transferred also the rattle which he carried. This procedure was continued until all the men had danced. Some were awkward, and their frantic efforts to imitate a pipe produced great merriment. It was considered a test of courage for a man to brave the ridicule of the assembly and seat himself where he would be asked to dance the pipe dance. In the early days the men who danced this wore no clothing except the moccasins, which were necessary to protect the feet.

A characteristic of the music of this dance is that a sharp, short beat of the drum is frequently given, followed by an instant of silence. When this drumbeat is heard the dancer pauses in whatever attitude he may chance to be and remains motionless until the drumbeat is resumed. This is indicated in the transcription of the first pipe dance song. The drumbeat is very rapid, and the dancer is expected to keep in perfect time with it.

No. 171. "O′gima" [1]   (Catalogue No. 408)

Sung by Ĕ′NIWÛB′E

VOICE ♩ = 208
DRUM ♩ = 138
(Drum-rhythm similar to No. 2)

Ha ni wa ya hi ne ha ha ni wa ya hi ne ha

Wa - ba - ca o - gi - ma ya ho na Wa - ba -

ca o - gi - ma ya ho na

WORDS

Waba′ca............................ Waba′ca, name of a Sioux chief
o′gima .... chief

Analysis.—In the several renditions of this song Ĕ′niwûb′e introduced the names of four chiefs, belonging to three different tribes: Waba′ca, a Sioux; Na′ögade′, a Winnebago; and Kaga′giwayan′ and Wasi′kwade′, of the Chippewa.[2] The mention of these names does not signify that the chiefs were actually present at the dance, but that the Chippewa remembered them on an occasion of pleasure.

---

[1] This song is analyzed with Unclassified Lac du Flambeau Songs, p. 242.
[2] Compare repetition of names in Song of the Peace Pact (No. 44).

The melody is simple in structure and contains only the tonic with the third and fourth. This tone material (minor third and fourth) is found in only two songs of the series of 340 (see No. 157 in Bulletin 45, and No. 11 of the present work). Attention is directed to the rapid tempo of both voice and drum, also to the pauses following the explosive tones.

No. 172. "Little Plover"   (Catalogue No. 281)

Sung by ODJĬB'WE

VOICE ♩ = 160

DRUM ♩ = 96

(Drum-rhythm similar to No. 19)

Dji - tcis - ki - wen   a   gi - mu - sĕ   kai   yo we ni

kai   yo we ni   kai   yo we ni   kai   yo we ni

WORDS

djitcis'kiwen'...................... little plover, it is said
gi'bimusĕ'[1]...................... has walked by

Analysis.—The singer stated that in this dance the men frequently imitated the motions of the plover, when singing this song.[2] The melody, which is short, consists of two distinct parts, the first in double, the second in triple, time; the former contains five measures and the latter four measures. Each part of the song has its own rhythm and tone material, the first containing the descending fifth from the dominant to the tonic, and the second the descending fourth from the tonic to the dominant to the lower octave. It is interesting to note in connection with the statement of Gardiner (quoted on p. 7) that the note of the plover is a descending minor third, that 38 per cent of the intervals are descending minor thirds.

The song contains only two upward progressions; two other songs having similar characteristics are Nos. 6 and 38 in Bulletin 45. The nine renditions of this song recorded show no variation.

---

[1] The second syllable of this word was omitted by the singer.
[2] See pp. 101, 201, 203.

No. 173. "Why?"   (Catalogue No. 282)

Sung by ODJĬB'WE

VOICE ♩= 192
DRUM ♩ = 96
(Drum-rhythm similar to No. 19)

We - go - nĕn nin - dan - gwe   wen - djĭ - ni - mi - yûñg

ga   wen - djĭ - ni - mi-yûñg   ga   wen - djĭ - ni. - mi - yûñg

WORDS

wegonĕn'..................... why
nindan'gwe................. my (female) friend
wĕn'djĭni'miyûñg'.......... do we dance?

Analysis.—Six renditions of this song were recorded. In a majority of these the last tone of the transcription was omitted, the singer returning to the first measure with no interruption of the time (see No. 125). It will be noted that the next to the last measure of the song is abrupt and unfinished, but the singer found no difficulty in beginning the repetition of the song on the proper pitch. The song is characterized by the emphatic syllable *ga*, given with a prolonged tone on the descending intervals of the tonic triad.

MĬDE′ SONGS

No. 174. Mĭde′ Burial Song (a)   (Catalogue No. 283)

Sung by NA′WAJI′BIGO′KWE

VOICE ♩ = 152

Recorded without drum

Gĭ-ga-ma - dja   ya   gĭ-ga-ma - dja   ya   gĭ-ga-ma -

dja   ya   gĭ-ga-ma - dja   gĭ-ga-ma - dja

gĭ - ga-ma - dja   ya   gĭ-ga-ma - dja   ya   gĭ-ga-ma -

dja   a   o - de - nañg   gĭ-dĭ-no - se   sa   gĭ-dĭ-no -

se   ya   gĭ - dĭ-no - se   gĭ-dĭ-no - se

gĭ-dĭ-no - se   sa   gĭ-dĭ-no - se   ya   gĭ - dĭ-no -

se   gĭ-dĭ-no - se   ya   gĭ-ga-ma - dja

WORDS

gĭ′gamadja′.................. you shall depart
ode′nañg′.................. to the village
gĭ′dĭnose′.................. you take your steps

This and the song next following were recorded by a prominent
member of the Mĭde′wĭwĭn on the White Earth Reservation; they were

said to be used during the burial of a member of that society.   There is a peculiar gentleness in both these melodies.   They are cheerful, yet plaintive, and are worthy of attention as features of the ceremonies connected with what is commonly designated "a heathen burial."

Analysis.—A persistent rhythmic unit characterizes this song.   The second measure of this unit is given in triple time and then in double time.   As in most Mĭde′ songs, the words are continuous, but this song contains none of the ejaculations used in songs intended to produce definite results by means of " spirit power " (see Bulletin 45, p. 43).   The melody is interesting, though simple in structure, and is characterized by the interval of the fourth, as noted in many songs which contain the idea of motion.   (See No. 22.)

No. 175. Mĭde′ Burial Song (b)   (Catalogue No. 284)

Sung by NA′WAJI′BIGO′KWE

VOICE ♩ = 160
Recorded without drum

Nĕ - ni - wa   ha   ni-ba-wi - da   ha   Nĕ - ni - wa   ha

ni-ba-wi - da   ha   Nĕ - ni - wa   ha   ni-ba-wi - da   ha

Nĕ - ni - wa   ha   ni-ba-wi - da   Nĕ - ni - wa   ni-ba-wi - da

ha   Nĕ - ni - wa   he   gi-ga-wa-ban-dan   ni - au   e   he

Nĕ - ni - wa   ha   ĕ -nĕn-da-man ĕ   hĕ   Nĕ - ni - wa   ha

ni-ba-wi - da   ha   Nĕ - ni - wa   ha   ni-ba-wi - da

WORDS

Nĕniwa'....................	Nĕniwa' (name of a man)
ni'bawida'..................	let us stand
gi'gawa'bandan'...........	and you shall see
niau......................	my body
ĕnĕn'daman'...............	as I desire

Analysis.—This song is in the same key as the preceding and has the same peculiar ending. The rhythmic unit shows a slight variation in the middle of the song, but clearly influences the entire rhythm. The song contains only the tones of the minor triad and fourth.

Moccasin Game Song

No. 176　　　(Catalogue No. 285)

Sung by WILLIAM POTTER

VOICE ♩ = 108
DRUM ♩ = 108
(Drum-rhythm similar to No. 125)

Analysis.—This song is harmonic in structure, major in tonality, and contains only the tones of the tonic triad and sixth. The rhythm was steadily maintained throughout the six renditions. At Waba'-cĭng a song rendered by a member of a Canadian band of Chippewa, temporarily residing there, was recorded, which resembles this so closely that it may be considered the same song, although it is in 3–4 instead of 2–4 time. (See No. 144.) That singer said it was a dream song, by means of which success in the moccasin game was secured. In his rendition the metric unit of the voice was slow and that of the drum rapid. In the rendition by the White Earth singer, a man accustomed to the ways of civilization, voice and drum were in the same tempo. The comparison is of interest, as the singers were widely separated in locality and in general development.

Love Songs

The two songs next following were sung by Mrs. Julia Warren Spears, sister of Hon. William Warren, author of the History of the Ojibway, and sister of Mrs. Mary Warren English (see p. v). Both Mrs. Spears and her sister are women of marked ability; they are lineal descendants of Richard Warren who came over in the *Mayflower*. Mrs. Spears is mother of Mrs. Charles Mee, who has greatly assisted the writer in securing material on the White Earth Reservation.

The following description of the songs was given by the singer, Mrs. Spears, who also translated the words:

When I was a girl 15 years old, living on Madeline Island in Lake Superior, I had a friend and playmate, a very pretty Indian maiden. She was the daughter of a chief, an only child, and she was always singing these songs. I learned them from her and have never forgotten them. The first is sung when the maiden sees the young Indian brave for the first time and they fall in love with each other. In her happiness she sings that song. The other is when her lover leaves her to travel a long distance, and being very lonely she sings the sad little song.

Mrs. Spears learned these songs more than 60 years before they were recorded by the phonograph. The writer heard them sung by Mrs. Spears at intervals during a period of several years and the renditions never varied in any respect.

(Catalogue No. 286)

No. 177. "I Have Found My Lover"

Sung by Mrs. Julia Warren Spears

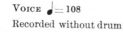

Voice ♩ = 108

Recorded without drum

Niä nin-dĭ - nĕn-dûm niä nin-dĭ-nĕn -dûm me - ka-wi -

ä - nin nin - i - mu - cĕn *sa* niä nin-dĭ-nĕn - dûm

WORDS

niä [1]	Oh
nin′dinĕn′dûm	I am thinking
niä	Oh
nin′dinĕn′dûm	I am thinking
me′kawia′nin	I have found
nin′imucĕn′	my lover
niä	Oh
nin′dinĕn′dûm	I think it is so

Analysis.—This song is purely melodic in structure, the melody moving freely along the tones of the tonic triad. Other songs composed or sung by women are Nos. 31, 39, 40, 112, 127, 151, 178. The rhythm of the first six measures is somewhat changed in the second section of the song. The range of the melody is of interest in con-

---

[1] A woman's exclamation of surprise.

nection with the fact that it was sung correctly and with pleasing
tone by a woman more than 70 years of age.

No. 178. "He Is Going Away" (Catalogue No. 287)

Sung by MRS. JULIA WARREN SPEARS

VOICE ♩ = 54
Recorded without drum

Wa - sa - we - ka - mi - kañg   wa - ǐ - ja - cǐ nin - i - mu - ce wa - ǐ - ba wa - ǐ - ba wi - ta -gwǐc - ǐn - sa

WORDS

wa′sawe′kami′kañg.................. to a very distant land
wäǐja′cǐ............................ he is going
nin′imu′ce......................... my lover
wa′ǐba............................. soon
witagwǐc′insa..................... he will come again

Analysis.—In structure this song differs widely from the one next
preceding. Instead of beginning on the twelfth and ending on the
tonic, it begins on the dominant above the tonic and ends on the
dominant below the tonic; it is melodic instead of harmonic; it begins
in double, instead of in triple, time; and instead of the simple tones
of the tonic triad we find a tone-material which has been but rarely
noted. The melody contains only the first, second, fifth, and sixth
tones of the major key. This tone-material is found in only five other
songs of the entire series (see No. 53). Other songs said to have
been composed or sung by women are Nos. 31, 39, 40, 112, 127, 151,
177.

Songs for the Entertainment of Children

No. 179. Song of the Game of Silence

(Catalogue No. 448)

Sung by John W. Carl

Voice ♩ = 192

Recorded without drum

A - go-djĭn a - go - djĭn e - kwa-teg ko-koc-ne-wa-ba-mû na -

bo - zi - de me - ma - gi - ci - a - si - wa - ge *he* we - mĭ - tĭ -

go - jĭ - wûg - e *he* ma - mi - ga - di - wûg - e *he* ma - mis-kwĕ -

wa - pi - ni - ni - di - wûg - e *he* dû - nĭ *e* *he* dû - nĭ *e*

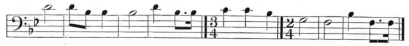

he dû - nĭ *e* *he* *he* da - gĭ - tcĭ - gam - e - we - na *he* da - gi -

tci - gam - i - we - na ĭc - kwe - a - cĭn - ge *he* en - dĭ - ji - dji - tci -

gwa - kwen - dji - ge - yan *e* *he* bĭ - ji - we - kû - wi - ä

bĭ - ji - we - kû - wi - ä na - ma - ha - na - na - ga - na na - ma -

ha - na - na - ga - na kwa-kwac-kwan-da-mo kwa-kwac-kwan-da-mo *sĕp*

WORDS

ago'djĭn............................	it is hanging
ekwateg'...........................	in the edge of the sunshine
kokoc'newa'bamû'.................	it is a pig, I see
na'bozide'.........................	with its double (cloven) hoofs
mema'gidĭsĭ'adisiwage'[1]...........	it is a very fat pig
we'mĭtĭgo'jĭwûge'..................	The people who live in a hollow tree [2]
ma'miga'diwûge'...................	are fighting
ma'miskwĕwa'pina'diwûge'.........	they are fighting bloodily
dûnĭ'..............................	he is rich
da'gĭtcĭgam'ewena'................	he will carry a pack toward the great water

(The rabbit speaks)[3]

ĭc'kweäcĭnge'.......................	at the end of the point of land
en'dĭjidji'tcigwakwen'djigeyan'....	I eat the bark off the tree
bĭjiwe'kûwiä'......................	I see the track of a lynx
nama'nahaninda' nagana'	I don't care, I can get away from him
kwa'kwackwandamo'..............	it is a jumping trail (referring to a rabbit trail by which the singer will travel to safety)
sĕp! (an interjection without meaning)	

This song was recorded by Mr. John W. Carl(see pp. 83, 130), a graduate of Haskell Institute. Mr. Carl's mother, a Chippewa, sang two of the Mĭde' songs contained in Bulletin 45 (serial Nos. 78, 79). Until he was 10 years of age Mr. Carl lived the typical life of a Chippewa child in a tribal camp. He stated that he had a distinct recollection of this game.

The "game of silence," which consisted in keeping still as long as possible, was played by the children at the suggestion of the older members of the family. It is said to have been called frequently into requisition when the adults wished to discuss matters of importance. A pile of presents was placed in the center of the wigwam— beaded moccasins, belts, and arrows of attractive design. These were to be the reward of keeping perfectly still for an indefinite period of time. The game was usually played in the evening, and if the children fell asleep before the spell was broken it was customary to renew the contest as soon as morning came and the family were waking. The child who first spoke or laughed was regarded as ingloriously defeated, while he who held out the longest received the spoils.

When the game was started this song was sung by some one with an active imagination. The indicated words are not arbitrary. Still more startling situations might be invented and the narrative continued still longer. The words of the song as rendered are in four distinct sections with no apparent connection between them. To the

---

[1] This word and the next to the last word are slightly changed to conform to the music.

[2] This term probably refers to the French, who lived in log cabins.

[3] This refers to a familiar folk-tale in which the rabbit defied the lynx.

child mind is first presented the vision of a pig—a very fat pig—
hanging in a tree. Next is shown the Frenchmen in gory conflict,
followed instantly by the rich man, who carries a pack toward the
great water. Where can he be going and why does he travel alone?
But with another lightning transition we are on familiar ground.
The rabbit is speaking. We all know how he jeered the lynx from his
place of safety on the point of land, extending far into the water.
He nibbled the bark off the tree and said he was not afraid, because
he knew of a rabbit track that led from that tree right away through
the brush. It was a jumping trail. We know that kind of trail.
Sĕp! The singer has stopped. What child laughed? The story
ended so *suddenly!* It was a very funny story. We watch the fire
with blinking eyes. "A pig in a tree." Yes, yes! It is warm in
the wigwam. The little dogs snuggle cosily. "The fighting Frenchmen." We saw a Frenchman once. It is fair to yawn if you do not
make any noise. Let us have part of that blanket. There is a bow
that goes with the red arrows in the pile of presents. Perhaps we
will get it. But we wish—wish—we might have—really seen—the
very fat pig—in—the—tree.

Curled in the blanket with their little dogs the Indian children are
asleep.

Analysis.—The tonic triad forms the framework of this melody,
part of which is above the tonic and part below it. All the tones of
the octave except the seventh occur in the melody. The rhythm is
lively and well-sustained though the song contains no rhythmic unit.

The next song accompanies one of the folk-tales (*a'dizo'ke*) told
to the children. The Chippewa have other folk-tales which belong
more especially to the older people; these are the stories of We'nabo'jo
(see Bulletin 45, pp. 92, 206). There are also stories of giants, or
cannibals, called *wĭn'dĭgo.* All these stories are of indefinite length,
it even being said that the full narration of the doings of We'nabo'jo
requires an entire winter, the story being begun each evening where
it was left the previous evening. In contrast to these are stories
similar to the one under consideration, which are brief and concise.
On the Red Lake Reservation the writer was told stories which were
said to be native but which were in reality a Chippewa version of
such well-known Hans Andersen stories as "Little Claus and Big
Claus." The story of Cinderella also was related with slight adapta-
tion. It is probable that these stories were introduced many years
ago by the wives of traders who came from Canada. It is said that
many of these were women of culture and that they often told stories
to the Indian children. These stories were found on no other reservation. Several of the stories told to children have been given to the
writer on three reservations in Minnesota and also on the Lac du
Flambeau Reservation in Wisconsin, the versions differing in detail

but retaining the same outline.   Many of these stories contain one or more songs, which are always said to be sung by the characters of the story.   These songs are therefore a form of musical expression ascribed to animals, the actors in the stories almost without exception being animals indigenous to the region.   Among the most persistent stories is that of the Coon and the Crawfish, which follows:

There was once a coon who lived in the country of the crawfish and made them a great deal of trouble.   At last the crawfish started to make war on the coon.   They said they were going to kill him.   An old female crawfish warned them against this and said that the coon was so cunning he would surely kill them.   She showed them her fingers, which the coon had bitten, and said that he had destroyed whole villages of crawfish.   But they would not listen to her.   They still said they were going to make war on the coon, so the old "woman" went into the water and stood there to see what would happen.

The coon was lying beside the road when the crawfish came along, singing their war song.   He seemed to be asleep.   Gathering around him and still singing their song, the crawfish pinched him with their claws; sometimes he winced as they did so, pleasing the crawfish very much.   But the song was interrupted.   The coon suddenly jumped up, crying, "Why are you disturbing my nap?"   Then he ate all the crawfish—every one of them.

The old "woman" standing up to her neck in the water saw it all; she was safe and the coon could not get her.   She laughed to see that what she said had come true.

The song as recorded contains the words "*e'sĭbûn* is dead."   In that version of the story the coon is represented as feigning death.   Another singer sang the song using the words "*e'sĭbûn* cringes," in which version the coon pretended to be asleep.

No. 180. Song of the Crawfish   (Catalogue No. 449)

Sung by ODJĬB'WE

VOICE ♩ = 108
Recorded without drum

E - si - bûn   ni - bo

WORDS

e'sĭbûn............................. coon
ni'bo............................... dead

Analysis.—This song contains only the first, second, fifth, and sixth tones of the minor key (see No. 53).   The interval of the fourth is prominent in the formation of the melody; this has been noted also in other songs concerning animals (see No. 22).

Songs—*White Earth Reservation*

This group contains 2 social songs (Nos. 168, 169); 3 love songs (Nos. 170, 177, 178); 2 pipe dance songs (Nos. 172, 173); 2 Mĭde′ songs (Nos. 174, 175); 1 moccasin game song (No. 176); and 5 songs for the entertainment of children (Nos. 51, 52, 53, 179, 180).

MELODIC ANALYSIS

TONALITY

	Number of songs	Serial Nos. of songs
Major	9	53, 168, 169, 172, 173, 176, 177, 178, 179
Minor	6	51, 52, 170, 174, 175, 180
Total	15	

BEGINNINGS OF SONGS

	Number of songs	Serial Nos. of songs
On twelfth	3	168, 166, 176
On fifth	4	172, 174, 178, 179
On eleventh	1	51
On tenth	1	52
On third	1	173
On octave	2	169, 170
On second	1	180
On tonic	2	53, 175
Total	15	

ENDINGS OF SONGS

	Number of songs	Serial Nos. of songs
On tonic	10	51, 52, 53, 168, 169, 170, 172, 173, 176, 177
On tonic fifth	5	174, 175, 178, 179, 180
Total	15	

MELODIC ANALYSIS—continued
TONE MATERIAL

	Number of songs	Serial Nos. of songs
Fifth five-toned scale	2	51, 52
Major triad	1	177
Major triad and seventh	1	173
Major triad and sixth	3	168, 172, 176
Major triad and fourth	1	169
Minor triad and fourth	1	175
Octave complete except seventh	1	179
Octave complete except seventh and sixth	1	174
Octave complete except second	1	170
First, second, fourth, and fifth tones	1	53
First, second, fifth, and sixth tones	2	178, 180
Total	15	

ACCIDENTALS

	Number of songs	Serial Nos. of songs
Songs containing no accidentals	15	51, 52, 53, 168, 169, 170, 172, 173, 174, 175, 176, 177, 178, 179, 180
Total	15	

STRUCTURE

	Number of songs	Serial Nos. of songs
Harmonic	3	172, 176, 177
Purely melodic	10	51, 52, 53, 170, 173, 174, 175, 178, 179, 180
Melodic with harmonic framework	2	168, 169
Total	15	

FIRST PROGRESSION

	Number of songs	Serial Nos. of songs
Downward	10	51, 52, 170, 172, 173, 174, 176, 177, 179, 180
Upward	5	53, 168, 169, 175, 178
Total	15	

RHYTHMIC ANALYSIS

PART OF MEASURE ON WHICH SONG BEGINS

	Number of songs	Serial Nos. of songs
On accented part	11	51, 53, 168, 172, 173, 174, 175, 176, 177, 178, 180 ·
On unaccented part	4	52, 169, 170, 179
Total	15	

RHYTHM OF FIRST MEASURE

	Number of songs	Serial Nos. of songs
Songs beginning in 2–4 time	11	51, 52, 168, 172, 173, 174, 175, 176, 178, 179, 180
Songs beginning in 3–4 time	4	53, 169, 170, 177
Total	15	

CHANGE OF TIME

	Number of songs	Serial Nos. of songs
Songs containing change of time	14	51, 52, 53, 168, 169, 170, 172, 173, 174, 175, 177, 178, 179, 180
Songs containing no change of time	1	176
Total	15	

RHYTHMIC UNIT

	Number of songs	Serial Nos. of songs
Songs containing rhythmic unit	6	168, 172, 173, 174, 175, 180
Songs containing no rhythmic unit	9	51, 52, 53, 169, 170, 176, 177, 178, 179
Total	15	

COMPARISON OF METRIC UNIT OF VOICE AND DRUM

	Number of songs	Serial Nos. of songs
Metric unit of voice and drum the same	2	51, 176
Metric unit of voice and drum different	4	168, 169, 172, 173
Recorded without drum	9	53, 169, 170, 174, 175, 177, 178, 179, 180
Total	15	

RHYTHMIC UNITS OF CHIPPEWA SONGS

The purpose of the following section is to place the rhythmic units of the several classes of songs in convenient form for observation. The analyses on pages 51–58 note some melodic and rhythmic resemblances between song-groups which have an underlying idea in common. The study of resemblances can be carried still further by comparing the rhythmic units of songs of related groups.

RHYTHMIC UNITS OF MÍDE′ SONGS[1]

No. 1 (Bull. 45)   (Catalogue No. 189)

No. 2 (Bull. 45)   (Catalogue No. 238)

No. 3 (Bull. 45)   (Catalogue No. 239)

No. 5 (Bull. 45)   (Catalogue No. 240)

No. 6 (Bull. 45)   (Catalogue No. 241)

No. 7 (Bull. 45)   (Catalogue No. 54)

[1] See pp. 34, 51.

No. 8 (Bull. 45)   (Catalogue No. 55)

No. 10 (Bull. 45)   (Catalogue No. 237)

No. 11 (Bull. 45)   (Catalogue No. 61)

No. 12 (Bull. 45)   (Catalogue No. 62)

No. 13 (Bull. 45)   (Catalogue No. 63)

No. 14 (Bull. 45)   (Catalogue No. 65)

No. 15 (Bull. 45)   (Catalogue No. 66)

No. 17 (Bull. 45)   (Catalogue No. 123)

No. 39 (Bull. 45)   (Catalogue No. 30)

No. 61 (Bull. 45)   (Catalogue No. 69)

No. 62 (Bull. 45)   (Catalogue No. 70)

No. 63 (Bull. 45)   (Catalogue No. 254)

No. 64 (Bull. 45)   (Catalogue No. 67)

No. 65 (Bull. 45)   (Catalogue No. 56)

No. 68 (Bull. 45)   (Catalogue No. 59)

No. 69 (Bull. 45)   (Catalogue No. 60)

No. 70 (Bull. 45)   (Catalogue No. 64)

No. 84 (Bull. 45)   (Catalogue No. 194)

No. 85 (Bull. 45)   (Catalogue No. 195)

No. 86 (Bull. 45)   (Catalogue No. 197)

No. 87 (Bull. 45)   (Catalogue No. 199)

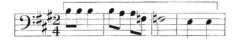

No. 88 (Bull. 45)   (Catalogue No. 200)

No. 89 (Bull. 45)   (Catalogue No. 236)

No. 90 (Bull. 45)   (Catalogue No. 248)

No. 91 (Bull. 45)   (Catalogue No. 253)

No. 92 (Bull. 45)   (Catalogue No. 255)

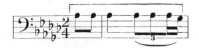

No. 93 (Bull. 45)   (Catalogue No. 256)

No. 154 (Bull. 53)   (Catalogue No. 306)

No. 155 (Bull. 53)   (Catalogue No. 304)

No. 174 (Bull. 53)   (Catalogue No. 283)

No. 175 (Bull. 53)   (Catalogue No. 284)

RHYTHMIC UNITS OF DREAM SONGS [1]

No. 109 (Bull. 45)   (Catalogue No. 245)

No. 110 (Bull. 45)   (Catalogue No. 246)

No. 111 (Bull. 45)   (Catalogue No. 213)

[1] See pp. 37, 52.

No. 112 (Bull. 45)   (Catalogue No. 206)

No. 115 (Bull. 45)   (Catalogue No. 209)

No. 116 (Bull. 45)   (Catalogue No. 210)

No. 118 (Bull. 45)   (Catalogue No. 212)

No. 121 (Bull. 45)   (Catalogue No. 261)

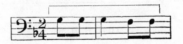

No. 94 (Bull. 53)   (Catalogue No. 394)

No. 95 (Bull. 53)   (Catalogue No. 398)

No. 97 (Bull. 53)   (Catalogue No. 433)

No. 98 (Bull. 53)   (Catalogue No. 434)

No. 99 (Bull. 53)   (Catalogue No. 399)

No. 101 (Bull. 53)   (Catalogue No. 422)

No. 102 (Bull. 53)   (Catalogue No. 395)

No. 103 (Bull. 53)   (Catalogue No. 396)

No. 104 (Bull. 53)   (Catalogue No. 397)

No. 128 (Bull. 53)   (Catalogue No. 289)

(1)

(2)

No. 131 (Bull. 53)   (Catalogue No. 324)

No. 134 (Bull. 53)   (Catalogue No. 320)

No. 135 (Bull. 53)   (Catalogue No. 323)

No. 140 (Bull. 53)   (Catalogue No. 310)

No. 141 (Bull. 53)   (Catalogue No. 311)

No. 142 (Bull. 53)   (Catalogue No. 312)

No. 143 (Bull. 53)   (Catalogue No. 313)

No. 147 (Bull. 53)   (Catalogue No. 291)

No. 153 (Bull. 53)   (Catalogue No. 322)

Rhythmic Units of War Songs[1]

No. 125 (Bull. 45)   (Catalogue No. 215)

No. 127 (Bull. 45)   (Catalogue No. 230)

No. 128 (Bull. 45)   (Catalogue No. 271)

No. 129 (Bull. 45)   (Catalogue No. 276)

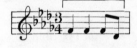

No. 130 (Bull. 45)   (Catalogue No. 277)

No. 131 (Bull. 45)   (Catalogue No. 114)

No. 132 (Bull. 45)   (Catalogue No. 116)

No. 155 (Bull. 45)   (Catalogue No. 140)

[1] See pp. 40, 53.

No. 161 (Bull. 45)   (Catalogue No. 167)

No. 1 (Bull. 53)   (Catalogue No. 392)

No. 2 (Bull. 53)   (Catalogue No. 371)

No. 3 (Bull. 53)   (Catalogue No. 346)

No. 4 (Bull. 53)   (Catalogue No. 387)

No. 5 (Bull. 53)   (Catalogue No. 391)

No. 6 (Bull. 53)   (Catalogue No. 384)

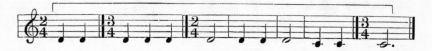

No. 8 (Bull. 53)   (Catalogue No. 338)

No. 11 (Bull. 53)   (Catalogue No. 358)

No. 12 (Bull. 53)   (Catalogue No. 359)

No. 13 (Bull. 53)   (Catalogue No. 13)

No. 15 (Bull. 53)   (Catalogue No. 360)

No. 16 (Bull. 53)   (Catalogue No. 361)

No. 17 (Bull. 53)   (Catalogue No. 362)

(1)

(2)

No. 18 (Bull. 53)   (Catalogue No. 343)

No. 19 (Bull. 53)   (Catalogue No. 333)

No. 20 (Bull. 53)   (Catalogue No. 332)

No. 21 (Bull. 53)   (Catalogue No. 370)

No. 22 (Bull. 53)   (Catalogue No. 372)

No. 23 (Bull. 53)   (Catalogue No. 382)

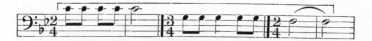

No. 24 (Bull. 53)   (Catalogue No. 373)

No. 25 (Bull. 53)   (Catalogue No. 374)

No. 26 (Bull. 53)   (Catalogue No. 375)

No. 27 (Bull. 53)   (Catalogue No. 376)

No. 28 (Bull. 53)   (Catalogue No. 369)

No. 29 (Bull. 53)   (Catalogue No. 341)

No. 30 (Bull. 53) (Catalogue No. 329)

No. 32 (Bull. 53) (Catalogue No. 385)

No. 33 (Bull. 53) (Catalogue No. 335)

No. 34 (Bull. 53) (Catalogue No. 336)

No. 35 (Bull. 53) (Catalogue No. 342)

No. 36 (Bull. 53) (Catalogue No. 367)

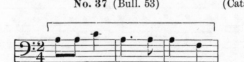

No. 37 (Bull. 53) (Catalogue No. 389)

No. 38 (Bull. 53) (Catalogue No. 366)

No. 39 (Bull. 53)   (Catalogue No. 348)

No. 40 (Bull. 53)   (Catalogue No. 365)

No. 42 (Bull. 53)   (Catalogue No. 330)

No. 44 (Bull. 53)   (Catalogue No. 352)

No. 45 (Bull. 53)   (Catalogue No. 390)

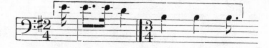

No. 46 (Bull. 53)   (Catalogue No. 354)

No. 47 (Bull. 53)   (Catalogue No. 355)

No. 63 (Bull. 53)   (Catalogue No. 423)

No. 64 (Bull. 53)   (Catalogue No. 424)

No. 65 (Bull. 53)   (Catalogue No. 425)

No. 66 (Bull. 53)   (Catalogue No. 432)

No. 80 (Bull. 53)   (Catalogue No. 437)

No. 81 (Bull. 53)   (Catalogue No. 393)

No. 83 (Bull. 53)   (Catalogue No. 406)

No. 85 (Bull. 53)   (Catalogue No. 415)

No. 86 (Bull. 53)   (Catalogue No. 419)

No. 88 (Bull. 53)   (Catalogue No. 411)

No. 89 (Bull. 53) (Catalogue No. 412)

No. 90 (Bull. 53) (Catalogue No. 416)

No. 91 (Bull. 53) (Catalogue No. 417)

No. 92 (Bull. 53) (Catalogue No. 418)

RHYTHMIC UNITS OF LOVE SONGS [1]

No. 134 (Bull. 45) (Catalogue No. 99)

No. 135 (Bull. 45) (Catalogue No. 101)

No. 136 (Bull. 45) (Catalogue No. 104)

No. 138 (Bull. 45) (Catalogue No. 107)

[1] See pp. 41, 53.

No. 139 (Bull. 45)   (Catalogue No. 110)

No. 140 (Bull. 45)   (Catalogue No. 262)

No. 163 (Bull. 45)   (Catalogue No. 161)

No. 164 (Bull. 45)   (Catalogue No. 155)

No. 105 (Bull. 53)   (Catalogue No. 400)

No. 106 (Bull. 53)   (Catalogue No. 401)

No. 108 (Bull. 53)   (Catalogue No. 431)

No. 109 (Bull. 53)   (Catalogue No. 442)

No. 110 (Bull. 53) (Catalogue No. 443)

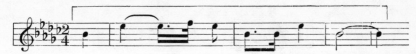

No. 112 (Bull. 53) (Catalogue No. 445)

No. 157 (Bull. 53) (Catalogue No. 300)

No. 159 (Bull. 53) (Catalogue No. 302)

No. 160 (Bull. 53) (Catalogue No. 303)

Rhythmic Units of Moccasin Game Songs [1]

No. 142 (Bull. 45) (Catalogue No. 112)

No. 172 (Bull. 45) (Catalogue No. 171)

No. 174 (Bull. 45) (Catalogue No. 150)

[1] See pp. 44, 54.

No. 125 (Bull. 53)   (Catalogue No. 410)

No. 126 (Bull. 53)   (Catalogue No. 427)

No. 162 (Bull. 53)   (Catalogue No. 293)

RHYTHMIC UNITS OF WOMAN'S DANCE SONGS[1]

No. 177 (Bull. 45)   (Catalogue No. 132)

No. 180 (Bull. 45)   (Catalogue No. 141)

No. 181 (Bull. 45)   (Catalogue No. 153)

No. 184 (Bull. 45)   (Catalogue No. 177)

[1] See pp. 45, 55.

RHYTHMIC UNITS OF BEGGING DANCE SONGS [1]

No. 115 (Bull. 53)   (Catalogue No. 438)

No. 116 (Bull. 53)   (Catalogue No. 439)

No. 118 (Bull. 53)   (Catalogue No. 441)

RHYTHMIC UNITS OF PIPE DANCE SONGS [2]

No. 171 (Bull. 53)   (Catalogue No. 408)

No. 173 (Bull. 53)   (Catalogue No. 282)

RHYTHMIC UNITS OF SONGS CONNECTED WITH GIFTS [3]

No. 152 (Bull. 45)   (Catalogue No. 92)

No. 153 (Bull. 45)   (Catalogue No. 93)

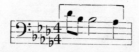

[1] See pp. 47, 56.   [2] See pp. 48, 56.   [3] See pp. 49, 57.

No. 189 (Bull. 45)   (Catalogue No. 168)

No. 123 (Bull. 53)   (Catalogue No. 435)

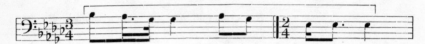

No. 124 (Bull. 53)   (Catalogue No. 436)

RHYTHMIC UNITS OF SONGS FOR THE ENTERTAINMENT OF CHILDREN [1]

No. 197 (Bull. 45)   (Catalogue No. 272)

No. 127 (Bull. 53)   (Catalogue No. 447)

No. 180 (Bull. 53)   (Catalogue No. 449)

RHYTHMIC UNITS OF UNCLASSIFIED SONGS [2]

No. 146 (Bull. 45)   (Catalogue No. 105)

[1] See pp. 49, 57.   [2] See p. 50.

No. 147 (Bull. 45)   (Catalogue No. 109)

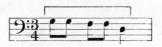

No. 192 (Bull. 45)   (Catalogue No. 160)

No. 194 (Bull. 45)   (Catalogue No. 163)

No. 195 (Bull. 45)   (Catalogue No. 164)

No. 67 (Bull. 53)   (Catalogue No. 428)

No. 68 (Bull. 53)   (Catalogue No. 429)

No. 119 (Bull. 53)   (Catalogue No. 404)

No. 120 (Bull. 53)   (Catalogue No. 405)

No. 121 (Bull. 53)   (Catalogue No. 413)

No. 122 (Bull. 53)   (Catalogue No. 414)

No. 165 (Bull. 53)   (Catalogue No. 294)

No. 166 (Bull. 53)   (Catalogue No. 316)

No. 167 (Bull. 53)   (Catalogue No. 297)

No. 168 (Bull. 53)   (Catalogue No. 268)

AUTHORITIES CITED

BAIRD, S. F., BREWER, T. M., AND RIDGWAY, R. North American birds. Boston, 1874.

BAKER, THEODOR. Über die Musik der nordamerikanischen Wilden. Leipzig, 1882.

BARAGA, FREDERIC. Dictionary of the Otchipwe language, pt. II. Montreal, 1880.

BARRETT, S. A. Dream dance of the Chippewa and Menominee Indians of northern Wisconsin; in Bull. Pub. Mus. Milwaukee, vol. I, art. 4. Milwaukee, 1911.

BOAS, FRANZ. Chinook songs; in Jour. Amer. Folk-Lore, vol. I. Boston and New York, 1888.

BREWER, T. M. See BAIRD, BREWER, AND RIDGWAY.

BROWER, J. V., AND BUSHNELL, D. I., jr. Mille Lac. St. Paul, 1900.

BUSHNELL, D. I., jr. See BROWER AND BUSHNELL.

CHURCH, GEORGE EARL. Aborigines of South America. London, 1912.

CRINGAN, A. T. Description of Iroquois music; in Archæological Report, App. Rep. Min. Education Ontario. Toronto, 1898.

CULIN, STEWART. Indian games; in 24th Rep. Bur. Amer. Ethn. Washington, 1907.

DAY, CHARLES R. Chapter on musical instruments, in Mockler-Ferryman, Up the Niger. London, 1892.

DORSEY, J. OWEN. Siouan sociology; in 15th Rep. Bur. Amer. Ethn. Washington, 1897.

ELLIS, ALEX. J. See HELMHOLTZ.

FILLMORE, JOHN COMFORT. Primitive scales and rhythms; in Mem. Int. Cong. Anthr. Chicago, 1894. See FLETCHER.

FLETCHER, ALICE C., aided by FRANCIS LA FLESCHE. A study of Omaha Indian music. With a report on the structural peculiarities of the music by JOHN COMFORT FILLMORE, A. M. Arch. and Ethn. Papers Peabody Mus., Harvard Univ., vol. I, No. 5. Cambridge, 1893.

FOLWELL, W. W. Minnesota, the North Star State. Boston, 1908.

GARDINER, WILLIAM. The music of nature. Boston, 1838.

GILMAN, BENJAMIN IVES. Hopi songs. Boston, 1908.

GRAM, WILLIAM. See STONE.

HANDBOOK OF AMERICAN INDIANS NORTH OF MEXICO. Bull. 30, pts. 1 and 2, Bur. Amer. Ethn. Washington, 1907 (pt. 1); 1910 (pt. 2).

HELMHOLTZ, H. L. F. The sensations of tone (translated by Alex. J. Ellis). London, 1885.

HEWITT, J. N. B. Orenda and a definition of religion; in Amer. Anthr., N. s., vol. IV, No. 1, 1902.

HOFFMAN, WALTER JAMES, M. D. The Menomini Indians; in 14th Rep. Bur. Amer. Ethn. Washington, 1896.

———. The Midē'wiwin or "Grand Medicine Society" of the Ojibwa; in 7th Rep. Bur. Amer. Ethn. Washington, 1891.

HORNBOSTEL, ERICH M. VON. Über die Musik der Kubu; aus dem Phonogramm-archiv der psychologischen Instituts der Universität Berlin. Frankfurt am Main, 1908.

HRDLIČKA, ALEŠ. Physiological and medical observations among the Indians of southwestern United States and northern Mexico. Bull. 34, Bur. Amer. Ethn. Washington, 1908.

INDIAN TREATIES. A compilation of all the treaties between the United States and the Indian tribes now in force as laws. Washington, 1873.

INDIAN TREATIES AND LAWS AND REGULATIONS relating to Indian affairs, compiled and published under orders of the Department of War. Washington, 1826.

JACKSON, W. H. Descriptive catalogue of the photographs of the United States Geological Survey of the Territories for the years 1869 to 1873, inclusive. Washington, 1874.

KEATING, WM. H. Narrative of an expedition to the source of St. Peter's River, vols. I–II. Philadelphia, 1824.

LACOMBE, ALBERT. Dictionnaire de la langue des Cris. Montreal, 1874.

LA FLESCHE, FRANCIS. See FLETCHER.

MARSDEN, WILLIAM. The history of Sumatra. London, 1811.

MOCKLER-FERRYMAN. See DAY.

MYERS, CHARLES S., M. A., M. D. In Reps. Camb. Anthr. Exped. Torres Straits, vol. IV. Cambridge, 1912.

———. The ethnological study of music; in Anthropological essays presented to Edward Burnett Tylor, etc. Oxford, 1907.

RAMSEY, GOV. ALEXANDER; in U. S. Ind. Affs. Rep. for 1850.

RICHET, CH. (EDITOR). Dictionnaire de physiologie. Paris, 1895–1909.

RIDGWAY, R. See BAIRD, BREWER, AND RIDGWAY.

RIGGS, S. R. Grammar and dictionary of the Dakota language; in Smithson. Contrs., vol. IV. Washington, 1852.

ROYCE, C. C. Indian land cessions; in 18th Rep. Bur. Amer. Ethn., pt. 2. Washington, 1899.

SCHOOLCRAFT, HENRY R. Oneo'ta, or characteristics of the Red Race of America. New York, 1845.

SPECK, F. G. Ceremonial songs of the Creek and Yuchi Indians. Anthr. Pub. Mus. Univ. Penn., vol. I, No. 2, 1911.

STONE, WITMER, AND GRAM, WILLIAM. American animals. New York, 1902.

TORRANCE, G. W. Music of the Australian aborigines; in Jour. Anthr. Inst. Great Britain and Ireland. London, 1887.

WARREN, WILLIAM W. History of the Ojibways. St. Paul, 1885.

WEAD, CHARLES KASSON. Contribution to the history of musical scales; in Rep. U. S. Nat. Mus. 1900. Washington, 1902.

ZÖLLNER, HEINRICH. Einiges über sudanesische Musik; in Musikalisches Wochenblatt. Leipzig, 1885.

INDEX

[NOTE.—In instances in which only a few songs of a certain kind are found in Bulletin 45, or in which these are of special importance, the numbers of such songs are given below, each preceded by an (*).

For a list of the songs contained in this volume, see pages XI-XIX, and of the authorities cited, pages 333-334.]

335

Page

Page